The Varieties of
Temporal Experience

The Varieties of Temporal Experience

Travels in Philosophical, Historical,
and Ethnographic Time

Michael Jackson

Columbia University Press

New York

Columbia University Press
Publishers Since 1893
New York   Chichester, West Sussex
cup.columbia.edu
Copyright © 2018 Columbia University Press
All rights reserved

Library of Congress Cataloging-in-Publication Data

Name: Jackson, Michael, 1940– author.
Title: The varieties of temporal experience: travels in philosophical,
historical, and ethnographic time / Michael Jackson.
Description: New York: Columbia University Press, [2018] |
Includes bibliographical references and index.
Identifiers: LCCN 2017049990 | ISBN 9780231186001 (cloth) | ISBN
9780231186018 (pbk) | ISBN 9780231546447 (e-book) Subjects: LCSH:
Time perception. | Time—Psychological aspects. Classification: LCC
BF468 .J33 2018 | DDC 153.7/53—dc23
LC record available at https://lccn.loc.gov/2017049990

Cover design: Lisa Hamm

Cover image: John Bevan Ford, *Amokura goes fishing*,
series: *Te Aitanga a Kiwa (The Progeny of Kiwa)*.
Courtesy of the Ford family / © The Trustees of the British Museum.

References to websites (URLs) were accurate at the time of writing.
Neither the author nor Columbia University Press is responsible for URLs
that may have expired or changed since the manuscript was prepared.

Contents

Preface

In 2016 I attended an anthropology conference in the UK to give a plenary address on "The Varieties of Temporal Experience." The conference organizers hoped that the theme—Footprints and Futures: The Time of Anthropology—would "provide a forum for critical reflection on time, temporality and chronicity as these play out in different settings." This hope was realized for me in a way I could not have anticipated. Although I had no personal connection with Northumberland, it was near enough to Yorkshire for me to feel that I had come back to the place my grandfather left 110 years ago, seeing no future for himself in England and taking a chance of a new life in New Zealand.

Fred Longbottom was born in an industrial suburb of Halifax in 1877 and went to work in the mills when he was ten. Only two other kinds of gainful employment were open to him—the army or the police. He joined the West Riding Constabulary only to quit when ordered to baton charge mill workers striking for safer working conditions and better pay. When a friend announced that he was immigrating to New Zealand, Fred followed suit. He arrived in Wellington, New Zealand, in 1906, was persuaded to give policing another go, and spent the rest of his life in a small Taranaki town where he alone could determine how he would do his job. In the years after his retirement in 1943, I became a beneficiary of his stories, absorbing his values and often feeling that I was a child of his times as well as my own.

Unlike Alfred Schutz, who writes that "the world of predecessors is by definition over and done with" and "has no open horizon toward the future," I have always felt that my grandfather's world and mine are coterminous and that whatever I do in my life is connected to what he sought to do in his. This feeling that my lifetime overlaps with his may explain why I am drawn to people who work with their hands, why I atavistically affiliate myself with labor rather than capital, and why I believe that sound ethnography is less a matter of philosophical acumen than of social skills in the field and care and craft in writing.

On a walking tour through Durham, my guide was a man who left school at 16 to "go down the pit." After the miners' strike of 1984–1985, a series of pit closures put Joe and tens of thousands of other miners out of work. In 1983, Britain had 174 working mines; by 2009 only 6 remained, and Joe did not hesitate to draw comparisons between the blighted economies and depressed mining towns of northeast England and indigenous communities in the Global South—places of unemployment, drink, hard drugs, and enduring bitterness against those who had conspired to destroy traditional livelihoods. Joe found a new lease of life by resuming his education and was now researching a PhD in the mining village where he grew up. "I'm not much good at theory," he told me. "It's a bit of a stumbling block, really, because what I'm interested in is the experience of these men, from the years they worked in the pits, and the raw deals they've had in life." I told Joe that if theory (whatever that may be) helps in this task, then well and good; if it doesn't, if it just serves to create an effect or lend authority to one's writing, then to hell with it. "Can I quote you on that?" Joe asked.

As we continued on our way, I was reflecting on the difficulty of writing narrative prose that, while philosophically engaged, avoided the kinds of alienating abstraction and systematizing that tend to render thought sufficient unto itself.

As if he had read my mind, Joe led me across the road to a pub called the ColePitts whose painted sign depicted a bucolic landscape with a Galloway pony hauling a coal wagon out of a mine and agricultural workers at harvest in an Elysian field. The pub was at the end of a row of houses built for middle-class buyers, and its name had nothing to do with coalpits but derived from the owners' surnames. "It's typical of how the bourgeoisie fashion 'their' heritage out of images that properly belong to those they oppress and exploit," Joe said. "I sometimes think that their power is as hollow as the wealth they hold and hoard and that they must constantly draw on the vitality of the underclass to give it meaning."

I now followed Joe down an alley where you could still see the coalholes, with their wooden shutters, built into the brick walls behind the row houses. Joe explained that the miners would get a "free" portion of coal, even though it was deducted from their wages, and he imitated the action of a coal man, heaving a sack onto his shoulder from the tray of a truck, and tipping it into the coalhole. I had a sudden flashback to the coal man in my home town, grubby with coal dust, wearing a leather jerkin, and going through the same motions in the shed at my grandparent's house, and remembered filling the coal scuttle, lugging it into the kitchen, and setting it down beside the coal range.

Joe described the system that bonded the miners to the mine owners. If you broke your bond and attempted to relocate to a mine where the wages or working conditions were better, the owners could evict you from your house. If you shopped anywhere other than the Tommy shop owned by the mining company, you could be evicted. If you stirred up trouble, you'd be evicted, or would have to work for three months without pay. "How a miner's family survived under these conditions does not bear thinking about." But I was thinking not of debt bondage but of the bonds that connect us to others across space and time, transcending age, gender, history, culture, and even death. As we walked on toward the Miners' Hall in North Road, built in the 1870s from pennies donated by the two hundred thousand miners in the Northumberland-Durham area, Joe talked of the double binds that came of trying to improve your lot. "If you became an overseer," Joe said, "you'd be materially better off, but in escaping the twelve-hour shifts at the coalface, you lost the respect of the miners; you were no longer one of them, nor were you any better off in their eyes than the owners whose stooge and instrument you had become." *This is what my grandfather experienced when he joined the police force*, I thought, *and this betrayal of my origins is something I too experience.*

The stone gates on Red Hill were topped by stone sculptures of miners, and on our right were white statues of the founding fathers of the Durham Miners Association (1869). All were dressed like owners. Ahead was an impressive red brick building, with the forthcoming miners' gala advertised on a big banner hanging from its high windows. Harry explained that the miners had been determined to negotiate on a level playing field. Their building would have to be as grand as any that the owners lived in; their dress and demeanor had to be equal to that of their adversaries; the toilets and facilities in the building had to be the best money could buy. No doffing caps or touching forelocks here. No one would look down on, or look up to, anyone.

Joe now showed me the memorial to the eighty-one miners who died in a gas explosion in the Easington Colliery in 1951. There were wagons filled with coal, and a miner, his back to a derailed wagon, the heels of his boots (with broken toes) dug into the ground, hoisting the iron wagon and its load of coal back onto the track. *What happened to men who broke their backs and destroyed their bodies toiling underground?* I wondered. Only ten minutes before we had passed the old workhouse, where the destitute and broken were doomed to eke out their days in meaningless work. So shameful was it to wind up in the workhouse that badly behaved children were admonished, "You'll end up in the workhouse if you go on like that." I was struck, in Joe's account, as I had been as a boy listening to my grandfather's stories, by the fact that upward mobility was seldom contemplated, and you lived in dread of downward mobility even though you already occupied the lowest rung on the social ladder.

It was strange returning to the conference after my time with Joe. I had been drawn back into my own prehistory, to be sure, but I had also become painfully aware of the problem of reconciling lived experience with the abstractions and interpretations to which academics dedicate so much time and energy. Like George Orwell, I had an aversion to stuffing one's sentences with extra syllables, using "pretentious diction" (as if "Latin or Greek words are grander than Saxon ones") and creating an inflated style in which "a mass of Latin words falls upon the facts like soft snow, blurring the outlines and covering up the details." In many human societies classical, formal, or respect languages coexist with plebeian, vernacular, or demotic forms, and these linguistic codes correspond to important social distinctions between classes, age groups, and kinship categories. After the Norman conquest, French became the language of the ruling elite, and in due course Latin became the official language of monasteries and universities. We are still haunted by this division, even though the English language is hybrid. Every sentence we speak or write involves words that belong to the discourse of those in power and words borrowed from the lifeworlds of the powerless.

Though our choice of language reflects the audience we seek to reach, the people we want to impress, and the social group we aspire to belong to, it is important to remember that all language implies a gap between the speaker and the experiences of which he speaks. For Theodor Adorno, reification is a form of forgetting. When Orwell remembers, as I did in Durham, how a coal man would deliver coal, he observes that "it is only very rarely, when I make a definite mental effort, that I connect this coal with that far-off labour in the mines. It is just 'coal'—something that I have got to have; black stuff that arrives mysteriously from nowhere in particular, like manna except you have to pay for it. You could quite easily drive a car right across the north of England and never once remember that hundreds of feet below the road you are on the miners are hacking at the coal. Yet in a sense it is the miners who are driving your car forward." Though these lines were written in 1937, the same forgetfulness informs our lives today. We rarely connect the privileges and pleasures of our middle-class lives with the deprivation and suffering of the countless individuals whose names we will never know, whose lifeworlds we will never enter, yet whose toil is the very condition, historically and presently, of the possibility of our own existence. Moreover, just as Orwell's coal seemed to arrive mysteriously from nowhere, so we erroneously assume that our lives unfold within the bookends of birth and death, beginning *ab nihilo*, at the moment of our conception, and ending with our last breath. It is necessary to be reminded, as I was during my days in Durham, that we inherit history not simply as acquired knowledge but as vital matter, so that we live the lives of those who came before us in the same way that we shape the lives of those who will come after us. Our distance from forebears and successors is as relative as the distance between ourselves and our contemporaries. It is never absolute. We may like to think that our time is discontinuous with theirs and that our home spaces are ours alone, but we also exist in the penumbra of *their* time and *their* places. Although Alfred Schutz insisted that only people "within the reach of my direct experience" can be said to share with me "a community of space and a community of time," I prefer the view I encountered in Maori New Zealand, Aboriginal Australia, and West Africa—that our face-to-face encounters may be experientially less meaningful than the felt presence of predecessors, successors, and contemporaries. Thus one's own life is always set in the matrix of life itself, the lineage to which one belongs, the name one carries and will pass on, the blessings one receives from one's ancestors and strives to bestow on one's children, so that every good deed is praised for bringing credit to one's clan and not oneself.

These observations touch on the phenomenon that Freud refers to as "the uncanny" (*Unheimlich*): that occasional and unnerving sense of not being at home in the world in which one has made one's home. Like the experience of déjà vu, something or someone strange feels strangely familiar, or something or someone familiar suddenly feels alien. In this respect, the uncanny echoes what Saint Augustine called *falsae memoriae,* and the English physician A. L. Wigan described as a "sentiment of pre-existence."

The emotion of the uncanny is, as Freud says, one of ambivalence, since one does not know whether a truth has been revealed or one's mind has been deceived. This is what occurs in bereavement. A loved one is dead and buried, yet her voice is still heard and her presence felt, despite her physical absence and the knowledge that she has gone forever. It is the same with the phenomenon of phantom limb pain when, following an amputation, a person will continue to feel the presence of his missing limb even though the evidence of his eyes tells him it is not there. The cortex misreads signals from the sites of the amputations.

Walter Benjamin argues that "the presence of the original is the prerequisite to the concept of authenticity," and that the original possesses an aura that a memento or photograph cannot reproduce. By implication, reproductions of the real create the same estrangement and disturbance that an actor feels when simulating steamy passion before a camera. Cognitively, he or she knows this is not real, but nevertheless his or her body becomes *really* and shamefully aroused. Benjamin's argument might therefore give a phenomenologist pause, for we are often as moved by a reproduction, a false memory, a staged drama, or a fake artwork as we are by a genuine article, a real event, or an independently verified recollection. By the same token, what actually happened in the past may be no less existentially compelling to a person than what he imagined happened, or dimly remembers, or deliberately reinvents in the name of creative license.

This phenomenological emphasis on how the stories we tell, the thoughts we entertain, and the actions we undertake *transfigure* our experience of reality and ameliorate our lot underpins my approach to religion, history, and cultural anthropology and demands a mode of writing in which "happening truth" and "story truth" are given equal weight, despite the fact that they are seldom congruent.

In using these terms, Tim O'Brien seeks to capture the paradox that war, for example, is "just another name for death, and yet [as] any soldier will tell you, if he tells the truth . . . proximity to death brings with it a corresponding proximity to life. After a firefight, there is always the immense pleasure of aliveness. The trees are alive. The grass, the soil—everything. All around you things are purely living, and you among them, and the aliveness makes you tremble."

My struggle to do justice to both happening truth and story truth explains my fascination with the gap between our cultural representations of temporality and the extraordinary variety of our experience of being-in-time—an issue broached by Edmund Leach fifty-five years ago when he asked how we come to have a verbal category of *time* at all and how that category links up with our everyday experience.

My own inclination is to bracket out conventional distinctions between history and historicity, history and biography, and history and myth in order to explore in a phenomenological vein the indeterminate *relationship* between objective and subjective modes of apprehending time consciousness.

While historical inquiry may establish the true identity of Jesus of Nazareth, or the time of his birth and death, it must be remembered that whatever such research brings to light, the truth of Jesus is to be found in the hearts and minds of individual believers, none of who will share exactly the same experience of him. Consider, too, James Joyce's *Ulysses*. The novel chronicles the meanderings, musings, and meetings of Leopold Bloom in the course of a single Dublin day, 16 June 1904. Though Joyce took great pains to ensure that his descriptions of Dublin were historically accurate, the title of his book makes it clear that Bloom's voyages were also mythical. Nowhere is this clearer than in the passage where Bloom ponders the relation between his age and the age of Stephen Dedalus. After convoluted calculations that begin with the fact that "16 years before in 1888 when Bloom was of Stephen's present age Stephen was 6," we are drawn back to the mythical time of Methuselah and to the question of what events might nullify these calculations, namely, "The cessation of existence of both or either, the inauguration of a new era or calendar, the annihilation of the world and consequent extermination of the human species, inevitable but unpredictable." If culturally or historically specific modes of reckoning identity are always entangled with lived experience and existential aporias, then we may doubt the standpoints of both Marshall Sahlins and Gananath Obeyesekere in their debate over whether cosmological or pragmatic considerations caused Hawaiians to kill Captain James Cook on February 14, 1779, for in such matters it is never a question of either/or but of the relative significance attaching to elements within a *constellation* of several copresent points of view.

Whereas the historian surveys the past from a detached perspective, analyzing sequences of events, identifying causes and effects, remarking continuities and discontinuities, and constructing precise chronologies, historicity draws attention to our immediate experiences of being-in-time and the way the past, present, and future *appear* to us. From this phenomenological perspective, temporality connotes both our immediate experience of duration as well as the metaphorical and mundane ways in which we conceptualize that experience. To evoke Walter Benjamin's notion of the now (*jetzeit*), our lives unfold in a force field (*kraftfeld*) wherein traces of the past and anticipations of the future combine and permute in ever changing ways. More radically, Lauren Berlant calls our attention to the affective properties of being present that make the now seem "virtually ahistorical, fleeting, fantasmatic." If, as Michel de Certeau suggests, "modern Western history essentially begins with differentiation between the present and the past," we might say that temporality covers experiences in which such differentiation is irrelevant or has been lost. There are echoes here of Henri Bergson's notion of "inner duration," in which our consciousness is continually oscillating between multiples states that we tend to reify as present, past, and future, but are in reality, "an organic whole." Long ago events come so vividly to mind that they seem to have just happened; time hangs fire in a moment of danger and speeds up in the face of an approaching deadline; an aroma or passage of music instantly transports us to another time; spellbound by a story, we lose all track of time; the future fills us with such dread that we hesitate to bring children into the world. At the same time, historical events—the Holocaust, the crucifixion of Christ, the killing of Imam Hussein, the Atlantic Slave Trade, the Fukushima nuclear disaster, the devastation of a traditional way of life—come to figure more compellingly in one's experience than events that occurred yesterday.

In extremis, chronology collapses, and only a sense of duration endures. Writing in her great memoir about those who survived Stalin's Gulag, Nadezhda Mandelstam observes that "it was a feature of almost all the former camp inmates I met immediately after their release—they had no memory for dates or the passage of time and it was difficult for them to distinguish between things they had actually experienced themselves and stories they had heard from others. Places, names, events and their sequence were all jumbled up in the minds of these broken people, and it was never possible to disentangle them." In his work on the testimonies of Holocaust survivors, Lawrence Langer speaks of this as a movement from chronology to duration. One's life is reduced to a series of events that have no connection to the life one lived before the Holocaust or to any life one may hope to live thereafter. "Testimony may *sound* chronological to an auditor or audience," Langer writes, "but the narrator, a mental witness rather than a temporal one, is 'out of time' as he or she tells the story." This sense of being out of time is, of course, a corollary of the sense of being no*where*.

The terms *past* and *future* are clearly relative to our social, emotional, and ethical preoccupations in the here and now rather than any externally defined timeline. In *Pig Earth*, John Berger recounts how he was walking in the mountains with a friend of seventy. As they walked along the foot of a high cliff, the French peasant remarked that a young girl had fallen to her death there whilst haymaking on the *alpage* above. "Was that before the war?" Berger asked. "In 1833," his friend replied. E. E. Evans-Pritchard relates a similar anecdote in his classical ethnography of the Nuer. "How shallow is Nuer time may be judged from the fact that the tree under which mankind came into being was still standing in Western Nuerland a few years ago!" The exclamation mark is telling. It suggests that Evans-Pritchard has not been able to overcome a Eurocentric assumption that preliterate people conflate mythology and history because their only means of reckoning time—through counting back ten to twelve generations—creates the *illusion* that "valid history ends a century ago."

Rather than see history as valid and myth as illusory, Hayden White, inspired by Michael Oakeshott, emphasizes the artificial and literary character of both genres. One explanation for this conflation of history and literature is that remembering and dreaming, which mediate both genres, are notoriously inconstant. Hence Gaston Bachelard's famous observation that "we are never real historians, but always near poets". Most importantly for White, however, is not the question of verisimilitude but the question of how the past is deployed. As a store of accumulated experience or accepted facts, tradition may be drawn upon to warn against repeating past mistakes, to give legitimacy to present practices, to teach lessons to the young, or lend weight to one's opinion.

Although, from an objectivist standpoint, the past has a causal effect on the present simply because it is prior, from a phenomenological standpoint effects may precede causes and, to all intents and purposes, "bring about the past." Thus, when a resentful younger brother in Sierra Leone complains about being "a slave" to his elder brother's will, or an unhappy wife refers to herself as "a slave" in her husband's house, or a sixteen-year-old schoolgirl expresses the opinion that "anyone who does not try to be educated will be just like a slave," we glimpse not only how "the" historical past (in this case "domestic slavery") is strategically and rhetorically deployed to explain quite different social and biographical circumstances but also how these contemporary allusions to slavery effectively bring the phenomenon into being. This was also brought home in Margaret Mead's famous "rap on race" in 1970 with James Baldwin, who repeatedly reminded Mead that if history "were the past, it would not matter," but for African Americans "history is not the past, it's the present"; slavery is not a historical fact, it is a lived experience, happening *now*.

Clearly, our sense of being-in-time has inner and outer horizons, and we move continually and contrapuntally between them. William James observes that "experience" is double-barreled and admits of no absolute division between the experiencing subject and the object of his or her experience. Experience encompasses the irreversible reality of aging and the inevitability of death, as well as fantasies of rejuvenation and rebirth that fly in the face of these facts. While young lovers may feel they have all the time in the world, the old may quail at the thought of "time's wingèd chariot hurrying near." The gambler may lose all track of time, taking refuge in a "zone" in which the tribulations of his or her everyday life momentary disappear from consciousness. But being-in-the-now is an unstable state, and at any moment one may be brought to one's senses, repossessed by one's dismal past or overwhelmed by grim thoughts of one's immediate future.

Whether one's life is regulated by circadian rhythms, phases of the moon, the rising and setting of stars, the cycle of the seasons, the swing of a pendulum, the rate of radioactive decay of ^{14}C, or caesium seconds, lived time encompasses *more* than is measured in these ways, and it is this "more" that a phenomenology of temporality seeks to describe.

Varying subjective responses to the same phenomenon tend to reflect what a person is thinking, feeling, and doing at any given moment in time. Evans-Pritchard observed that the Nuer pastoralists have no word in their language equivalent to our word *time* as something that can be squandered or saved. They do not experience their lives as a fight against time or as requiring coordination "with an abstract passage of time, because their points of reference are mainly the activities themselves." Evans-Pritchard speaks of ecological time to capture the difference between the monotony and routine of the dry season and the more intense activities ("frequent feasts, dances, and ceremonies") of the rains. In the modern West, waiting is sometimes associated with a sense of having no future, of having too much time on one's hands, while hyperactivity is often taken to be a sign of vitality, like the business man in Antoine Saint-Exupéry's *Little Prince* who is so busily engaged with "matters of consequence" (counting the stars) that he feels himself to be someone of much greater importance than a curious child or star-gazing dreamer.

Just as our sense of duration is constantly varying in relation to our immediate purposes, so our experience and discourse switch constantly between past, present, and future referents. Although Kuranko stories are framed as taking place "once upon a time," skilled narrators make recurring allusions to real places in real time in order to give these fantastic tales contemporary relevance. And when recording Dreaming narratives during fieldwork among the Warlpiri, I was constantly struck by the way narrators spontaneously slipped from third to first person, as if these epochal stories made sense only when integrated with the narrator's autobiographical experiences of the sacred sites and ancestral journeys referenced in the myths. We make history in the same measure that it makes us, and we inevitably make or remake the past in the light of our present concerns.

The art historian and anthropologist Aby Warburg spoke of the afterlife (*nachleben*) of the past, by which he meant the uncanny perseverance of images, gestures, expressions, and ideas over time and across different societies. Thus the snake in Australian Aboriginal myth, Aztec cosmology, ancient Greek healing rites, Minoan art, and Pueblo dance suggest an enduring human preoccupation with rain and fertility, health and healing, and life after death. Although the exact threat to life's continuance and abundance may differ from time to time, place to place, or person to person, death is always a matter of time. And both death and time are inextricably connected with narrative and ritual, for in narrating or enacting events that occurred in the past we can transform the experience of passing into nothingness to an experience of passing into another state of being.

Nevertheless, it is important to stress that different "regimes of historicity" and diverse "tones of mental life" may be found in every person and every society, and that context is what determines which will be brought to the fore and which will be suppressed. For example, traditional Aboriginal conceptions of the Dreaming suggest a timeless and circumambient condition in which ancestral, animal, and contemporary beings are continually morphing, one into the other. Yet archaeological evidence suggests that the Dreaming is not as ancient and unchanging as it appears to be, and contemporary conceptions of the Dreaming often reflect the legal demands of reclaiming "traditional land" under the terms of Australian Land Rights legislation, in which case the Dreaming tends to be conflated with past time and firstness in order to confirm prior ownership and belonging.

Because variations *within* a population or person are as great as variations *between* populations or persons, one cannot define either cultures or individuals in terms of a single prevailing modality of time consciousness despite the allure of such anthropological binaries as hot/cold, stationary/cumulative, and cyclical/linear.

In West Africa, divinatory and musical talents often come to a person in the course of a feverish episode of illness, usually during childhood. The jinn that enter a person's life in this manner can be summoned at any time thenceforth and bestow oracular power. But when a diviner explains how he acquired his skills, he may refer *back* to such childhood events while acknowledging that the jinn are timeless beings and that during a divinatory séance the distinction between what happened in the past and what is occurring now is experientially annulled. The same is true of ancestors. Summoned in a sacrifice or appearing in a dream, an ancestor is nominally and palpably present; at other times, the same ancestor is out of sight and out of mind. In other words, consciousness oscillates between quite

different ways of apprehending one's being-in-time, and it would be fool-
ish to reduce temporality in any one society or any one person to a single
static mode of experience. Rather, we need to speak of polyontologies, of
multiple regimes of historicity, across and within cultures as well as within
the consciousness of a single person. As easily as he'd slip from acoustic to
electric guitar, or guitar to harmonica, Bob Dylan would move from realist to surrealist imagery. So it was with time, in one song singing that his
name "it is nothing, my age it means less," yet invoking history as exact
testimony ("Oh the history books tell it / they tell it so well / the cavalries
charged / the Indians fell"), only to declare, "I was so much older then, I'm
younger than that now"—which seems logically impossible yet phenomenologically makes perfect sense, at least to me.

Consider the place of dreams and dreaming in traditional Africa. During my fieldwork in northern Sierra Leone, villagers would sometimes
recount vivid dreams in which a deceased family member appeared to
them. This was not construed as *remembering*, or dismissed as a figment of
the *imagination*, but taken as *evidence* of the existence of the dream figure
elsewhere in present time. My friend Sewa Koroma explained this phenomenon of *fo' koe* (lit. "dead thing" or the "action of the dead"), as follows:
"The dead are always there, they see everything, they know exactly what is
happening. The dead are your *sabu* ('cause')." Sewa prays to his ancestors
(*bimba forenu*) every morning, asking them to "beg God" to open a path
so he will be blessed, before greeting his late father. "My dad is still alive,"
Sewa explained to me. "It's just that I am not seeing him. I only see him in
my dreams, like once a month or every two or three months I see him in a
dream, but I know he's around me. I have a picture of him in my room.
There's one thing he never wants any of his kids to do, and that is drink
alcohol. When I go out and drink alcohol, as soon as I come home and step
into my room and see that picture, I have to run out of the room again. I
want to go and take the picture and put it away, like in my cupboard or
box, but I know I have alcohol in my system so I cannot touch the picture.
I have to wait for days, days, to take that picture and put it somewhere, so
I can walk into my room and not see it straightaway. I know it's just a
picture, but it's like it's him seeing me, what I'm doing, you know. You see,
I've got all these beliefs. And when I stop drinking, pray to him, ask him for
forgiveness, I know that's the only thing I'm doing that my dad's unhappy
about."

It is not that Sewa's "belief" eclipses his knowledge of his father's death or lessens the grief he feels over his father's passing. Rather, the conviction that his *relationship* with his father remains vital to him (*ni le wola*) bolsters his spirits in a foreign environment where he is often racked with guilt at having left his natal village, abandoned his birthright, and sought a new life in England. While it may be logically fallacious to infer that the force of an experience proves the existence of what is experienced, Sewa's insistence that his father is "still alive," like Christians who speak of God as a living presence in their lives, are choosing beliefs not on the basis of their rationality but on the basis of what the beliefs make possible in their lives—a sense of community or solidarity with others, a sense of confidence in themselves, and a sense of connectedness that survives death and separation.

Time may not be unreal, as John McTaggart famously declared, but it is so various that it is impossible to unequivocally define it. At any given moment one cannot be sure whether one is blindly recapitulating a world one had no hand in making or actually creating a world one can call one's own. Our lives waver continually between these two extremes, sometimes moved by fates and furies we can neither comprehend nor control, sometimes appearing to be within our power to determine.

Ethnography offers one of the most edifying ways in which one can stretch the limits of being born, raised, and educated in one culture, just as history can potentially transport one to another time. However, as Johannes Fabian points out, both history and anthropology have invoked *time past* as a stratagem for denying coevalness to our prehistorical forebears and our distant contemporaries alike. Insofar as *their* time and *our* time are allegedly not one, their humanity and ours are essentially different. Yet ethnography holds out the possibility of seeing through this illusion of essential difference and identifying what is common to all humans despite appearances to the contrary.

Whether fieldwork is carried out in a remote African village or close to home, through face-to-face encounters or archival research, through history or through autobiography, and whether one writes fiction or nonfiction, for academic consumption or the common reader, the promise is not only that we will know ourselves as if for the first time *through the other* but that we will have, in the process, made it more possible to live *with one another* in the same world.

The present work is at once ethnographic and biographical. Its focus is on life in a minor key—the small things, contingent events, everyday habits, and mood shifts that sustain a sense of life endured rather than comprehended, lived rather than rendered explicable. My writing is realist in Saul Bellow's sense of the word ("Realism specializes in *apparently* unmediated experiences"). Bellow also speaks of realist writing as "victim literature" since it tends to depict people struggling against natural or social forces that they cannot fully explain or control.

Both "The Blind Impress" and "The Enigma of Anteriority" explore this Homeric theme, particularly as it finds expression in the fragment of Anaximander where it is suggested that things "suffer punishment and give satisfaction to one another for injustice according to the order of time." Herodotus shared the view that "history was essentially the interval, calculated in generations, between an injustice and its punishment or redress," and this notion is echoed in Walter Benjamin's messianic theory of history, with its emphasis on the infinite possibilities for redeeming the past in *the here and now*. The focus of "The Blind Impress" is the criminal career of John Joseph Pawelka, a self-styled "man against the world," whose name, in the annals of New Zealand crime, became practically synonymous with anarchy. The Pawelka manhunt was the most sensational news story of 1910, and the mystery of his escape from prison and subsequent disappearance has never been solved. In recounting the story of this disaffected son of Moravian migrants, I draw on historical and ethnographic research to describe Joe Pawelka's background, the radically different stories occasioned by his life, and the long-term repercussions of his criminal career for his family, both past and present. An autobiographical thread also runs through this book as I reflect on the relationship between Joe Pawelka's times and my own, his life and mine. While noting precise dates and times for events that occurred over one hundred years ago, I am most intrigued by the presentness of Pawelka's story—its relevance for understanding contemporary struggles to overcome stigma and marginalization and for what it reveals about the interplay of demotic stories, hidden histories, and media narratives in constructing allegories of national and moral identity.

"The Enigma of Anteriority" comprises a set of reflections on journeys up and down the two main islands of my natal New Zealand in 2008–2009. Revisiting old haunts and talking with old friends, I was inspired to ponder the hold our histories have over us and the limits of our freedom to renegotiate our relationship to the past. Blending ethnography, history, philosophy, and literature, "The Enigma of Anteriority" touches on the ways that personal stories are interwoven with social and historical events and shows how the ambiguity of our origins pertains equally to indigenous Maori invocations of *toi whenua* in making claims for recognition and social justice; the search by adopted children for their birth parents; the notion of childhood as "the formative years"; our current preoccupation with genealogical, geographical or genetic backgrounds; and the allure of myths and models of cause and effect.

Both these narratives pay homage to Svetlana Boym's argument against seeing exile and expatriation as all-or-nothing phenomena. Like the knight in a game of chess, we simultaneously move one square forward and one square off to the side. Despite the fact that we can only be physically present in one place at any one time, our consciousness is not so confined. Our minds wander constantly, and our dreams return us nightly to places we have left and people we once knew, so that we continue our lives in parallel to theirs even as we hive off in search of new horizons. We experience nostalgia for the past and the future. These stories, then, are testimonies to the "off-modern condition," its hidden histories, its oblique continuities, its multiple lives and multiples selves. As such, place and time become as arbitrary as the person who once thought of himself or herself as being indivisibly one.

The Blind Impress

And once you have walked the length of your mind, what
You command is clear as a lading-list.
Anything else must not, for you, be thought
      To exist.

And what's the profit? Only that, in time,
We half-identify the blind impress
All our behavings bear, may trace it home.
      But to confess,

On that green evening when our death begins,
Just what it was, is hardly satisfying,
Since it applied only to one man once,
      And that one dying.

—PHILIP LARKIN, FROM "CONTINUING TO LIVE"

Part One

Prologue

One sometimes happens on a scholarly essay that transcends the discursive conventions of the academy and leaves one stunned and moved. Such was the impact on me of reading Thomas Schwarz Wentzer's "I Have Seen Königsberg Burning," in which the author describes events that occurred before he was born as if he had experienced and suffered them at first hand. How is it, Wentzer asks, that someone else's story becomes in effect one's own? And to whom can we assign the authorship of such a story when it appears to possess an independent life, inherited and reinterpreted within a family generation after generation?

As the Red Army advances across East Prussia in December 1944, a German mother and her youngest children flee their farm near the Memel River, hoping to reach a Baltic port and possible evacuation to Scandinavia. The second youngest of these children, born in 1938, will outlive the war, marry, and become the father of Thomas Schwarz Wentzer. But in the unbearably cold winter of 1944–1945, living on soup made of potato peelings and passing the cairns of children who have died on the road, the family is unsure whether it will survive hunger, frostbite from temperatures that fall to minus 25 degrees Celsius, and the strafing attacks on their refugee column. Not long after crossing the frozen Vistula Lagoon, the front line cuts off their escape route and the family has to retreat.

Thirty kilometers to the north lay Königsberg, the historic capital of East Prussia. Four months ago the city was reduced to burning rubble by phosphorus bombs dropped from Allied bombers. Firestorms raged for three days, leaving 200,000 of the city's 320,00 inhabitants homeless. When the Red Army occupied Königsberg in April 1945, the 100,000 Germans who had not already fled were systematically expelled, and to this day the descendants of these refugees return to their ancestral city as tourists, nostalgic for a world that ended before many of them were even born.

Similarly indelible traces of a former life seem to have haunted Thomas's father, who often told his son that he had seen Königsberg burning. As a child, Thomas took this declaration on trust, trying to imagine the city as it once was. As a student of philosophy, he associated Königsberg with Kant and began to see the fire-bombed city as a symbol of the collapse of European Enlightenment, the annihilation of the dignity of man, the destruction of the Good and of the moral integrity of everything connected to German culture.

Ironically, Thomas's father never actually saw Königsberg burning. He probably appropriated his older sister's traumatic memories from the time she worked as a nurse in the city. Having escaped the one-thousand-degree firestorms that blew through the streets at over one hundred miles an hour—melting glass, boiling asphalt, and incinerating hundreds of thousands of human beings—Liesbeth fled east in the hope of being reunited with her family. Just as her direct experience of Königsberg in flames would be absorbed by her younger brother, his false memories were in turn taken up by his son. Finally, the same historical event was subject to so many biographical reworkings that no one could claim to know the truth of the event or to be the author of the story it occasioned. Each person made the event his or her own. Yet even when Thomas comes to doubt the veracity of his father's claim to have seen Königsberg burning, he does not doubt this reiterated phrase held such a profound meaning for his father that he has a filial obligation to ponder the meaning, however unfathomable it may be. Though not at liberty to discount his father's claim; he must respond to it, just as he feels obliged to respond to the horrific history of his homeland. Thomas quotes Walter Benjamin to convey this thought. "The past carries a secret index with it, by which it is referred to its redemption. Are we not touched by the same breath of air that was among those who came before us? Is there not an echo of those who have been silenced in the voices to which we lend our ears today? Have not the women, who we court, sisters who they do not recognize anymore? If so, then there is a secret appointment between the generations of the past and that of our own. For we have been expected upon this earth. For it has been given us to know, just like every generation before us, a weak messianic power, on which the past has a claim."

Thomas wrote his remarkable essay in response to a past that, in the form of his father's compelling testimony, made a claim on the son, and it is possible that the son was brought into the world in order for this claim to be redeemed.

Thomas's essay left such a profound impression on me that I felt that I now inherited it and had to find an adequate response to it. Something more was required of me than simply writing to the author and telling him how moved I had been by his essay. This more considered response involved a lot of thought, some of it disciplined, some idle. Initially, my mind went back to 1945, the year I began school in a small New Zealand town. At the very moment that Thomas's grandmother Selma and her four children were trudging across the snowbound wastes of East Prussia with tens of thousands of other displaced persons, starving, chilled to the bone, stigmatized by their ethnicity, their belongings in mud-soiled bundles or shabby suitcases, I was blissfully ignorant of the war, though some of my earliest memories were of my two uncles returning home on leave, the texture of their serge uniforms merging with the smell of the laurel hedge near my grandparent's front gate. Despite these gaps and contrasts, sixty years later one of Selma's grandsons, now a teacher of philosophy in a Danish university, and I, an anthropologist and writer living in the United States, would become close friends. This was not, however, the story I came to tell. I needed to find another way of treating the entangled relationship of biography and history. Thomas speaks of this relationship as something "I cannot escape from, being the person that I am, born in the mid-sixties of the last century, a German of all nationalities, coincidentally having been educated as a philosopher, having to deal with the facticity of the contingent necessities of my peculiar situation that are both so unique and yet so common to people like me."

Even if no chronicle of the past remains, and tyrants like Qin Shi Huang or Adolf Hitler burn the books that keep our memories of the past alive, the past persists, smoldering for years only to spontaneously combust one day in a moment of violence. Even if our unhealed scars are not mentioned and our history suppressed, the tradition of the dead generations continues to weigh like a nightmare on the minds of the living, affecting a parent's mood or the inflection of a voice, explaining a minor mannerism, an addictive tendency, a fatal flaw. Does a story one day *have* to be told—to shed light on this insidious field of shadow, this haunted landscape, those lost Edens? And can this story redeem what has been done or lift the curse that has been transmitted in silence across the generations?

"The Blind Impress" was born of these questions, and invites reflection on the complicated ways that history impresses itself upon us so that our individual lives are grafts of the lives of others whose sacrifices place us in their debt, whose errors we are blamed for, whose wounds we bind up and try to heal, whose questions we attempt to answer, and whose deferred dreams we feel called upon to realize on their behalf.

That Green Evening

He is sitting outside his garden shed. A panama hat shades his face. Hoes and rakes are propped against the wall; seed potatoes are spread out on superphosphate sacks. He lights his pipe and tosses the match away.

I was three when my grandfather retired from the police. He began telling me stories before I even understood what stories were.

"My, the living" (Yorkshire accent, rueful shake of the head), "to look at him you wouldn't think he could make anything but a nuisance of himself."

He pauses. Holds his pipe away from his face. Wipes a film of spittle from his lips with the back of his hand. The cabbage patch is spattered with white butterflies.

"Aye, there was only one thing 'e could do, could that lad, and that was make a public nuisance of himself."

My grandfather seems to brood for a moment on the failings and foibles of men, and I can smell blood and bone and hear the river stumbling through the bush.

In the years my grandfather is remembering, Saturday was late-night shopping. Farmers drove in from the boondock and stood along the footpath, backs to the street, smoking cigarettes and complaining about the falling price of wool. Wives went shopping. A lot of town boys resented the young farmers. Would get drunk and pick fights. One bloke in particular was an inveterate troublemaker. My grandfather was "forever being called out to deal with him." But telling this story, my grandfather doesn't mention the misdemeanor. It's the young man's pride that is at stake, not his guilt. When my grandfather arrests him outside the post office, he avoids taking him directly to the police station because this will mean going along the thronged main street. Instead, he takes an alleyway into a back street so the miscreant will not be seen and shamed.

In 1960, when my grandfather died, I went back to Inglewood for the funeral. After a Methodist service, the cortege set off for the cemetery. As our car turned behind the hearse toward the cemetery gates, I noticed a group of old men standing on the opposite side of the road, heads bowed, hats in their hands. One was the man whose public humiliation my grandfather had averted fifty years ago.

My uncles inherited my grandfather's fob watch, watch chain, and police baton. My legacy has been my grandfather's stories.

One story in particular he returned to time and time again. It was also a story about youth, and loss, and guilt and shame.

In 1910 a young man called Joe Pawelka was arrested in the Manawatu and remanded on charges of housebreaking, arson, and theft. His escape from police custody triggered the most intense manhunt in New Zealand since the military pursuit in the late 1860s of the Māori resistance leader Te Kooti. During the weeks that Pawelka was on the run, two men were shot dead, buildings were set on fire, shops and homes burgled, and panic engulfed a province. My grandfather was stationed in Levin at the time and was among police reinforcements brought to the Manawatu for the manhunt. Like many New Zealanders, he would remember "The Powelka Campaign" as the biggest news story of the year, with banner headlines fueling the general "hysteria" and "pandemonium." "Mad Orgy of Manslaying," *Truth* declared. "Wild Rumour and False Alarm."

Recaptured and brought to trial, Joe Pawelka got twenty-one years' hard labor for breaking and entering, theft, arson, and escape. Many people, including my grandfather, thought the sentence vengeful and unjust, and on the wintry August day in 1911 when Pawelka escaped from the Terrace

Gaol in Wellington, never to be heard of again, my grandfather was happy to conclude that poetic justice had been done.

Stories have a habit of generating stories. They come to nest, one inside the other, like Chinese boxes, each a window onto another's world. This is what happened to my grandfather's story about Joe Pawelka.

In 1973, after several years abroad, I came back to New Zealand with my wife and daughter and went to live in the Manawatu. Some of the places where Joe Pawelka had lived, worked, and taken refuge became as familiar to me as they had been for him, and three years later, when I published my first book of poems, *Latitudes of Exile*, I alluded to some of the connections that were beginning to take hold in my imagination.

This poem has been written before;
it has been written by men and women
who never read a line of poetry all their lives;
it has been said and imagined many times;
it is the poem of the labyrinth,
of the other way, of forgotten roads
and of the wheel of chance
and today, traveling the Pahiatua Track
to Scarborough, I think of Joe Pawelka
and what went wrong for him,
my grandfather's story of a hunted man
who vanished from the cells
in which he was condemned
for burning down a school,
housebreaking and escape,
for bothering his wife when a magistrate
ordered their separation,
who scrawled a note with the lead of a bullet
and signed it "a man against the world."

Like my grandfather, I always wanted to know what went wrong for Joe Pawelka and what became of him. This is not simply a question of what happened after he escaped and disappeared. More compellingly, it is a matter of the transformations his persona and story have undergone, of the way they have entered the diffuse and dimly lit world of our collective

imagination, blurring with countless other stories, pub yarns, and anecdotes until they resemble a kind of national self-portrait on which we work
tirelessly, unselfconsciously, and without much sense of the finished
picture.

This is why my search for Joe Pawelka came to encompass many lives,
including my own, and why his story is also a story about stories: an alle-
gory of events that outstrip his particular life, bridging the known and the
imagined, negotiating that open ground where the shadows of the past
define the fugitive shape of our future.

The Blind Impress

My plane came into Wellington over the strait, buffeted by high winds. I
peered out at raw-boned hills, the sea like saliva, black rocks strewn with
driftwood.

Driving in to the city, I remembered how empty my homeland could be.
So little outward sign of neighborhood. Colin McCahon's "landscape with
too few lovers." Was it Robert Morley who said he once visited New Zealand but it was closed?

Next morning the wind was coming off the sea, and the sky bruised.
Between rain squalls, a marine light flooded the glass facades of the downtown office buildings. Over breakfast in an espresso bar, I read the morning
paper. The first black vote in the South African elections had been cast in
Wellington, where Nomoza Paintin—an imposter, it later turned out—
lived in political exile. She called the moment euphoric. "I felt in the presence of my ancestors today," she said. "I felt I was voting for them."

I remembered the cold, rainswept streets where we marched in 1981,
chanting the ANC slogan *Amandla Ngawethu* against the Springbok Tour.
And as I made my way downtown to the National Library, my thoughts
went back to the street clashes, the cries of "Shame," the divided families
and troubled friendships that had brought so many New Zealanders to the
realization that violence was closer to home than they'd ever imagined. For
all our pacific imagery, egalitarian myths, and talk of racial tolerance, our
country had suddenly revealed itself to be a place of unhealed wounds and
growing inequality. In the ashen landscapes of the central North Island,
long dormant volcanoes were erupting. But the violence was also in our

houses and our hearts. We saw it in the faces of abused children and battered wives. We nurtured it in the anxious hope that our children would see no evil, hear no evil, speak no evil, and feel no evil. And we fostered it in the poverty and powerlessness that drove many down the road of violence as the only road that would give them room to maneuver and confirm their worth.

Was New Zealand an accident waiting to happen? Had we kept ourselves too long in the dark about the passions and quandaries that governed us? In coming to terms with our hidden history, could we make peace with ourselves?

At the National Library, photocopying pages of the Wellington and Manawatu newspapers that carried the Pawelka story in 1910, I had no idea whether my journey back in time would provide any answers to these questions. But I held out the hope that by returning to one place where the questions had been raised I might better understand the long shadows they had cast in our lives.

* * *

Joe Pawelka's grandfather, Ferdinand Pavelka, migrated to New Zealand in 1873. He'd been a glazier in Stramberk, Moravia—a crownland east of Bohemia in the Austro-Hungarian Empire. A year after reaching New Zealand, Ferdinand sent for his wife, Rosina, and their five children. Rosina, then forty-three, would forever remember dipping her fingers in the Danube on the day they left.

The Pavelkas settled near Oxford, North Canterbury, where there was work building roads and felling and milling timber. In 1885, Ferdinand's second son, Jozef (soon anglicized to Joseph), married Louise (anglicized to Louisa) König, who had coincidentally come out from Moravia with her family on the *Stonehouse*—the same ship that brought Jozef's family to New Zealand.

Joseph's mother Rosina disapproved of Louisa and tried to prevent the marriage. In this close-knit Catholic family, the matriarch had the right to decree who belonged and who did not. Respect for her authority was practically synonymous with respect for God; she was the family's fountainhead of power and its moral arbiter. It was a grave matter for a son to go against his mother's wishes, and when Joseph married Louisa without his mother's blessing, the fiftyseven-year-old matriarch construed it, in part, as a violation of their faith. When Louisa's first child, Mary Rosina, died two months after she was born, Rosina declared the death to be a divine judgment on the ill-advised marriage.

John Joseph Thomas (Joe) Pawelka began life in the shadow of this loss. One wonders what passed through Rosina's mind when he was born on the first of August 1887, sixteen months after Mary Rosina's death. Did she consider him doomed as well? And when Joe's life took its tragic turn, did she conclude that he, who showed no more regard for God than his father had, was also divinely cursed?

In 1891, when Joe was four and his sister Agnes two, the family left North Canterbury and followed Joe's maverick Uncle John to the North Island where he had opened a butcher's shop in a bush settlement called Kimbolton. The break cannot have been easy. Among the Moravian migrants, kinship was the wellspring of a person's security and identity. It was also one's tie to the past. In choosing autonomy over these blood ties, Joseph was repudiating his mother's Old World domination and nostalgia, breaking away from the suffocating insularity of the immigrant community, and distancing himself from the Moravian church to which he had, in any event, never been devoutly attached. By marrying Louisa when he was twenty-four, he had begun an irrevocable process of estrangement from Rosina. Now aged thirty-one, he marked the finality of the separation by changing the spelling of his name from Pavelka to Pawelka.

Kimbolton stands on a windblown ridge above the Oroua River. When the Pawelkas traveled up the newly metaled road from Feilding in 1891, they would have looked out over a devastated landscape of surveyors' tracks, dead trees, splintered logs, stumps, slab whares and scorched earth. A country stunned into silence. No motors. Few forest birds. A dog barking in the distance. The bellowing of a bull.

Ranged along one side of Kimbolton's main street were a hotel, two stores, a post office, blacksmith's shop, library, public hall, stockyard, and school. Opposite was a wasteland of stumps and scrub.

The land, at £1 an acre, was being broken in. Intractable forests of totara, hinau, and rimu were felled and fired. Grass was sown among the ruins. Fences defined properties. Roads enclosed blocks.

But the broken land played havoc with those who claimed it. The Oroua shingled up and flooded with run-off from autumn rains. In winter, bush

tracks became quagmires, impassable even to bullock teams and horses. In summer, smoke from bush fires blotted out the sun, and dry winds stripped the topsoil from tenuous farms. In January 1898, one fire, fanned by gale-force winds from the west, razed a dozen Kimbolton homes and several shops before sweeping down into the Oroua valley and the ranges beyond. The acrid smoke blinded people for days. What impression this left in the mind of eleven-year-old Joe Pawelka one can only guess.

It is also hard to know exactly how immigrants from central Europe fared in this predominantly Anglo settlement. The Pawelkas' North Canterbury life had been governed by bonds of kinship and their Catholic faith. In Kimbolton, a Wesleyan church was built in 1891 (the year the Pawelkas arrived), but until 1912 there was no Catholic church, and a priest had to travel up from Feilding to say mass in Catholic homes. One old-timer, who had lived in Kimbolton since 1911, told me that the Catholic-Protestant division surfaced only on Sundays and during life crises: "The thing that used to amaze me was that people could go out and work together from Monday to Saturday night, but at midnight on Saturday the bloody blinds came down. And the same thing applied in the blimmin' cemetery. The Catholic part of the cemetery, the Protestant part of the cemetery, somebody else's part of the cemetery." Another younger informant, whose uncle was Protestant, remembered being told that Joe Pawelka's evasion of the law during the manhunt was "a Catholic conspiracy."

Most Kimbolton shops were owned by English, Irish, or Scottish settlers. Already ingrained was the New Zealand habit of joining clubs and forming committees as a way of defeating loneliness and creating some sense of social solidarity. But those who belonged to the cricket club, tennis club, football club, farmers' club, rifle club, and debating society, or were members of the school committee, coronation committee, concert party, and flag committee, were seldom foreign or Māori. The very names of the settlement—Birmingham first, then Kimbolton—memorialized connections with England. In 1897 Queen Victoria's Diamond Jubilee was celebrated enthusiastically, and local men enlisted to fight for Queen and Empire in the Boer War, convinced that the future of their colony was inextricably tied up with the motherland.

Joseph Pawelka worked as a gravedigger and casual laborer. In those years, grass harvesting was a major export industry. Every summer, cocksfoot, fescue, blue grass, and rye seed was harvested from the newly cleared land. Gangs of men with sickles moved across the stumpy paddocks, gathering sheaves and shocking them to dry. They threshed the grass with wooden flails on canvas sheets and lifted the canvas into the wind to winnow the chaff from the grain.

When Joe Pawelka left school in 1900 at age thirteen, he worked for a while with his father collecting seed, and then, at his mother's urging, apprenticed himself to his Uncle John. But John Pawelka had left Kimbolton by this time, and if Joe did learn butchery from his uncle, it must have been elsewhere.

At the height of the manhunt in 1910, a *New Zealand Times* reporter went up to Kimbolton to interview people about the fugitive. "Everybody I spoke to in Kimbolton seemed heartily sorry for Powelka," the reporter wrote, "and all with whom he had dealings say that Powelka was a thoroughly upright fellow who could be trusted with anything."

The reporter learned that Joe had attended the local school and been considered "a very smart boy" by his master, though he quit after Standard 7. References were also made to Joe's "very passionate" nature: "Even when a very small boy, his morose moods were a subject of comment."

In due course there would be talk, not of mood swings or a "bad temper," but of a "lunatic" with a "deranged mind," given to "mad fits." Are passion and insanity always too close for comfort? Can the good citizen only construe disregard for the law as evidence of some psychological aberration? If something goes wrong in a person's life, must we always look for some pathology in early childhood?

One story has it that Joe didn't get on with his father—that his father had a quick temper, too. "Old Joe, he had a terrific temper. It was passed on to young Joe. Joe got it from his father. Old Joe used to beat all the kids except the youngest, Helen. Agnes got plenty of hidings as a kid. Belted around the bum. And he was pretty nasty toward his wife at times. Though he was never aggressive in public."

According to this account, the ill feeling between father and son was "the reason Joe cleared out." Joseph may have been jealous of the intense bond between Louise and Joe, and one is tempted to see Joe as someone too much indulged by his mother, so that he grows intolerant of being crossed, harbors some smoldering resentment when he is forced out into the world at thirteen to fend for himself.

Here is a photo of Joe with his sister Agnes and brother Jack in 1903. They are outdoors, probably in the garden behind their house in Edwards Street. A table has been laid for tea in the shelter of a laurel hedge. There is an embroidered tablecloth. The china tea set is one the family brought out from Moravia. There is a vase of arum lilies under the table, and trampled grass. The scene has been carefully set: Agnes, wearing a bonnet, holding the teapot, ready to pour; Jack standing on one side of her; Joe sitting on a folding verandah chair on the other. Joe is wearing a serge jacket,

PLATE 1. ANNE HARRIS

waistcoat, and knickerbockers. His legs are crossed; he is balancing a cup and saucer on his knee.

What can one read in the face of this sixteen-year-old? He has tilted the straw boater back on his head. His mouth is set. His gaze seems uneasy, almost shifty. He has been toughened by hard work. He is someone who will not take kindly to being told what to do. Someone with a short fuse. Who will buck authority.

When I look at this photo, James K. Baxter's line about his childhood comes to mind—"the sense of having been pounded all over with a club by invisible adversaries"—and I have to caution myself not to see things in it that are not there, although sometimes the blankness and muteness of the past beg to be redeemed in the imagination of the living. As when, fifty-five years after the event, someone remembers "this awful mouth, vile mouth he had, cruel as though he'd fire at you as quick as look at you, you know he had that type, a bad look" . . . so claiming, as we all readily do, wisdom with hindsight.

* * *

In the winter of 1905, Joe Pawelka is working for a butcher in Dannevirke on the eastern side of the Ruahine range. He writes home to his mother:

My Dear Mother,

I suppose you are wondering where in the world I have got here in a place a little smaller than Palmerston. Since I came here I have got a job butchering in the town and intend to stick to it if I dont have a row with the boss This place is not so bad to live in and since I have been here I have met Cruden and his missus the Richardsons and the Gensons who are all living here. Cruden is as big a skiter as ever he was his Mrs has grown like her mother about as broad as she is long Well Mother how have you been getting on I hope you are quite happy and well and am not working too hard I suppose the kid gives you enough bother though Oh Mother what about the Photo you promised me I should like to have a separate one of the lot of you Agnes Jack and yourself Tell Agnes to get her Photo taken as soon as she can and you too mother for I often wish for a separate Photo of you all so try and satisfy my wish if you can I hope you got that Photo of mine all right I have been wondering weather it went astray or not Dear Mother I wonder whether you have been why I asked for my school certificate in such a hurry for the truth is I had a chance of obtaining a government billet as Guard on the Railway train at Masterton, but I would not take the billet on account of the wages too small If I had been 21 years of age I would have received 8 shillings a day to start but being young they would not give enough to suit me and so I threw it up I have been travelling about aimlessly ever since and as you see luck brought me here and I struck work at my own trade Dear Mother you always complained about Kimbolton being a cold place but I believe this is worse here I do not know if it is always like this but the weather is something terrible since I have been here I have seen three snow falls all ready. I suppose Kimbolton is nearly

as bad now too I am glad I am not in that miserable hole I wonder when I shall see
it again How is young Jack getting on I expect he is getting quite a big lump of a
fellow by this time and the baby too you havent told me its name yet Mother I feel
quite proud to have a little sister like that Have you got a Go Cart for her yet If not
write and let me know How are all the people getting on around you now I expect
~~you wou~~ if I were to go back I should find nearly all strangers in the town and all the
young fellows married by what I have heard on occasions The fools are mad and
dont know what they are doing never mind we have all got to go through the mill
once they find women out as well as I have they wont trouble their heads about them
How is Agnes getting on with the tailoring it is a good thing for her to learn some-
thing in that line it is far easier than going out to service Well Mother it is getting
dark and I cant very well see to write I would like to tell you a little more but I cant
see so I think I shall close this little letter I hope to hear from you as soon as possi-
ble so write immediately and let it be a long letter with any amount of news in it
Good by Dear Mother my best love to you and Agnes and Jack

> *from Your loving Son*
> *J Pawelka*

Written five weeks before his eighteenth birthday, the letter is from a solitary young man with little joy in his life. It is the one window we have on his world at this age. With the exception of his family, his hometown holds no redeeming memories for him. His father does not figure in his affections. His unhappiness has embittered him, making him cynical and judgmental. He has a habit of getting into arguments with employers and changes jobs often. And he has been wounded in love. The world is a dark, inhospitable place.

The Other Side of the Tracks

Henry James observed that for any writer "there is the story of one's hero, and then, thanks to the intimate connection of things, the story of one's story itself."

As I began to piece together the mosaic of Joe Pawelka's early life my thoughts went back to the small Taranaki town where I was raised. It was no more a "miserable hole" than Joe's Kimbolton, or any small town anywhere. There are thousands of Inglewoods in the world, and there is no reason to slight them. They contain as many happy and unhappy families as any city. Still, they're the kinds of places you don't want to get stuck in. And if you're young, and have known no other life, you have to get away. To find yourself. To come into your own.

There was another reason why my hometown became implicated in my attempt to understand Joe Pawelka's beginnings. Inglewood was built on Ngati-Maru land confiscated by the government in 1863 to punish the insurgent Taranaki tribes, defray the costs of the military campaign against the Te Āti Awa chief Wiremu Kingi, and provide land for settlers. Through one of those tragic ironies of which history is replete, at the very moment that the Ngati-Maru lands on the Upper Waitara River and its tributaries were being alienated, ethnic Poles in Northern Germany were being subject to draconian assimilation laws. Under the Prussian administration, Polish towns, streets, and family names were to be Germanized. The Polish language was banned in schools, land was seized, military conscription enforced. Resistance meant certain unemployment and the loss of one's civil rights. Together with others, already landless and exploited, the Poles chose to immigrate. Thus the dispossessed in one hemisphere unwittingly became dispossessors in another. When Inglewood first appeared on the map in the 1870s, its inhabitants numbered as many Polish as English families. The Poles were Catholic; the English were Protestant.

I grew up in a state house in the still largely Polish part of town. Our neighbors had names like Fabish, Dodunski, Bielski, Schimanski, and Kuklinski. And jokes were told about the curious mix of Polish and Anglo names: Drinkwater, Haverbier, Schicker, Biesiek.

Of course, the joking wasn't altogether innocent.

"Catholic wogs, stink like dogs."

The gibes of kids echoed the voice of age-old bigotry and intolerance, and from an early age I remember feeling that there was something amiss in the fact that the kids with Polish names were poor and attended the Catholic school, while most of my classmates were Protestant and Anglo. It was like that other division, hinted at but seldom spoken of, between Pākehā and Māori. In the whitebait season, black-clad *kuia* came up from Waitara with flax kits bulging with whitebait. They had *moko* on their chins and smoked pipes. They sat, shawls drawn around their shoulders, on benches outside the post office or on the curbstones. At night they vanished. But you never heard talk of confiscated land; only of some so-called superstition that made Māori afraid of Inglewood because it lay on the route Mount Taranaki would take when it returned from exile and rejoined the other mountains in the middle of the island.

* * *

I hadn't been back to Inglewood for many years. But in Wellington, racking my brains for anything that might help me understand Joe Pawelka, I found myself recalling my last trip home.

It would be wrong to say this trip was a pilgrimage. Yet, if the truth be told, who does not return to the neighborhoods and landscapes of childhood without a sense of nostalgia that deepens into a sense of loss?

Most of my old friends had moved on. The house in which I grew up had fallen into disrepair. And the town's familiar landmarks—the band rotunda, cenotaph, railway station, municipal library, and offices—were surrounded by new buildings and looked anomalous. As for the streets, they were as empty as ever, and it was only by reminding myself how our lives unfold and fall apart behind closed doors that I could believe that this place had the highest rate of violent crime in the nation.

It was early afternoon when I went into the Railway Hotel and ordered a beer. The barman was nobody known to me, so I took my drink to a corner table where the sun filtered through the painted DB sign on the windowpane like the amber light of cathedral glass.

I did not expect to run into anyone I knew, and was scribbling in my journal when Eddie Potroz came up behind me and clamped a heavy hand on my shoulder.

I recognized Eddie at once. The birthmark like a blackberry stain across one side of his face. His self-abnegating manner.

At first, our conversation was forced. As though we were sparring. Parrying blows.

"What are you doing now?"

"Keepin' outta trouble. How about you?"

"Getting around."

"I haven't seen you since, when was it?"

"It must have been our school reunion?"

"Yeah, that was it!"

We drank away the afternoon and shot some pool. We remembered how we used to play marbles together along the dirt footpath of Kelly Street or at school, incising a circle in the clay, the outline of an eye, and beating the other kids hands down. We used to swap glass mandalas and tors. And we always walked home from school together along the Manutahi Stream so we could wash and appraise our hoard in the icy water.

Eddie lived with his mother in a cottage behind a huge lawsoniana hedge. A passage ran through the house from front door to back. The floorboards sagged on rotting piles. There had been torn linoleum in the kitchen and sugar bags for doormats. But it was my second home, where I read the Superman and Captain Marvel comics my parents banned.

As we reminisced, we talked of our need for heroes. While other boys sought glory on the rugby field, our triumphs lay in larceny and subterfuge. On Prize Days, as some dignitary droned on about the virtues of team spirit and patriotism, we hatched subversive schemes to raid the tennis club for soft drinks and biscuits or climb the huge rhododendron tree in the middle of town and eavesdrop on the old codgers who spent their twilight years in its shade. Our friendship was forged in the shared if mistaken belief that we were misfits, and that nothing we could do would ever gain acceptance or win approval.

We were addicted to the movies. Hollywood licensed our sense of difference. We took our personae from the electric shadows as well as our names: Tom Mix. Flash Gordon. From B-grade films we learned how to smoke, fight, drink martinis with a sophisticated sneer, and wear a raincoat even when it wasn't raining. We never got the message that crime does not pay.

Eddie quit school when he was fifteen and went to New Plymouth. Though we were of an age, the fact that I was still in short pants and school uniform and he was riding a motorbike and flashing money around ended our intimacy.

But meeting again after so many years, the gap closed. Eddie told me how he'd got into trouble, converting cars, joyriding, "that sort of thing. Didn't harm no one." But he got caught and did time. He didn't like to talk about it much. It was like it had happened to someone else. Anyway, he had paid his dues. Now he was married, with two kids. That was all that mattered.

Looking back, I think our need for heroism was driven by a deeper need to dignify our sense of being different. We had to mythologize our marginality. We were duffers at school. We were no good at sports. We were, or thought we were, pariahs. It was the old story of not feeling accepted and not wanting to risk further hurt by seeking acceptance. In fact, you go out of your way to avoid the humiliation of being knocked back. So you withdraw. Or form an alliance with someone who feels as you do. For a while you gain a sense of spurious dignity in defiance, in going against the grain, in brooding on your sense of otherness. But it's a lost cause. You paint yourself into a corner and become more and more vulnerable as you secretly dream of acceptance by beating the others at their own game.

Perhaps this is why, even now, I have recurring dreams of our school cricket field on a summer afternoon, and see myself running in to bowl or feel my sinews strain as I crack the leather ball through the covers for a six. But, as with Eddie Potroz, there's little consolation in the memory of one's misdemeanors, and I have to go back to a winter morning when I was eight to focus on the one high point of all my school days.

Since ours was a small country school, almost everyone played together at recess. Usually Bedlam or Running Through.

Running Through began with a kid standing in the middle of the playground and trying to tackle someone as the whole school rushed from one side to the other. If you were tackled and brought down, you went into the middle. So the odds quickly turned against anyone running this gauntlet and getting through. On this particular day I was one of the last who had not been tackled. Those of us who had survived now lined up and faced the rest of the school. There seemed no way through the forest of jeering faces. But I hurtled across the playground, dodging, stumbling, wincing, and found myself within a couple of yards of the other side. At the very moment I thought I would make it, Jenkins and Mumby materialized in front of me. They were giants. Thirteen-year-olds still stuck in Standard 6. Front-row forwards in the first fifteen. Bigger and more belligerent than most of our teachers, they saw me coming, crouched and joined their arms—forming a barred gate against my progress. But then, as though lifted out of myself, I leaped over their locked arms, landed beyond them, and made it home. As I turned to take in what I had accomplished so miraculously, I met with looks of surprise and approval. Then they both came up to me, so tall they blotted out the sun, and shook my hand and said I was really something. It was my finest hour.

When I read of Joe Pawelka's ability to jump, how can I not remember this incident? And is it not also inevitable that when I try to imagine him I think of Eddie Potroz and what he had to say about acceptance?

"Dad did a bunk," Eddie told me once. "I used to think he was Christmas, but he was a shit. I never want to do to my kids what he did to Mum and me."

"Did you ever see him again?"

"Yeah, he dropped in from time to time."

Eddie's father was what my grandmother called "a bad seed." Perhaps he was one of the miscreants my grandfather had to put in the lockup from time to time, someone my grandmother grudgingly had to provide dinner and breakfast for. For all I know, it might have been my grandfather who put Eddie's father away.

There is something unforgiving about a small town. It's not simply the oppressive moralizing and inescapable gossip that condemns anyone who deviates from the straight and narrow. It's more to do with the impossibility of hiding anything, or of forgetting. I think of Eddie's mother, for instance, as she struggled to make ends meet. Neither the object of scorn nor of sympathy, she bore her misfortunes like a stigma, as irrevocable as Eddie's birthmark. And I think of Miss Therkelson, whose lover jilted her when she was seventeen. In despair, she threw herself from the top of a drowned quarry outside the town, and smashed her hip on the submerged carcass of an old truck. She limped around Inglewood for the rest of her life, her ugly injury a permanent reminder of something that would have been best forgotten. And I think of Cloris Goller, who had a child out of wedlock, and, in my grandmother's words, "lost her hold on goodness." She carried the burden of her "mistake" for as long as she lived and saw her daughter, Clover, grow up to be as beautiful as she had been, then follow in her footsteps, "duffed," we heard it said, "by some milkbar cowboy." What chance did one have, when every primary school child knew the "full story" and passed it on?

You were damned if you stayed, and you were often damned if you didn't. But at least in clearing out there was some hope of making a fresh start.

Joe Pawelka never escaped. Not in the way I did. Perhaps in the way Eddie did.

Joe's one surviving letter ends with the winter light failing. "I would like to tell you a little more," he writes to his mother, "but I can't see."

When we are young and confused, can we ever expect to see clearly? And when we are older and think we possess the clarity of hindsight, can we honestly say we remember the way things were?

I tell myself that it probably isn't a matter of seeing clearly at all, but of using the imagination to repair and augment our vision—which is always faulty. And what I imagine, when I think of Joe Pawelka and the town where I was raised, is a place where identities overlap and blur, a place where one is haunted by the thought that someone else's fate might equally have been one's own, where one man's loss is another's gain, or, like the icy pool where Eddie Potraz and I washed our mandalas, a place where colors run together and differences are eclipsed by what is shared.

Of the Woe That Is in Marriage

On his twenty-first birthday, 1 August 1908, Joe Pawelka was admitted to Palmerston Public Hospital with typhoid fever. Designated a "disease of complications," typhoid typically might cause intestinal ulcers, hemorrhaging, perforation of the bowel, peritonitis, and osteomyelitis. "Localisation and abscess formation could occur in any organ." In Joe Pawelka's case, it was found necessary to remove an abscess from one of his lungs. In order for the patient to be able to cough and so avoid drowning in his own fluid, he needed to be conscious during surgery. So Pawelka's three operations were done with local anesthetic. Three of his ribs and a portion of a lung were removed. His chances of surviving this trauma were fifty-fifty.

After five months in the hospital, he went home to Kimbolton where his mother nursed him back to health. Two years later, during the Pawelka manhunt, our *New Zealand Times* reporter would be told that Joe had been "a marvellous patient"—a remark that justified the conclusion that the determination and fortitude that brought Joe through his illness would now help him survive life in the open. Others expressed the opinion that Joe's mind had been "deranged" by the ordeal he had undergone in hospital.

After convalescing in Kimbolton for a couple of months, Joe began work at Banks & Co., a butchery on the Square in Palmerston. Four months later, on 3 July 1909, the shop manager, Leonard Hampton, sacked him because he "found him such a liar."

Ten days after being thrown out of work, Joe allegedly broke into Arthur Dixon's butcher's shop and stole 120 pounds of bacon and a steel. Three weeks later he burgled the house of a Palmerston lawyer, Harold Cooper, taking a pair of silver hairbrushes, a dinner suit, a shaving case, and a cigar case.

The following month, on 29 September, he married Hannah Elizabeth Wilson at Ashhurst. Lizzie was twenty-eight, Joe twentytwo.

Assuming they had not known each other before Joe's illness, they probably met in Palmerston sometime between March and August 1909. It was a brief courtship. Joe was in and out of work. And already, it seems, he was in trouble.

The couple rented a house in Palmerston at Church Street West, and Joe took up his old job at the abattoirs. Sometime during the first month of the marriage, Lizzie got pregnant. But, according to newspaper reports six months later, the Pawelkas' "married life was unhappy," and their "domestic affairs appear to have been very unpleasant." In early December, Lizzie filed a court application for "summary separation" and returned to live with her widowed mother in Ashhurst.

Joe's response was a rather pathetic attempt at suicide in a shallow pool in the Manawatu River. Brought before a local magistrate on 13 December, his counsel—ironically, the lawyer whose house he'd broken into four and a half months earlier—argued that Joe's severe illness had affected his general health. As if in compliance with this argument, in court Joe acted "in a very peculiar manner." After admitting his guilt, separation from Lizzie was ordered. Discharged without a conviction, he had to pay court costs as well as wife support of ten shillings a week, the first payment due 10 January.

About a week after his court appearance, Joe moved into a boardinghouse on Cuba Street.

Why did Lizzie walk out on Joe? What turned her against him?

Certainly they can't have known each other very well when they married. And it seems likely that Joe was guilty of petty larceny during the period when they were living in Church Street. Perhaps Lizzie was

PLATE 2. ANNE HARRIS

suddenly confronted with the sinister side of her husband. His possession of a revolver, which he seemed to regard as an extension of himself, may have hastened her decision to leave him. There is the possibility that he made violent threats, if not against her then against himself. Perhaps he was jealous of the hold her mother had over her. Perhaps he wanted to possess her utterly, like a bird in a cage.

His attempted suicide got him no sympathy. Instead, it saddled him with maintenance and court costs that he was probably hard pressed to pay.

But if Lizzie's decision was irrevocable, so too was his resolution. The callow eighteen-year-old who had written that marriage was for fools who didn't know what they were doing, and women not worth the trouble they brought, now found himself bereft. Unable to imagine or endure life without Lizzie, he began to fill the Church Street house with stolen furniture and furnishings, as if seeking to make good his emotional loss through material gain. Such a metaphorical fusion of feelings and things is familiar to most of us. After a death or divorce, people often squabble over the spoils as though, in laying claim to things, they will magically recover their sundered lives. Or, when a house is burgled, people feel sullied and bereft, as if their very bodies and souls had been invaded. Through what we *possess* we fetishistically establish our sense of who we *are*.

This may shed some light on why Joe Pawelka filled the house in Church Street with stolen furniture. The empty house embodied his loss. It also served as a sore reminder of the bourgeois world in which he had failed to find a place. If he filled his house with things taken from the family homes of others, perhaps, he imagined, his stolen happiness would be restored. Though he had failed to win Lizzie, perhaps the accoutrements of gentility would do the trick. When Hampton sacked him, he began stealing. Now that his wife had rejected him, and he had lost everything, he would stop at nothing to get her back. What did he have to lose?

* * *

Early on the morning of 25 February 1910, there was a "disturbance" in the house at 107 Church Street west. Apparently Lizzie had returned to the house with her mother to collect some of her belongings. Joe was also there, and they argued.

A constable was called to the house at 8 A.M. but saw nothing to justify action. Later in the morning, however, between 11 and noon, Lizzie went to the police station and laid a complaint against her husband. Joe followed her. At the police station, in Joe's presence, she claimed he had a revolver in his possession. Husband and wife were interviewed in separate rooms. Lizzie said she wanted police protection while she removed her belongings from the house. The police denied her request but promised to detain Joe while she went about her business.

Questioned by the police, Joe admitted having a revolver and offered to hand it in. As soon as Lizzie and her mother left the house, Constable King went there with Joe. After the pretense of a search, Joe said he could not find his revolver, so later that afternoon, between 5 and 6, Constables King and Barry returned to the house to search for it themselves. During their search they recognized paintings stolen over the Christmas holidays from several local homes. They placed Joe Pawelka under arrest and called in detectives to investigate further.

Early next morning, accompanied by Joe and some of the citizens who had been burgled, the police resumed their search of the house. It quickly became clear that almost everything in the house was stolen property, including Joe's revolver. Ira Gordon's bicycle was in the washhouse. The steel from Dixon's butchery was found in a kitchen drawer. Harold Cooper's dinner suit, dressing case, collar-box portmanteau, and set of razors came to light. Edward Kidd helped detectives identify furniture stolen from his house between Christmas Eve and 26 January—the period he and his family had been away on holiday. A Palmerston carpenter, Norman Metcalfe, who'd spent Christmas at Foxton with his family, identified items from his house. Then there was a clock belonging to James Robbie, who'd also been out of town during the Christmas break; tires and cigars from J. B. Clarkson's warehouse; and numerous articles taken on Boxing Day from Mrs. Hardley's residence: an oak table, a chair, cushions, pictures, table cover, brush stand and mirror, glass stand, vases, watch cases, carpet squares, hearth rugs, mats, fender, bedstead, silver, crockery, pots, and kettles. Finally, goods stolen from Helen McKay, an unmarried dressmaker, were found, including curtains, sheets, pillows and pillowcases, a table cover, quilt, cushions, possum skin rug, hammock, and sheepskin mats. The discovery of these items was particularly incriminating. Helen McKay's house at 1 Campbell Street was immediately behind the boardinghouse on Cuba Street where Joe Pawelka was living on 3 January 1910. That night, between midnight and 1 A.M., the McKay house had been willfully burned to the ground.

At 8 A.M. on 26 February 1910, Joe Pawelka was charged on five counts of breaking, entering, and theft from the homes of Kidd, Metcalfe, Robbie, and Hardley and from J. B. Clarkson's warehouse. When the first charge was read, Joe was heard to declare, "Oh, good God." When the second was read, his response was, "Good God Almighty." To the remaining three charges he made no reply.

He was remanded in custody until 7 March, when he was further charged with breaking, entering, and theft from Cooper's residence and Dixon's butchery. Finally, on 14 March, he was charged with breaking and entering the McKay house as well as arson. He was committed for trial at the next sitting of the Palmerston North Supreme Court on 23 March.

* * *

It is now part of the Pawelka legend that Joe's troubles stemmed from his broken marriage. Filling his house with stolen furniture and furnishings was, it is supposed, a desperate stratagem to please and impress Lizzie, whose mother thought her daughter had married beneath her. Though the Wilsons were also working-class migrants, in Mrs. Wilson's eyes her son-in-law was a mere butcher, lacking manners and prospects. If Joe was to win Lizzie's heart, so this argument goes, he would have to break the hold her mother had over her. Failing that, he would have to become worthy of her by giving her the material things that defined, for her and her mother, conspicuous membership of the middle class. Without the means to do this honestly, he resorted to theft. Or, at the very least, received or paid money for stolen property.

This comes close to Joe's own story: he claimed he'd purchased the furniture from Archie McRae, unaware it was stolen, and that had been the beginning of his troubles.

The stories are plausible. There seems no doubt that Joe was besotted by Lizzie and heartbroken when she spurned him. If he was desperate enough to try to drown himself as a way of winning her back, he would have been distracted enough not to think too deeply about his dealings with Archie McRae. And Lizzie was pregnant with their child. But his problems predate his marriage, and it is unlikely that Archie McRae was responsible for all the criminal acts with which Joe Pawelka was charged. The theft of Ira Gordon's bicycle and Arthur Dixon's steel, the 350 cigars stolen from Clarkson's warehouse, and the theft of such gentlemanly appurtenances as a cigar case, a shaving case, and dinner suit from Harold Cooper all seem to have been his doing. As for the fire that destroyed Helen McKay's house, the evidence is circumstantial but compelling: furnishings stolen from

McKay's on the night of the fire were found in Pawelka's Church Street house.

Perhaps like this fire, which smoldered for some time before bursting into flame, Joe Pawelka nursed resentments and grievances that he could no longer contain. Yet it is seldom possible to half-identify, let alone trace home, the blind impress all our behavings bear, and, often, all one can confidently demonstrate are the unforeseen consequences of an ill-considered act. Or draw comparisons between one's own life and that of another, endeavoring to find the common ground where an essay in human understanding might begin.

Manawatu

I remember it as a place of wind and rain. A landscape laid bare to the sky. Sodden paddocks, bitten by huddled herds. In winter, the stench of silage. Sheep dotted over dark green hills. I used to feel that the land had been emptied of life. Walking along a valley road, your footsteps echoed in the emptiness. Except for a creek spilling down a hillside, the whistling of birds, and the *maaa maaa* of a sheep, there was a cold silence.

For the Rangitāne people, the word *manawa-tu* conjures up the legendary figure of Hau-nui-a-Nanaia. Hau's stamping ground was the west coast, but when his wife, Wairaka, ran away with another man, Hau set off in pursuit. He traveled from Whanganui (large river mouth), to Turakina (thrown down) where he bridged the river with a dead tree. Footsore, he then came to the Rangitikei (day of trudging) where he rested overnight. Next day he journeyed south and came to the Manawatu River, flowing through a deep cleft (te Apiti) in the range and on across the flatlands to the sea. As he stepped into the cold water, Hau's breath was knocked out of him, whence Manawatu (breath stopped).

When I lived in the Manawatu I liked to think it was not only the coldness of the river that made Hau's heart miss a beat, but the light flooding through the gorge on a winter's day, as from a gate in the sky.

For the less mythologically minded, the region may be conceived as a parallelogram, with the Tararua-Ruahine ranges defining its eastern side, and the sore-footed Rangitikei River to the west. Draining this uplifted land are the Oroua and Pohangina Rivers whose parallel valleys open onto the plains of the Manawatu to the south.

For Joe Pawelka there were two cardinal points: Kimbolton, which over-looks the southern plain, and Ashhurst, under the axial range, hard by the entrance to the gorge. For six weeks now, these places will determine his bearings and define his limits.

* * *

The police cells where Pawelka is detained are notoriously cramped, unventilated, and unsanitary. Locally they are known as the Black Hole of Calcutta.

Ten minutes after noon on Saturday, 12 March 1910, Pawelka breaks out of the "black hole." Momentarily unguarded while being transferred to a more secure wing, he seizes his opportunity. Placing two buckets against the galvanized iron fence that encloses the exercise yard, he clambers up onto the roof and jumps down into the United Farmers' yard next door. There he takes an employee's bicycle and disappears onto Boundary Road.

The police immediately alert Ashhurst and warn Lizzie. It is thought that he will "resort to extreme violence upon her, by reason of her connec-tion with the circumstances which led to his arrest." But he heads north, along the main highway.

Eight hours after his escape, he is spotted near the Awahuri abattoirs, leading the police to suspect that he has taken shelter in the house of a Mrs. Wicks, "with whom he had been intimate before his marriage." By midnight he is in Bunnythorpe where he enters Rowe's store with a soft brown felt hat pulled down over his eyes and buys biscuits and lemonade. He pays with a pound note and asks if he can borrow some carbide for his bicy-cle lamp, which, Rowe observes, is tied to the handlebars with binder twine.

By dawn on Sunday he has reached the Kiwitea Stream just east of Feild-ing. He catches some sleep on a shingle bank shaded by willows, where the river loops back by the bridge. At 11 A.M. he walks along the streambed to a contractor's camp where he cadges a meal. He then returns to his hiding place.

That night he continues north on his stolen bicycle, stealing two loaves of bread, four pounds of uncooked beef, and some jam and syrup from a road contractor near Kimbolton. The police stake out the Pawelka house in Edwards Street. At 3:30 in the morning, the fugitive tries to slip past them, but is seen. Climbing onto his bicycle, he speeds away down the long hill from Kimbolton. The police, unable to stop him, fire shots into the air as he is swallowed up by the darkness.

Six hours later, a police sergeant finds telltale cycle tire tracks in the shingle by the Kiwitea Bridge. Then he sees Pawelka 150 yards ahead. Joe flees down the road toward Feilding. He goes along Derby Street onto East Street, thence to Aorangi, avoiding the town center. At Aorangi he turns down Cameron's Line in the direction of Awahuri. A quarter of a mile from the Awahuri abattoir, he abandons his bicycle by the roadside and strikes out across country. At 2:20 that afternoon, two constables standing under the verandah at the Awahuri store see him walk past. He has a handkerchief pulled up over his face, but is readily identified. When arrested and handcuffed he offers no resistance and says he will go quietly.

An hour and a half after his capture, he is brought before S. M. Thompson in the Magistrate's Court in Palmerston. Thompson orders him remanded in custody in the Terrace Gaol, Wellington, until 23 March.

At the time of his escape, Joe Pawelka was confused. At first he may have reckoned on help in Awahuri, possibly from workmates at the abattoirs. But then he traveled east, to Bunnythorpe, as if he had taken it into his head to go to Ashhurst and see Lizzie. At this point, however, he turned north for home. Thwarted by a police ambush in Kimbolton, he headed south again, winding up at Awahuri where he began.

It seems he has nowhere to hide. Worse, there is no one to whom he can turn. Perhaps he does not resist recapture because he has exhausted every possibility of remaining free. Indeed, one wonders whether anyone, apart from his family, is prepared to help him now. One feels that he is already beyond the pale, inspiring suspicion and fear more often than compassion. A telling detail in a newspaper account of his arrest is that he was wearing an overcoat stolen from a man called Anderson who worked at the abattoirs. Is he now feeling despised and rejected by friends, just as he felt abandoned by Lizzie? And is theft once more his way of avenging himself against those who turn their backs on him in his hour of need?

For a person badly hurt by life, even indifference may be experienced as a slight. More tragically, it may be taken as a sign of a conspiracy against one's right to justice and happiness.

Fires of No Return

The sky was like lead. The southerly beat about the city like the sea. Walking along the bay, I saw yachts torn like gulls from the hold of the harbor. The wind-sheered water was all scud and wake.

It was my fourth day in Wellington. At the National Archives, gale-force winds pummeled the building; rain was flung against the windows like scattershot. Driven inward, I worked in silence on criminal record books, depositions, and police files.

* * *

In 1910, Palmerston is a town of twelve thousand. Under cloudy skies, a New Zealand blue ensign snaps in the wind. The business premises along Rangitikei Street are built solidly of wood or brick. Wooden telegraph poles, cross bars studded with porcelain insulators, line an unpaved street. Some men in three-piece suits and hats stand on a street corner. Several women in straw boaters and long skirts cross the road. There is no evidence of motor vehicles; only drays and carts pulled by teams of horses and cyclists wearing cloth caps. The crimes and misdemeanors one reads about in the police court column of the *Manawatu Evening Standard* seem quaint: drunks using indecent language, bicycles without lights, truancy, vagrancy, petty theft, rigged scales and false weights, negligence in paying maintenance, cruelty to horses, failure to keep livestock under control.

Kimbolton is like a scaled-down version of Palmerston. The main street is rutted and stony. Wooden storefronts are emblazoned with the proprietors' names: R. U. Harden's Land Stock Financial & Commission Agent; Barlow Brothers' Plumbers & Tinsmiths; the Kimbolton Saddlery; C. J. Hansen's General Store; Lowes' Family and Commercial Hotel.

In the cleared valleys of the Oroua and Pohangina Rivers, scrub is reclaiming the ransacked hillsides. There are cottages, sheds, and hay barns along narrow gravel roads. Fences and grassed paddocks. A horse-drawn cart, loaded with a stack of milled boards, stands outside a farrier's. A dray carrying milk churns lurches down a metal road toward the cooperative butter factory.

It is Wednesday, 23 March 1910, and in Wellington Joe Pawelka has been in custody for nine days.

At 9:30 in the morning he is in a cell in the lockup at the Lambton Quay police station with another remand prisoner, waiting to be brought before the magistrate. The second prisoner is being held on charges of wife desertion.

The watchhouse keeper is twenty-six-year-old Constable J. J. Gallagher, promoted to the position only four months ago. Gallagher gives the cell key to Constable Mahoney, who takes the second prisoner to the watchhouse. But the lock on the cell door is faulty, and to compound the problem Mahoney fails to shoot the bolt home. Joe Pawelka slips out of the cell, scales a wall, and is free.

In the following days, newspapers report Pawelka heading northeast into the Wairarapa, where the police search is least intense, and making his way back to the Manawatu. But these reports are based on a single sighting, two days after Pawelka's escape, by a settler at Waingawa, three or four miles out of Masterton. The settler said that a man answering Pawelka's description called at his house and asked for food. After finishing his meal, the stranger rode away on a bicycle.

It is likely that this visitor was one of the thousands of vagrants or itinerant workers who drifted around the country in these years. If this is a case of mistaken identity, it will not be the last. In the weeks ahead, every nondescript stranger or derelict will be Pawelka, and the identity of the fugitive assimilated to that of the swagger who, since the depression of the 1880s and early 1890s, had become a familiar figure in the social landscape. One must remember that these were insular and isolated communities where footloose young men and vagrants were often the object of scorn and the focus of parochial fears.

According to Pawelka's own account, he knew the police would concentrate their search on the Wellington railway station and wharves, so he decided against making for the railway yards. Instead, he walked to Wadestown, forded a stream to Crofton, stole a bicycle, and rode north via Johnsonville. That night he slept in an old shed at Titahi Bay. Next day he went on to Paekakariki and late in the afternoon climbed into an empty cattle truck on a goods train going north. He got off at Longburn, four miles southwest of Palmerston, and hid there for a couple of days, surviving on bread, cheese, and tinned sardines he stole from Charles Perry's store on Saturday night. He also helped himself to cigarettes and a change of clothing. Then he made his way along the Manawatu River and up Stoney Creek to a prepared hiding place in the creek bed of McRae's farm.

How was he described?

According to Constable Gallagher the escaped prisoner had dark hair, black eyes, was clean-shaven, sallow, of slim build, and walked erect with a quick stride. Gallagher also recalled that Pawelka was dressed in light green trousers, a soft white shirt, blucher boots, a dark coat, but no hat or collar. A "wanted" poster, circulated the day after the escape, included a photo of the fugitive taken against a weatherboard wall.

Powelka is described as colonial born, twenty-eight years of age, standing 5 feet 10 inches in height, and weighing about 10 stone 10 pounds. He is of pale, sallow complexion, with a thin face, sunken cheeks, dark brown hair, dark eyebrows, and is usually clean-shaven. At the time of his escape he had about ten days' growth of hair on his face. He was dressed in brown tweed trousers and a soft shirt. He had no vest or cap, though since his escape he may have acquired these articles or changed his wearing apparel.

His age is given incorrectly. But something else is amiss. The complexity of Joe Pawelka's life has been reduced to a mugshot, a negative caricature. The frozen pose with its formal placement of the hands, the prisoner literally up against a wall, evokes an image of a body in death. Made over as a criminal type, he suffers our gaze and our judgment. His lived history, his background, his thoughts, his voice have been invalidated. Whatever unsettled and troubled his soul, the axis of his misfortunes now shifts to the world around him. Trapped inside the photo as in a cage, his only freedom now will be to become the person he has been made.

There is never any respite. On the run you are nerve-racked by lack of sleep and the unrelenting need for vigilance. There is no safe house, no haven. You can't simply lie low or sit still. It is like being lost. You are driven from cover, not only by fear of your pursuers closing in, but by the pain and disquiet in your own mind. You move to keep at bay the inner voices of your despair.

Joe Pawelka was living rough in an autumn that was already turning to winter. Preoccupied with finding food and clothing and the exhausting search for shelter and succor, he was also a man possessed by grief. He moved continually not only to evade capture but to shift the burden of his

PLATE 3. ALBERT WILLIAM ORGAN

loss. Alone and desperate, he seems to vacillate between imagining some kind of reconciliation with Lizzie and being overwhelmed by abject misery. Self-lacerating grief gives way to rage. He sees himself as unjustly used, an outcast, a voice crying in the wilderness. The society that has made him a pariah will now suffer for its sins. He has a score to settle. He will visit upon those who rejected him the hurt they visited upon him.

At 10:45 on the night of Saturday 2 April, nine days after Pawelka's escape, Jack and Pauline Kendall return to their house near Awapuni, west of Palmerston, after five hours shopping in town. Under a willow near the front gate they find a sugar bag of food stolen from the house. A duck, ten pounds of bacon, four pounds of cake, and a small loaf of bread are wrapped in one of Pauline Kendall's tablecloths. Nearby is a small leather bag containing a jar of pickles. Inside the house they find drawers ransacked and an empty larder. Jack Kendall's first suspicion is that two boys recently escaped from the Weraroa Training Farm are responsible.

As he goes back to the gate to retrieve a candle he left there, Kendall sees a man walking down the road toward the house. Later, he will tell the police that when the man saw him he dropped into a crouch with a revolver in each hand and said: "Your money, you—! It's your money I want!" The man was wearing a cap and old overcoat. Over his eyes and the upper part of his face he wore a mask made from one of Pauline Kendall's black silk blouses. His mouth was covered with a neckerchief. When Kendall explained that he'd spent all his pay in town, the armed man (who he now suspected to be Pawelka because of "a hissing tone which is a peculiarity of Powelka's utterance") allegedly declared, "You don't think they're loaded, eh?" and threatened to blow Kendall's brains out, brandishing the pistols in front of his eyes and rubbing his cheeks with the cold steel. Terrified, Kendall turned out his pockets.

When Pauline Kendall came out to see what was going on, Pawelka ordered her back to the house to fetch her purse. When he found it empty, the intruder lost his temper. "You think these are not loaded, do you?" he said, and promptly fired one of the revolvers within a foot of Pauline Kendall's head. She fell back against the fence, screaming, and went on screaming for two or three minutes until a cyclist suddenly appeared out of the darkness of the road. Immediately the intruder fell into a crouch, crept along the fence line, dropped into a ditch and disappeared.

Though Kendall knew Pawelka well (they'd both worked at the abattoirs and often broke their checks together on Saturday nights), there was considerable doubt over whether Kendall's identification of Pawelka's voice would be accepted by a court. Doubts were also cast on Kendall's story of being fired at.

But what bothered me, reading accounts of the holdup, was why Pawelka's mates seemed so afraid of him, so ready to incriminate him. In a sworn statement to the Supreme Court, Jack Kendall would declare, "I knew who he was as soon as I saw him . . . it was a very clear night . . . it was not dark . . . I have no doubt as to the identity of the man. I could have told him a mile off." Though Pauline Kendall, in her testimony, said she had known Pawelka "by sight three or four months," she also "had an idea it was Joe Powelka because of his figure. He sort of crouched down all the time." Yet it is unlikely that Jack Kendall could have so readily recognized the man who approached his gate in darkness with his face covered. By his own admission, Kendall could not clearly remember whether the intruder's overcoat and cap were gray or green. And despite having first concluded that boys from the Weraroa Training Camp had raided his wife's larder, he later told the police that his first thought had been, "Here comes Joe Powelka for a feed!" If this was true, why not give the fugitive a feed? If he was a workmate, why not talk to him, if only to press upon him the need to give himself up? Why not at least listen to his story?

If Joe Pawelka's own testimony is to be believed, he was never at Awapuni on the night in question, but shooting rabbits near his camp at McCrae's farm on Stoney Creek. He avowed that Awapuni was not on his beat: if he traveled between Longburn and Bunnythorpe, he skirted Palmerston to the north using the Boundary and Kairanga Roads.

* * *

In Wellington I began reading Mikal Gilmore's *A Shot in the Heart* and was at once struck by parallels with Joe Pawelka's story.

Much of Mikal Gilmore's book concerns his brother Gary, who gained international notoriety in 1976 and 1977 by challenging and ordering the state of Utah not to stay his execution after he had been found guilty of murder and sentenced to die. In his memoir, Mikal Gilmore searches for "a decisive turning point," a moment in Gary's story "where everything went wrong," "an instance that gave birth to my family's devastation." He asks whether this moment might be located "inside Gary's life" or "outside him . . . in the secret darkness of his own father's history." In the end he has to conclude that there are no simple answers, only interminable arguments and useless speculations. But then Mikal Gilmore turns to a different sort of question. No longer seeking to identify "each terrible link in that fateful chain," he asks instead "where could we have altered this history," how could the fateful chain have been broken and other links forged? In effect, his question turns our attention from what we cannot change to what we can.

In his last interview on Utah's death row, Gary Gilmore mentioned the name of a teacher called Tom Lyden who taught him in Portland, Oregon, when he was in eighth grade. Joseph Lane Grade School had been a tough school, and when Gary Gilmore started there he already had a delinquent history as a rebel, thief, and troublemaker.

The day Gary Gilmore was executed by firing squad and made his blood atonement, Tom Lyden, who'd been following the story on the news, got a call from the man who'd conducted this last interview. Lyden was surprised to hear that Gary had remembered him. He was even more surprised to learn that the condemned man had mentioned Lyden not only as the teacher he had most valued and respected, but as one of the few people he had reached out to for help. But rather than rue the extra step he might have taken twenty-five years ago with Gary Gilmore, Lyden, now principal at another school in Portland, thinks of a boy in his school who is giving his teachers trouble, and at a staff meeting the following day, Lyden tells the boy's teachers about the phone call he'd received. "Gary told somebody that he once had an eighth-grade teacher whom he'd held his hand out to, and that teacher didn't quite reach for it. He said he thought that perhaps that teacher could have made a difference in his life. That teacher was me. Now, what are you going to do about this youngster?"

* * *

It is Tuesday 5 April, three days after the Kendall holdup. On this night, there are three major fires in Palmerston, and Pawelka will be blamed for them all.

The fire bell is first rung at 8 P.M. At the Boys' High School in Feather-ston Street, a lavatory window is smashed and a fire lit that spreads quickly through the wooden building. As the brigade is fighting this blaze, another breaks out in the newly renovated storage, packing, polishing, and uphol-stery rooms of W. Pegden on the Square. The brigade rushes to Pegden's, only to be summoned at 10:30 to yet another fire at the temporary premises of Millar and Giorgi's draper's shop, fifty yards away. With a horse-drawn fire engine and an inadequate supply of water under pressure, the volun-teer brigade can do little more than contain the fires.

Almost immediately rumors circulate that the fires are the work of an arsonist, and it is quickly agreed that Pawelka is "the person responsible for the conflagrations." Various citizens claim to have seen him in various parts of town, and by midnight Palmerston is, in the words of one newspa-perman, "practically reduced to a state of terror." In this uneasy atmo-sphere, women leave their homes on the outskirts of town to stay with friends, and men arm themselves with revolvers. At the same time, police reinforcements are brought in from Wanganui and Hawera.

Yet even in this panic there are voices urging caution and calm. Observes a reporter for the *New Zealand Times*, "persons with a good knowledge of Powelka declare that he is not half as eccentric as has been made out, and that in some respects he is a man of more than ordinary intelligence. Men who have worked with him are of the opinion that his object in returning to the district is to avenge himself on his wife for having acted in such a way as to cause his arrest in the first instance."

* * *

In the early hours of the morning after the fires, Pawelka dumps the Day-ton bicycle he'd stolen from the driveway of a house near the High School and steals a horse and saddle. After crossing the Fitzherbert Bridge, he makes for the Pahiatua Track. Late in the afternoon, in failing light, he rides up to a store a couple of hundred yards from the Pahiatua railway sta-tion and asks for some fuses. The store has none, and Pawelka rides away.

Two mounted constables from Palmerston then spot him on the Bal-lance Road and go in pursuit. Pawelka's horse has been ridden hard and is lame from having lost two shoes. With Constables King and Macleod clos-ing on him, Pawelka abandons his horse and plunges into Matthews Bush along the Mangahao River. King glimpses the fugitive running among stumps and logs with a revolver in his hand. Pawelka is wearing a green slouch hat, a dark green tweed overcoat, and yellow leggings stolen from Millar and Giorgi's on the night of the fire. King fires at the fleeing man, but he is quickly gone.

Seeing no point in following Pawelka into the bush, King rides off to get reinforcements.

A search, beginning at first light the next day, yields nothing. It is assumed Pawelka broke through the police cordon in the night and will be making for Dannevirke where he once worked in Brighouse's butchery. Most likely, however, he emerged from the bush onto the Ballance Valley Road and made his way to Woodville where he laid low until late on the night of 8 April.

The Pahiatua district now experiences the same panic that seized Palmerston. Armed settlers volunteer to help the police search. Rumors spread like wildfire.

"The theory is gaining ground," observes a reporter for the *New Zealand Times*, "that some person other than Powelka is assisting to increase the present condition of unrest, as it is considered impossible for one individual to have done what is alleged to have taken place in the city and neighbourhood."

* * *

At the end of the day I wrote down in my journal some of the things that seemed now to be falling into place.

When Joe escapes, wanted notices go up on police bulletin boards around the country. The gaunt face is both bewildered and belligerent. What chances he had to define his own identity, to tell his own story, have been lost. He is already the bogeyman parents use to frighten their errant children into line. He is doomed to travel a road that has been decided for him. But he will embrace this destiny with a vengeance. If he cannot prove his innocence, he will perversely embrace his guilt. If he cannot love, he will attract hate. He will fulfill everyone's worst expectations. Rather than be condemned by others, he will now condemn himself.

Not once during the fortnight after his escape does he turn for home. He sees himself as a man alone against the world. The change is presaged in his suicidal gestures. When crossed in his desire to be accepted, he imagines his own annihilation. There is no mystery in this. If one's need for recognition is not met through affection, it will often be sought through disaffection. We all know children who, unable to get love from their parents, turn to eliciting hate. If Joe Pawelka cannot gain recognition through conforming to social convention, he will gain it through defiance. In so far as the law diminishes him, he will become a law unto himself. He will turn the tables on the world that has turned against him. So he burns down a high school, destroying a symbol of the decent education to which he once aspired. Then burns down a furniture warehouse and draper's shop, symbolically destroying the trappings of the social class that has spurned him.

Fugue

Returning from exile is a bit like returning from the dead. You half expect to reenter the same world you left, but the connective tissue has gone; both you and the place with which you identify have changed. Strange as it may seem, this sense of loss can be more devastating than any homesickness you experience when away.

When I came back to Wellington, the city felt both alien and familiar. The concrete ziggurats and glass towers that stood shoulder to shoulder in the narrow downtown streets did not entirely eclipse my memories of what had once stood there. But I was aware that a new generation now occupied the space I had once considered mine. This had the effect of making me feel I was invisible, and I moved about like a revenant.

This sense of being displaced in a place I still thought of as home influenced the way I saw Joe Pawelka. At times, it was as though the line between me and Joe had become blurred, and with this blurring went an erasure of the line between present and past.

One evening at Les and Mary Cleveland's house in Brooklyn, where I was staying, Les dug out a reel of film he'd shot twenty-nine years ago. He'd never developed it. He had taken the photos in the summer of '65 when he and Mary came to stay with me and my first wife Pauline in the southern Wairarapa. Vince O'Sullivan and his wife, Tui, were also with us. Three couples very much in love.

Now, after all this time, Les had decided to develop the film.

The photos he brought out of his darkroom were grainy, gray, and scratched. This only increased their power. It was like opening up a grave and finding no evidence of decay. The shock of seeing these snapshots overwhelmed me. They were windows onto a time I had reworked in memory. But now a faithful likeness of Pauline, who died in 1983, had reappeared, and it was like a door opened for a moment onto a field of light and then slammed shut.

Here we are, sitting outside the Lake Ferry Hotel in the sun, except for Mary, who must have taken the photo. In another photo we are in the bar holding glasses of beer and peering at Mary behind the camera. Other photos capture us sitting together in long grass, somewhere near the Pinnacles, eating lunch. Here is this beautiful young woman laughing at the camera, and a callow young man, myself, beside her, draining a bottle of DB Brown, oblivious.

I remembered Michaelmas daisies shimmering in the lilac Wairarapa light. Of long evenings, walking country roads. The smell of pinestraw and river water. For twenty-nine years I had remembered these things . . . but the faces had become a blur.

Would there be anything like this—a photograph, a letter—that would give me a glimpse into Joe Pawelka's life?

* * *

Since Joe's escape, Lizzie and her mother have, on police advice, stayed every night in the Ashhurst Hotel. It is still widely believed that Pawelka is bent on vengeance, and has "declared his intention of shooting his wife and mother-in-law and various other people at Ashhurst."

At 9:30 in the morning of Saturday 9 April 1910, Lizzie and Hannah return home.

Hannah Wilson's house is "in a lonely part of Ashhurst"—the spur of a river terrace that overlooks the Pohangina Valley and the Ruahine range beyond.

Most mornings, when they get back to the house, Lizzie and her mother check to see that everything is as they left it. It is also their custom to look under the beds.

This morning, however, they remove their hats and go straight into the yard to fix the well rope. Lizzie hears a noise in the house. She thinks it might be the cat, but wants to make sure. She asks her mother to go and investigate. Hannah Wilson walks into the kitchen and finds herself face to face with her son-in-law.

Joe is standing with his back to the fireplace. "Don't be afraid, Mother," he says.

He doesn't get a chance to say anything more. In a panic, Hannah Wilson runs screaming toward her neighbor's house. Joe bolts, clambers over a fence, and seeks the shelter of the river flats below the house.

When the police arrive five minutes later and search the place, they find Pawelka's heavy fur-lined coat hanging on the back fence. It was an expensive coat. Joe bought it when he was living with Lizzie. She'd argued that they couldn't afford it, but he'd bought it anyway. To impress her? To transcend his background?

In the pockets of the coat are some .22 cartridges and detonator caps as well as the piece of wire with which Joe had picked the backdoor lock.

Inside the house, it is found that Hannah Wilson's bed has been slept in. But, against the assumption that Pawelka occupied it, Constable Watts argues that when he inspected the house just before daybreak there was no sign of life.

What is Joe Pawelka thinking? What draws him back to the one place that is going to be most closely watched? What dire necessity overcomes all sense of caution and makes him take this risk?

One clue is a note he scrawls with the lead of a bullet and leaves in a milk billy on the gatepost of the Grammars' house on the outskirts of Ashhurst. A boy called Robert Elliott, who lives with the Grammars, finds the letter stuck in the billy when he goes to fetch the milk on Sunday morning. The billy lid is closed, and the note is in a sealed envelope. Robert Elliott gives it to Mrs. Rhoda Grammar, who then gives it to another boy, Stanley Liddicoat, who had dropped by the house that morning, to take to the police.

The grubby scrap of paper is addressed to the manhunters of Ashhurst. It reads:

To my fellow-men—After hearing a remark passed by one of the party this afternoon, to the effect that I am supposed to have burned down a house in town last night, I do hereby solemnly swear before my God Almighty that it is an untruth. At the time this man said the house was on fire—9 P.M. he said—I was on the outskirts of Woodville. I might also state that a good many of the happenings of late that

*have been blamed on to me are false. I also heard P. Hanlon say while within one
yard of me that I shot at my wife this morning. That also is a foul lie, and he went
near getting a bullet for his pains. Excuse this writing, for I have only a pointed bullet to scrawl with. Signed, J. POWELKA, a man against the world.*

* * *

The misspelling of the name Pawelka calls the authenticity of the note into
question. But when the note gets produced as evidence at Pawelka's trial, the
signature and handwriting are authenticated. Pat Hanlon was Joe Pawelka's
brother-in-law and Joe and Lizzie had been married in his home. According
to newspaper reports, Hanlon had been living in fear of the fugitive ever
since his escape. The fire referred to destroyed a two-story house in Palmerston on the night of Friday 8 April.

We can infer that "last night" is 8 April, "this morning" is 9 April when
Joe tried to see Lizzie, and "this afternoon" is the afternoon of the same day.
In all likelihood, therefore, the note was placed in the billy under cover of
darkness on the night of Saturday 9 April. The Grammar's house, on the
main road to Palmerston, was isolated. Pawelka could have passed the gate
on his way to town.

But Joe Pawelka's note is addressed to a community where he can expect
little support. Eighty-five years later, informants would tell me that some
Ashhurst people left food at their front gates at night for the fugitive, but
almost everyone's allegiance is to Pawelka's wife and mother-in-law. Only
in Kimbolton and the Pohangina Valley "where he was well known, and
where he was also liked" is there any sympathy for him. Yet he will not
head home. He will return to the place where he is feared and despised,
driven, it seems, by some imperative need to explain himself, to clear things
up, and to win back his wife's affection.

Shots in the Dark

The rain does not cease all day. After fleeing the Wilson house in Ashhurst,
Joe Pawelka may have made his way up the Pohangina Valley and taken
shelter in a hay barn. Then he may have come south across country, following Stoney Creek. More likely, he waited until after sunset at 5:30, returned

to Ashhurst, left his note in the billy can, and walked toward Stoney Creek along the railway line.

The question is, did he then return to his hiding place on Stoney Creek or press on toward Palmerston in search of food and a raincoat?

Stoney Creek is a small Scandinavian settlement just east of Palmerston; today it is known as Whakarongo.

At 6:45 in the evening a man knocks on the door of the church and asks for a Mr. Grover. The stranger is given directions to Grover's Store and post office next door. At the store, the stranger explains that he is a policeman engaged in the search for Pawelka. He stands out of the light, as if not wanting to be recognized, and asks for an overcoat.

Three-quarters of an hour later, someone breaks into Amelia Farland's house at 128 Ferguson Street, Palmerston, and steals two loaves of bread, one pound of butter, a tin of tea, two pounds of sugar, a billy can, a bottle of pickles, and a green skullcap. The key to the back door is also taken, and from a house opposite, an overcoat goes missing.

Was Joe Pawelka the man at Grover's Store who an hour later broke into Amelia Farland's house four miles away?

It is possible that copycat criminals are at work. At Ashhurst, a young offender named Richard Collis has already exploited "the Powelka pandemonium" by impersonating a special constable. He "borrows" an overcoat, field glasses, and money and is given lodging for a week before clearing out with all his debts unpaid.

At 9:45 at 61 Ferguson Street, Leonard Hampton, master butcher and manager of Banks and Company's butchery in the Square, comes home from work on his bicycle to find a trip wire stretched across his driveway.

Last year, Joe Pawelka worked at Banks's butchery for four months before Hampton sacked him because he "found him such a liar." Aware that Joe Pawelka knows that he always brings his takings home on Saturday nights, Hampton comes to the conclusion that Pawelka is seeking revenge. But when Hampton goes to the police, he is told that they are unable to send anyone to the house and he returns home.

Searching his orchard the next day, Sunday 10 April, Hampton finds evidence that someone has camped there. Convinced that it must be Joe Pawelka, Hampton mounts vigil outside his house in the shadows of a willow and a macrocarpa. At about 7 P.M., after a half-hour wait in darkness and rain, he hears the thud of someone jumping a fence. Then he sees a man cross the road, enter his driveway, and latch the gate behind him.

In a sworn statement, Hampton—like Kendall the previous Saturday—will claim to have positively identified the intruder, although he does not see his face and never gets close to him. "The figure appeared to me [to be] Joseph Pawelka . . . that was the impression in my mind. He was wearing a three-quarter overcoat, a dark one . . . It was the way he straightened himself up and walked across the road that made me think it was Pawelka. It was a pretty bad night at the time and it had just started to rain."

Hampton waits until the intruder has gone into the shadows, then runs to the police station. Six men are dispatched immediately and quickly surround the house.

Police Sergeant McGuire and Detective Quartermain now approach the house from the front.

John Patrick Hackett McGuire has been in Palmerston only forty-eight hours, following a transfer from Lambton Quay, Wellington. Born and bred on the West Coast, he is forty-one and married with no children. But he is lacking in experience of practical police work, having served in Wellington as a clerk, his duties confined to "quill driving." He is unarmed. Quartermain is also from Wellington. The *New Zealand Truth* refers to him by his nickname, Demon, speaking scathingly of him as a city man, a fingerprint expert, with no experience of fieldwork or the bush. Unlike McGuire, Quartermain is armed.

In the pitch darkness, McGuire accosts and grapples with the intruder near Hampton's front door. The man is wearing a mask and a large hat. The two men wrestle their way across a gravel path to the front lawn where they tumble to the ground. The intruder stands up. A shot is fired. McGuire, lying on the ground, is hit in the stomach, just above the navel. He cries out, "I'm hit!"

The track of the bullet is upward and to the left—a fact hard to reconcile with a shot being fired by someone standing over him.

Quartermain, who is "but a short distance away," will later say he fired two shots toward "the flash of Powelka's revolver," which gives rise to a rumor that it may have been he, not the intruder, who fatally wounded McGuire. Interviewed in hospital, McGuire says he "could not actually say it was Powelka," and cannot say for certain whether he was shot by the intruder or by Quartermain." Hampton, who supposed the intruder was his former employee, would not "kiss the Bible to it" either.

As word of the shooting spreads, Palmerston is a "maddened, frightened community" gripped by "hysterical fever." In the darkness and steady rain, old firearms—short-barreled rifles, fowling pieces, ancient revolvers—are requisitioned and handed out to civilian volunteers who form a cordon stretching a mile and a half around the Ferguson Street block. People cannot sleep. Shop owners leave their lights burning. Some hotels remain open all night. And reporters file their stories, declaring Pawelka to be a "mad man and thoroughly desperate," a "criminal lunatic" who has "terrorized a whole countryside." "The town is in a fearful state of excitement," one reporter writes. "The cry is 'Powelka! Powelka!' all day, and no one talks of anything else." At Ashhurst "the residents are in a great state of alarm." Mrs Pawelka is said to be "terrified."

That night and the next morning, Pawelka is seen everywhere. He is sighted on the Rangitikei Line, near the flourmill, in North Street and at Awapuni. A woman in Terrace End reports a batch of scones and two loaves of bread taken by the fugitive. Concludes the *Manawatu Evening Standard*, "these and other alarming rumours . . . show that Powelka was hovering 'round Palmerston, and that something serious could be expected when night fell."

But if Pawelka was the intruder at Hampton's house, he probably fled the scene of the shooting at once, cutting across paddocks toward the Manawatu River, using the cover of raupo swamps and lagoons in the Hokowhitu area. At his trial, however, Pawelka would vehemently deny having been anywhere near the scene of the crime and during subsequent prison visits would protest his innocence, telling his family that he was in Tokomaru the night of the McGuire shooting, though he could not prove his alibi.

* * *

When McGuire is shot, an old schoolmate and close friend joins in the search for Pawelka. Michael (Mick) Quirk is a hairdresser and tobacconist from Pahiatua, thirty-six and unmarried. His father and brother are both on the police force.

On the evening after the shooting of McGuire, Mick Quirk and another volunteer, Walter Henry Overton, are patrolling the streets of Palmerston.

Overton is licensee of the Princess Hotel in Terrace End. He is thirty-five, an ex-artilleryman.

At 7:30 Overton is walking along a footpath at Terrace End with Sergeant Bowden from Feilding. Suddenly, out of the darkness they hear cries of "Powelka! Powelka!" and see a man walking toward them with a revolver in his hand.

Overton and Bowden turn a powerful acetylene car headlight on the man, now fifteen yards away, and challenge him:

"Who are you?"

The man does not answer.

"Stop!"

There is no response.

"Stop or I'll fire!"

The man, dazzled by the glare from the lamp, stoops and lowers his head.

Overton fires, and the expanding bullet blows the back off Michael Quirk's head.

Overton, certain he has shot Pawelka, shouts, "I've shot him, he's mine!"

Moments later, aware of his tragic mistake and realizing that Quirk had not responded to his challenge because he probably thought Overton was the fugitive, Overton is "stunned" and "completely prostrated."

At the inquest the next day, he appears "broken up throughout the proceedings."

Orders are now given to disarm and disband the vigilantes. At the same time, the government doubles its reward to £100 for information leading to the capture of John Joseph Thomas Pawelka, described as having a large scar near his left shoulder blade, a scar on the side of his left kneecap, and pinched features. He is said to be wearing a dark gray coat, dark vest, greenish tweed trousers, a light well-worn shirt (torn in front), and blucher boots.

On the same evening, and at almost the same time Quirk is shot, a man with two revolvers accosts an old woman and child in Church Street. Ten minutes later, Alfred Richards, a farmer from Stoney Creek, is driving along East Street toward Ferguson Street when he is held at gunpoint by a man who rummages in his cart for food. Richards has had dealings with Pawelka at the abattoirs and at butchers' shops. He is certain his assailant is Pawelka. Then, at Baldwin's Avenue, one street away from East Street, a

Mr. M. E. Leybourne, a commission agent, encounters a man with a revolver. When Leybourne asks the man if he is scouting for the fugitive, the man declares, "I am Pawelka! Not another word or you are a dead man," and presses the revolver to Leybourne's forehead before walking away.

In due course, the Leybourne stickup will be shown to be the work of a prankster. But in Palmerston the imagined now defines the real.

In truth, Pawelka was probably well away. At the time Quirk was shot and killed, Pawelka was positively identified by two constables twenty miles away as he approached the lower Gorge Bridge from the direction of Woodville. This was about 7 P.M. When ordered to stand and put his hands up, he ignored the demand. He was again challenged before one of the constables fired two shots at him. The constable was convinced he had killed the fugitive, but next day it was found that the bullet had hit the woodwork of the bridge. It was supposed that Pawelka climbed over the side of the bridge and worked his way upstream under cover of darkness.

It is always in darkness that he is observed and identified.

Whatever the facts, this is the pattern now: every stranger at the door on a dark, rainy, windswept night will be Pawelka, and every case of burglary or arson will be blamed on him. Even allowing for the likelihood that copycat criminals are at work, newspapers will report that Pawelka has "fired another unbalanced individual to emulation."

*　*　*

The following day, Tuesday the 12th, Pawelka is again sighted, this time on the railway line near Bunnythorpe. It is three in the morning, the sighting is for less than a minute, and Constable Flannagan will report that Pawelka looked "worn out and dejected."

When Flannagan fired a shot, the man made off toward the Bunnythorpe School grounds, abandoning a swag containing both cooked and raw meat. A few hours later some pickles and dried fruit were stolen from a farmer's outhouse on the Ashhurst road half a mile away. And as day broke, another farmer, getting out his cows, surprised Pawelka lying on the ground.

Again it is a day of high winds and rain. In Palmerston, people feel "it is absolutely unsafe for anyone to move about except in the most thickly trafficked places." Excitement, according to the local newspaper, "is rising to a

great pitch." As for Pawelka, the search for him goes on in falling temperatures, hurricane-force winds, and driving rain. The general view is that he
will head home to Kimbolton, traveling at night and sleeping by day, keeping to the Oroua River valley where there is bush cover. Several constables
are stationed in the Kimbolton area; others scour the Oroua.

When he worked at the abattoirs, Joe had a reputation for great strength.
He could lift a three-hundred-pound side of beef with ease or pick up two
ninety-pound carcasses, one in each hand. And people in Kimbolton often
recounted how athletic he had been, how well he could jump. Now, however, Joe's mother is convinced that her son's health will not stand up to the
ordeal of living rough and being on the run. She says, "He will be found
dead before the search continues much longer."

In Kimbolton, a reporter finds the locals solidly in support of him.
Small-town New Zealand is possessed of deep and parochially loyal ties.
While Ashhurst goes in fear of him and stands behind his estranged wife
and in-laws, Kimbolton closes ranks to defend him. "Those who know
Powelka well say they have absolutely no fear of him, and do not believe he
has fired on anybody," one newspaperman reports.

> Everybody I spoke to . . . seemed heartily sorry for Powelka, and all with
> whom he had dealings say that Powelka was a thoroughly upright fellow,
> one who could be trusted with anything. There seems to be no doubt in the
> minds of many people as to the author of the Palmerston shooting affray.
> Naturally the youth's parents are terribly cup [sic] up about the affair. They
> are old and respected residents of Kimbolton, and there seems little doubt
> that they would be glad to see Powelka captured, because he is evidently
> being blamed for many an ill deed that he has not committed. "Everything
> is attributed to him," said a local resident yesterday, and the statement was
> correct in every way.

But many who know Pawelka take the view that he will not go home,
but double back to Ashhurst and try again to see his wife. "Rumour has it,"
one newspaper reports with unintended poignancy, "that Powelka is very
much attached to his wife."

Recaptured

I had reached a point in my research where I needed to see the places I'd been reading about and try to recapture in the landscape itself the mood of what had happened there. So I rented a car and headed to the Manawatu.

As I drove north, the light drained from the sky and the darkness came up out of the land. I felt I was traveling not through space, but time. I drove through country towns where mud-splattered utes were parked against the curbs and groups of disgruntled young men dressed in shapeless clothing stood and stared. I drove down a highway where white crosses and wreaths marked the site of fatal accidents.

As I approached Palmerston North, my preoccupation with Joe Pawelka gave way to memories of my own. As I slowed between the plane trees along Fitzherbert Avenue, I felt a tightening in my chest as though my body were registering things my consciousness could not yet grasp. I had lived nine years in this city, surrounded by waterlogged paddocks, oppressed by lowering skies. A good half of my first marriage; the best years of my daughter's childhood. Now, coming back, I was thrown.

I had not expected this. I drove as in a dream, drawn toward the house where I had once lived.

The paint on the weatherboards and windowsills was peeling. The front porch was shaded by the native trees I'd planted almost twenty years ago. In the driveway where my daughter once played, a little girl was sweeping the concrete with a yard broom. I felt I could have got out of the car and walked back into my previous existence.

I drove quickly away, passing through Terrace End—the same windswept and treeless avenue where Henry Overton shot Michael Quirk.

In the distance, the backbone of the Ruahines was a smudge of dark green under a colorless sky.

It was the middle of the afternoon, but the light was already failing. There were dark stands of macrocarpas in the paddocks, and a band of white light over the range, as in one of McCahon's canvases. North, overnight, snow had dusted the peaks of the Ruahines. In the south, sunlight flooded the plain, momentarily touching the domes and hillocks of the Tararua foothills.

At Ashhurst, I found the site of the Wilson house on the corner of Salisbury and Wyndham Streets. There was nothing to see, nothing to give the imagination purchase or provide a link to the lives of those who once lived there.

I turned the car and drove slowly back to the center of town, reliant now solely on my research notes to reconstruct the events that unfolded in the stormy darkness of 17 April 1910.

* * *

For five days the search for Pawelka is hindered by equinoctial gales and heavy rain, and the fugitive lies low, probably in the Longburn area where six pounds of steak and four pounds of German sausage are stolen from the Manawatu Meat Company's shop on Friday the 15th. A sou'wester hat and oilskin coat are also taken from the butcher's house. Almost certainly Joe Pawelka travels from Longburn to Palmerston on Saturday afternoon, buying three pounds of his favorite cream crackers, one pound of cheese, and four pennyworth of matches from Cox's store in Ferguson Street before heading yet again toward Ashhurst. The rain has not let up.

A reporter in the *New Zealand Times* writes of this irrational refusal to escape from the region where he is hunted. Why is he compelled to return over and over again to the very place where he is most likely to be caught? The reporter can only suggest "a deranged mind."

* * *

It is the coldest night of the year. In Ashhurst, in windswept darkness before dawn on Sunday 17 April, one policeman has Mrs. Wilson's house under surveillance; two others are watching Pat Hanlon's house; two are patrolling the town.

The policemen outside Hanlon's house in Winchester Street are hidden in the shadows of a macrocarpa hedge. Constable John J. Gallagher is from Wellington. He had been responsible for security at the lockup in Lambton Quay when Pawelka escaped on 23 March and is determined to repair his damaged reputation. His companion is a probationer called Callery.

At 4 A.M., in driving rain, Gallagher and Callery see a man cross a side street and head toward Hanlon's paddock. When they call on him to stop, he dives over a fence (they hear the ting of the fencing wire), dropping some water biscuits and bottles of stout. Callery fires a shot after the fleeing man.

Gallagher reports the sighting to the constables on patrol who notify Constable Thompson at the Wilson house.

Because the man was seen coming from the direction of Scott's farm (about a quarter of a mile from the post office) and could have easily doubled back there after diving over Hanlon's fence, the police decide to search the farm buildings.

It is now 6:30 A.M. Watts and Thompson inspect the cowshed. Thompson checks the hayloft. Then, joined by two civilian searchers, they move on to the neighboring farm.

Currie's cowshed is across the road from the Grammar's house where Pawelka left his note, written with the lead of a bullet, signed "a man against the world." The cowshed is a large weatherboard building with eleven bails on either side of a central aisle. The aisle is uncovered and open at either end. Above the bails are haylofts.

Thompson takes the loft on the left. Gallagher takes the one on the right, using a haycart to clamber up. The other searchers remain below.

Thompson finds nothing and calls across to Gallagher, "Do you see anything?"

Gallagher can't see much in the bad light and strikes a match. He discerns a man lying full length between the loft wall and a heap of hay. The man has a revolver in his hand; an empty bottle of stout lies nearby. With considerable sangfroid, Gallagher shouts down to the others, "There is no one here."

Gallagher descends into the yard, holding up his hand to caution silence.

While the searchers work out their plan of attack, a railway clerk named Bryce is sent to fetch an acetylene bicycle lamp.

When everything is ready, Callery and the second civilian searcher, Sheridan, remain below. Sylvester and Watts take one end of the loft, while Gallagher and Thompson take the other. Thompson has the lamp. He turns it on Pawelka as he and Gallagher rush forward. Pawelka raises his revolver, but Thompson knocks his hand up into the air and disarms him. There is a short struggle as Pawelka is handcuffed. Then he is helped down from the loft.

As the party set off toward the Ashhurst police station, Pawelka mutters, "You bloody cowards!" He walks in a shuffle, making some of his guards think he might be drunk. Once he tries to trip Gallagher and struggles to get away. "Do you think I'm a coward?" he says, and, indicating his handcuffs, adds, "If so, take these off, and I'll show you."

"It's all right, Joe," Gallagher says. "You wouldn't shoot a man."

Thompson then says, "No? Who shot poor McGuire?"

Pawelka allegedly turns his head to Thompson and asks, "Who fired the first shot, you bastards?" But at his trial, Pawelka will declare angrily that this is a police lie.

At the police station he is searched. Apart from the two revolvers in his possession when captured at Currie's cowshed (a .32 and a .380 Harrington), he has ammunition, eight detonators, several pennies, eight threepenny bits, four candles of various lengths, a sock, a new but soiled shirt with a Millar and Giorgi label, a chisel, some notepaper, a copy of Saturday night's *Manawatu Evening Standard*, a couple of postal notes, and eighteen penny stamps. Most telling, when one considers that he has been captured in the town to which his affections have doomed him to return so many times, is the discovery of a photo of his wife and his mother-in-law in his pocket.

The police recognize the postal notes, stamps, and stout as stolen from the Ashhurst railway station where there had also been a failed attempt to blow the safe earlier in the night.

Pawelka's captors are surprised that the fugitive does not look like a man who has been on the lam and living rough for twenty-four days. He is clean-shaven, except for a small moustache, and his hair is combed. He is wearing the sou'wester hat and black oilskin coat stolen from Longburn the previous day over a grey three-quarter coat. Under the coat he has an ordinary suit of clothes, one sock (the other is in his pocket), and his now-famous green riding pants and yellow leggings. There is no evidence on his leggings or clothing that he has been fording rivers.

Had he made himself presentable before yet another bid to see his wife?

Whatever his appearance, he is a man in despair.

"This is hell upon earth," he says to his captors. "Why didn't you put a bullet into me? Put one now, and they will think I did it myself. I wanted to see my wife, and then I would have put a bullet into myself. She is an affectionate wife. My wife has led me to this. My heart is broken. I can feel nothing."

At about 9 in the morning, the prisoner is taken to Palmerston by car. Once he struggles to throw himself from it, as if the impulse to escape now blurs with the impulse to do away with himself. At Palmerston he is stripped and given hot coffee and blankets. In his cell he collapses and weeps, but most of the time he paces up and down and asks for his wife, "speaking affectionately of her." He is told she will not come. He does not sleep, but stands all day at the cell door looking out through the spy hole. When a local doctor visits him and offers him a sleeping draught to calm his nerves, Pawelka asks that he be given poison instead "to finish himself off."

He blames a Shannon man called Archie McRae for all his troubles, alleging that McRae sold him the stolen furniture that was found in his Church Street house, though a year later, in a letter written to Lizzie from prison, Joe would confess that McRae was not "solely responsible for stealing the furniture," implying that he *had* been guilty. And as if determined to make the most of this confession and appear praiseworthy in her eyes, he added that he had not divulged McCrae's name to the police because his accomplice was married and had two children.

These shifting stories suggest that for Joe Pawelka truth was simply the most expedient lie.

The thing about inveterate liars is the difficulty they have remembering their lies. This is their fatal flaw: sooner or later, they incriminate themselves through inconsistency. But they also reveal themselves. So we learn the truth about Joe Pawelka in his confabulations: his desperate need for approval and affection; his vilification of those who did not mirror him, who failed to meet his overweening needs. This is why, even as he sought to win back his wife, he made threats against her and cursed her for abandoning him.

Given his emotional desperation, it is difficult to judge him. When one thinks of all the crimes against humanity that have been done in the name of Truth, one wonders if the consequences of mendacity and deceit have been any more terrible.

In any event, what one person will call a lie, another will deem a truth.

Perhaps what matters is not the descriptive truth of words, but whether the words sustain us and help us survive.

* * *

Twenty-four hours after being recaptured, Pawelka begins his journey back to Wellington. Handcuffed to Gallagher and Callery, and escorted by several constables returning to the capital, Pawelka sits in a second-class railway carriage with the shades drawn. Already he has been charged with the murder of McGuire. Other charges are pending.

In Wellington he is arraigned in the Magistrate's Court. His appearance gives away his state of mind. His hair is dishevelled. His collar is turned up for warmth. One newspaper reporter writes that the prisoner's eyes wandered restlessly and uneasily around the room, that he looked "fatigued, as if he had had quite enough."

He is charged with breaking and entering Dixon's butchery on or about 6 August 1909 and stealing a butcher's steel valued at ten shillings. The trial date is set for 26 April and he is remanded in custody.

Pawelka tells his counsel that he is not guilty of murder. He repeats his story about McRae being the cause of all his troubles. He declares that the only thing he is sorry for is that he did not shoot McRae and that if ever he got out again he would.

No Quarter

On 29 April 1910, twelve days after his arrest, Joe Pawelka is taken back to Palmerston for trial.

A large crowd is at the station to meet the Wellington train. Pawelka, manacled and escorted by police, appears fit and well. He is wearing a soft white shirt and green tie. As he is led away, someone calls from the crowd, "You're a hero, Pawelka," and the hero smiles.

Later, entering the packed courtroom handcuffed to his captors, Gallagher and Callery, he appears confident and even defiant, walking "almost majestically" to the dock.

As the thirteen indictments are read, a chain is forged from the theft of the butcher's steel on 13 July 1909 to the fires in Palmerston on the night of 5 April.

The trial sessions continue into June. Proceedings are reported in detail by the press. Millar and Giorgi, making the most of the free publicity, run half-page advertisements in the *Manawatu Evening Standard* for a "Great Sale of Salvaged Stock" from the fire that Joe Pawelka is accused of starting. Between court hearings, Pawelka is returned, heavily manacled, to Wellington's Terrace Prison.

At each of his appearances in court he listens carefully, smiling when an absurd charge is read and occasionally asking for pencil and paper to take notes. On 6 May, when charged with the murder of Sergeant McGuire, he gives a "convulsive start" but pleads not guilty in "a clear voice, sharp and emphatic."

It is not until 30 May that the evidence has been heard and reviewed. In his summing up, Mr. Justice Cooper points out that in the case of the McGuire shooting the evidence is circumstantial. Ominously, however, he compares the accumulated evidence to a rope, "each strand of which, though not strong enough to stand alone, yet contributed to the strength of the whole."

When the jury comes in, a hush falls over the courtroom. Joe Pawelka, "labouring under great excitement," eagerly scans their faces.

There is reasonable doubt. He is found "not guilty" of murder.

But the tension of the trial has brought him to the limits of his endurance, and he is taken from the courtroom in a state of collapse.

When the trial resumes on 1 June, Pawelka is obviously distressed. He demands that the police permit him to appear before the court in his dress suit. The request is refused on the grounds that the suit was stolen. In court he looks "worn and weary." His manner is described as "peculiar." The police suggest he is "shamming" and "feigning insanity."

To the ten charges of breaking and entering, theft and escape from custody, he pleads guilty. To the charges of arson, he pleads not guilty, even though he was captured in clothing stolen from Millar and Giorgi's draper's shop and his fingerprints were found on broken glass from the burned-down high school. Evidence that Pawelka was guilty of robbery under arms (the Kendall holdup) is considered too flimsy to sustain an indictment.

The trial ends on 5 June, five weeks after it began. Three days later, Pawelka comes up for sentencing. He stands before the court neatly dressed and clean-shaven.

Asked if he has anything to say before sentencing, he declares: "I am very sorry for the offences I have committed, and for which I appear before the Court. I hope you will be as lenient as possible with me. I committed some of the offences because I had to exist. Although I was found guilty of the furniture stealing, I no more stole the furniture than you did, sir!"

"Then you should not have pleaded guilty," Justice Cooper replies.

"I couldn't do anything else. The man I bought it off could not be found. I had receipts for it, but they could not be found either."

At this moment Pawelka falls back in a faint, and a glass of water is brought for him. He drinks, then in an almost inaudible voice attempts to tell his story. "I have had a very hard life, and have practically been on my own since I was thirteen years old. As for the charge of murder, I—"

"You were acquitted of that."

"I know, but people say I'm still guilty. I swear I was never near the place. I would sooner hang than be thought guilty."

With nothing more to say, Pawelka waits while Justice Cooper prepares his remarks.

> It is a very painful thing to have to pass sentence on a man as young as you are for a series of very serious crimes. But I have to do my duty. I have to protect the public against such offences. It may be that your early life has had something to do with your relapse into crime, but you have certainly during the past twelve months committed as many crimes (I am only referring to those crimes to which you have pleaded guilty and of which you were found guilty) as an ordinary criminal commits in the whole course of his life. You commenced your career of crime on the first November with the theft of a bicycle, and followed it by a series of offences of the most serious description—breaking and entering and stealing goods from the houses of various persons in this district. You have pleaded guilty in all to seven charges of breaking and entering from December last until February this year before your first escape from custody. On twelfth March you escaped. Then came another series of offences committed by you. You have pleaded guilty to five more charges of breaking and entering and have been found guilty of arson. I have a report which indicates that no doubt you have an ill-balanced mind. You attempted suicide before your first arrest. I have to do what I can to protect you against yourself, and I have to do more. I have to protect the public against you.

As the sentences are handed down, Pawelka seems stunned. When he hears the first sentence of seven years, he groans. He receives the second and third in silence. After pronouncing a cumulative sentence of twenty-one years, Mr. Justice Cooper observes that Pawelka is a habitual criminal, implying the possibility of indefinite detention.

* * *

Even before the sentence, sympathy for Pawelka had been growing. On the day Joe Pawelka was recaptured, the *New Zealand Truth* observed that he had already been "condemned without trial," and there was every possibility that some "mad-headed civilian or reward-seeking policeman might obviate the necessity of placing him in the dock." The conduct of the manhunt also came in for criticism. The *Christchurch Press* compared it to a hunt for a mad dog that would have driven any man to deeds of violence. Now, with the sentence passed, the *New Zealand Times* reproached the judge, calling the heavy sentence worse than a death sentence, "a clumsy attempt to wreak vengeance on a half-demented offender." One contemporary observer wrote: "Never in the history of New Zealand has there been such an agitation as that which followed the sentencing of Pawelka."

Dozens of letters to newspapers called the sentence cruel and inhuman. Protest meetings were held and trade unions took up the case. Delegations to the minister of justice asked that the sentence be reduced to fourteen years. Only the *Manawatu Evening Standard*, speaking on behalf of the region that had borne the brunt of the manhunt, declared the sentence fair. In an editorial of 10 June, one reads: "There is certainly a very humane and growing tendency to regard moral perversion more in the light of a disease and to prescribe reformative treatment rather than retributive punishment, but until the principle is completely recognised, judges have merely to administer the law as they find it."

Even in the Manawatu, not everyone shared this view. Pawelka committees were formed in Palmerston and Wanganui to press for a reduction in the sentence. And two men were brought before the court in Palmerston for coming to blows over the question as to whether Pawelka was rightly or wrongly treated.

All this was symptomatic of a deep division in New Zealand at the time. The poor who migrated to New Zealand in the late nineteenth century had hoped for freedom from want and exploitation. This engendered the strongly egalitarian ethos that survives in New Zealand even today, despite neoliberal governments. It is still considered unseemly to draw attention to yourself; you neither brag about your abilities or properties nor put others down. New Zealand even has a word for the vice of braggadocio, a word you don't hear so much these days—skiting. But in the early 1890s, with the economy coming slowly out of recession, the gap between workers and the well-to-do was widening. At one extreme were bankers, merchants, manufacturers, runholders, and wealthy farmers with their chambers of commerce, agricultural and pastoral associations, and elite social clubs. At the other extreme was an underclass struggling for living wages, bearable hours, and decent working conditions. Between these extremes was a burgeoning white-collar society of small businessmen, clerks, doctors, lawyers, and self-employed tradesmen whose values and aspirations were, by and large, those of the rich, not the poor. For a while, the poor saw unionization as an answer, and in 1891 trade union membership rose to a peak of about 23 percent of the population. The destitute and poor also made their voices heard in less legitimate protests: street marches in the cities, and, in rural areas, sheep stealing and rick and barn burning. By 1910, when Pawelka was tried and sentenced, trade unions were strong. A successful strike by miners at Blackball in 1908 had inspired watersiders, shearers, laborers, and clothing workers to consider "direct" action in the "class war," and members of these labor organizations saw Joe Pawelka as a victim of the class whose slogans about law and order disguised a double standard. The wealthy and educated got justice; the poor and uneducated lost out.

Thus Joe Pawelka became New Zealand's first avatar of that mythical figure that John Mulgan called *Man Alone*—a man of the working class, a bushman, a rugged individualist, an underdog, a law unto himself. We would recognize him again in 1941 when the Kowhitirangi farmer Eric Stanley Graham ran amok, and in 1962 when George Wilder broke out of New Plymouth Gaol and went bush.

But though poverty and powerlessness may have been the soil in which the seeds of Joe Pawelka's discontent took root, it would be a mistake to reduce the meaning of his life to that stony ground where he was born and raised.

Joe Pawelka abhorred cowardice, was driven by a need to prove himself the equal of any man, and had a bone to pick with the world. As a boy he fashioned a revolver from a sawn-off .22 rifle and became a crack shot. At one time he thought of becoming a policeman or railway guard. He was an

avid reader of such penny dreadfuls as *Deadwood Dick*. He felt lonely, abandoned, hard done by, and thwarted in his ambitions. But such dreams and
adversities have been shared by thousands who did not share his fate.

It is the particular way in which Joe Pawelka lived his fate that I find
fascinating. The question of how a person acts when robbed of the power
to act.

"We are not lumps of clay," Sartre writes in his biography of Jean Genet,
"and what is important is not what people make of us but what we ourselves
make of what they have made us."

Was there a lesson to be learned from Genet who, when deprived of his
freedom and made a scapegoat for the anxieties of others, embraced this
lack of freedom as though he himself had willed it—deciding, as he put it,
"to be what crime had made of me—a thief"?

* * *

Joe Pawelka was sentenced in early June 1910. Six weeks later his daughter
was born in Ashhurst. Lizzie, who had reverted to her maiden name, chris-
tened the child Iris. Father and daughter would never see each other, and
for two generations the Wilsons would expunge the name Pawelka from
their lives.

Joe Pawelka was held in a condemned cell at Wellington's Terrace Gaol
and kept under constant surveillance. It was intended that he should move
to a new wing of the prison as soon as construction was complete.

His family came to see him often. Joe always complained that Lizzie had
not got in touch with him and would ask when he was going to have a
chance to see his daughter. Louisa, who had visited the Wilsons in Ashhurst on several occasions, knew Lizzie would never consent to see Joe.
And Lizzie refused to allow him to see Iris either.

For a while Joe feigned sickness. Then he seemed to reconcile himself to
his fate and accept the constraints of prison life.

Indeed, it seems that he immediately set out to win the hearts of those
guarding him. He gave no trouble, was docile, conformed to prison discipline, and became a model prisoner.

Escape seems to have been the last thing on his mind, and to his jailors
escape was impossible. The strict watch of the day and night was relaxed,
and as Pawelka made progress physically, actually benefiting by the regular

hours of jail life, it was deemed necessary that the prisoner should learn a trade—tailoring or boot making. Pawelka chose the latter. The result was that the prisoner now mingled more freely with his fellow inmates, and from their daily intercourse Pawelka began to be regarded as a hero. Every prisoner was an admirer and wished Pawelka all sorts of luck. The eastern wing was completed, and in due course Pawelka shifted his quarters from the condemned cell. He was an omnivorous reader of light fiction, and his vice of cigarette smoking was indulged him. Even his jailers sympathized with him because of the term of imprisonment he had to serve.

* * *

A fortnight after the birth of his daughter, Joe Pawelka revealed his hidden hand. A twelve- or fourteen-foot double galvanized iron fence had been erected around the new wing. With the help of another prisoner, Joe slipped into the space between the two fences and waited for nightfall. Unfortunately for him, his absence from the boot shop was noticed almost at once and he was found and returned to his cell.

A week later he tried again to break out. Using a hacksaw blade, he sawed through the one-inch iron bars that protected his eighteen-inch cell window. It was only by chance that a warder caught him in the act of wriggling out. His cell was searched, and several more hacksaw blades were found (of a type used in the prison workshop), together with a rope ladder and a suit of black street clothes, presumably smuggled in by one of his prison visitors.

He was now watched both night and day and denied all privileges.

Undeterred, he attempted his third escape three days later.

On 17 August, the criminal court was in session, and several of Pawelka's jailers had to attend. That day Pawelka was placed in a small triangular yard supervised by an armed warder in a watchtower. A moment's inattention was all he needed. He leaped onto a ledge—a blind spot beneath the watchtower—scrambled over a corrugated iron roof, and dropped into the street. Again luck was against him. The wife of an ex-jailer spotted his arrow-marked prison uniform and raised the alarm. A quarter-hour after his escape he was found hiding under a cottage in Woolcombe Street not far from the jail.

He was placed in a condemned cell again, a light kept burning at night. There were two fifteen-by-twelve-inch gratings to this cell, each covered by a shutter. The shutters allowed warders to observe him at any time, and instructions were posted that Pawelka was to be checked every fifteen minutes.

The two condemned cells were in poor repair. Indeed, in Pawelka's cell one of the barred observation windows could not be locked. Before first light on Sunday 27 August, Joe removed one of the windows from its frame, got out into the corridor leading to the jail office and crossed into the kitchen yard. There he scaled a wall, clambered across the kitchen roof, and dropped eight feet onto a small hill outside the prison overlooking the Terrace.

The escape was well timed. It was Sunday. It was dark. And it was pouring rain. Pawelka had waited until an orderly officer checked his cell at 6 o'clock before making his move. But his escape would have been impossible without complicity. The screws that held the window in its frame had been removed by inmates during a renovation of the cell block three or four months before. When the prison workers reinstalled the window, they embedded it in blanket fluff and clay and created dummy screws with paint and putty. Also in Pawelka's favor, the door to the kitchen yard had been opened at 4:45 A.M. to allow the prison cooks access to the kitchen. Possibly another door leading from the corridor outside Pawelka's cell to the single officer's quarters had also been left open when the officer's cook passed through with a cup of tea for the chief warder.

Warder Eric Wallace raised the alarm a few minutes after 6 A.M. After checking the prisoner, he had gone to padlock a gate to the penal yard. But hearing a "sharp noise," he had retraced his steps. Pawelka was gone.

His shoes were outside the cell door. Inside the cell were his arrow-marked cap and blankets, together with some cigarette butts and three books: *Pickwick Papers, America at Work,* and *No Name.*

The day broke wet and windy. Sixty police were brought in for the search. They scoured the Wellington hills, searched houses, trampled gardens, kept a watch on the waterfront, and set up roadblocks on the main roads out of the city, but apart from a single report by a milk-delivery boy who said he'd seen a figure in white making for the Botanical Gardens before dawn, there were no sightings, no clues.

In the weeks that followed there was talk of Pawelka being taken aboard a schooner bound for Australia, of Pawelka drowning in Wellington Harbor, and of Pawelka being given his freedom when he agreed, in the absence of the official hangman, to execute a condemned Māori murderer called Kaka.

Rumor and rain covered his tracks.

Part Two

Carlo Ginzburg begins his study of truth, falsity, and fiction in the writing of history by evoking the Minoan labyrinth designed by Daedalus for King Midas of Knossos to contain the ferocious half-human, half-bull Minotaur. "The Greeks tell us that Theseus received a thread as a gift from Ariadne. With that thread he found his bearings in the labyrinth, located the Minotaur, and slew him. The myth says nothing about the traces that Theseus left as made his way through the labyrinth."

For Ginzburg, it is the thread of narrative that enables us to "orient ourselves in the labyrinth of reality." As for traces, the root meaning of the ancient Greek ἱστορία (*historía*) is "tracking"—an art of divining events that have left traces, or spoors, but are no longer accessible in their entirety, either in objective reality or in memory.

I began my second stint of research on Joe Pawelka after returning to New Zealand from the United States to attend my father's funeral, and the labyrinthine archive in which I had hoped to find traces of Joe Pawelka now became a metaphor for my personal search for bearings. If the coherence of written history depends on a story line, the meaning of my own life story depended on the meaning I could find in my father's life, and this awareness of how one life implicates another undoubtedly shaped the course my new fieldwork.

My most pressing concern was to trace members of the Pawelka family. So far I had wound up in archives and cemeteries. Like the winter day I walked over a windswept hill near Kimbolton where lichen-covered graves huddled among laurels, box, and yew. There was a cold wind blowing across the Oroua valley, threatening rain, and I did not stay long. And I found no Pawelkas; only a lopsided white wooden cross with the name Agnes Elizabeth Hansen painted on a strip of tin. Joe Pawelka's oldest sister had died only nine years ago.

In Wellington, Richard Hill, the official police historian, had urged me to get in touch with Ray Carter. Ray was a retired senior constable who had interviewed members of the Pawelka family when researching his history of the Palmerston North police district, and he might give me some leads. I wrote to Ray Carter, mentioning my grandfather and my long-standing interest in Joe Pawelka, and in reply Ray invited me to visit him when I was next in Palmerston North.

* * *

Following Joe Pawelka's trail into the land of the living made me unsure of my ground and brought to mind many of the anxieties I had felt when embarking on my first fieldwork in Sierra Leone twenty-six years ago.

Ray's house was white stucco, with a neat lawn and concrete driveway. The front door was a pane of frosted glass, a tulle curtain inside. I pressed the doorbell nervously.

Ray seemed not at all suspicious. He led me into the sitting room and invited me to sit down. A copy of the *Manawatu Evening Standard* lay open on the coffee table. The front page story was about a kidnapping at gunpoint and high-speed car chase through the Manawatu. Ray was surprised I hadn't heard about it. There was so much violent crime these days, he said. Things were going from bad to worse. In his entire police career he had carried a firearm only once. But now . . .

"It was the same in my grandfather's day," I said. "He carried a truncheon. He said that if you carried a gun you had to be ready to use it, and he didn't want to risk that."

"Nowadays the Armed Offenders' Squad is out all the time," Ray said.

We chatted for a while about the stresses of police work. Then Ray took a slip of paper from a conjurer's table and passed it to me.

It gave details of my grandfather's police service, including his six years between 1908 and 1915 stationed in Levin. Fred Longbottom. No.: 1267. Born: England 21 October 1877. Sworn: 26 June 1906. Retired on pension: 13 December 1943.

Ray explained that a new police station had just been opened in Levin. He had assembled a large collection of old photographs for the occasion, but hadn't been able to lay his hands on a photo of my grandfather. Perhaps I had one I could send him?

"I suppose he took a lot of flak because of his name," Ray said.

"Being called Longbottom can't have been any more bothersome than being called Michael Jackson," I said. I told Ray that I envied my grandfather's thick skin. When friends urged him to change his name by deed poll to Long, he wouldn't hear of it.

"In the force they called him Longy," Ray said.

As we reminisced, I began to relax. I realized how fortuitous it was that my grandfather had been a cop. It made it easier for me to broach the subject of Joe Pawelka.

When Ray offered to make coffee or tea, I said I'd like a cup of tea, and followed him into the kitchen where he put on the kettle and emptied some biscuits out of a packet. When I asked Ray about the conjuring table in the other room, he explained that he was secretary of the local magic club.

I told Ray that my grandfather had been a constable in Halifax at the time Harry Houdini made his famous tour of England. He'd been in Bradford in 1901 when Houdini escaped from a locked cell in the police station. My grandfather admired Houdini and used to tell me stories about his various stunts and athletic feats.

"An interesting coincidence," I said, "was that Houdini was on tour in Australia in March and April 1910, performing his escapes from handcuffs and straitjackets at the same time Joe Pawelka broke out of prison and did his vanishing act."

Ray confessed that he had not dug very deeply into the Pawelka story. After all, it had been just one item among many that he'd had to research for his history of the Palmerston North police district. But he had gone up to Kimbolton in July 1985 and interviewed Joe Pawelka's sister.

"I think Agnes got fed up with reporters over the years," Ray said. "She'd been so pestered by people wanting to know what happened to her brother that she clammed up."

When talking to Agnes, Ray had been careful not to pry. He neither referred to her brother's crimes nor to his escape from prison. He'd been forewarned that he'd be shown the door if he did. But the conversation went well, and Ray felt that Agnes trusted him. When her son Jack came to take her to a doctor's appointment in Feilding, Agnes invited Ray to come back some time and talk with her again.

But Ray never did go back. A few weeks later, his wife died of cancer. And Agnes died the same month, aged ninety-six. Ray remembered the exact date because it fell so soon after his wife's death.

"It was the same with my interview with Jack Hansen," Ray said. "I began to interview him, but never followed it up."

But he did learn something that might interest me. Sometime during World War I, Joe's parents received a photo of a group of soldiers clipped from a newspaper. There were about thirty soldiers in the photograph. They were in a desert somewhere. Around one of the soldiers in the back row a circle had been drawn. The family were unable to decipher the postmark on the envelope, and there was no letter to indicate who had sent the photo or why.

I asked Ray if he minded if I took some notes.

He didn't mind; he was only sorry he couldn't help me more. He'd felt the same when Joe Pawelka's granddaughter came to see him, asking if he could tell her something about her grandfather.

I was astounded. "His granddaughter?" I exclaimed. At this moment my *historical* research suddenly entered present time. What had been a fixed record of past events, replete with gaps and unanswerable questions, instantly became a world of real people in which my place and position would be radically redefined.

Early in 1984, Ray was visited by a woman who'd traveled up from Wellington with her son. She told Ray that only two weeks before she had learned of the identity of her grandfather. Her name was Anne Harris, and her mother's maiden name was Iris Wilson.

Although Ray had taken only a passing interest in Joe Pawelka, he had been stunned to discover not only the existence of Joe's granddaughter but the fact that an old friend with whom he'd traveled to England and France thirty years ago for a scout jamboree was Anne's ex-husband.

After I had copied Anne's address and telephone number into my note-book, our talk drifted away from Joe Pawelka. Ray pointed out photos of his wife on the china cabinet and mantelpiece. Then he showed me a photo of himself in dress uniform, with the governor-general pinning a medal to his chest. It was the Queen's Medal, he explained. He received it the year he retired. It was an odd thing. For years he and his wife used to scan the birthday honors list and joke about his name not being included. Then one day he picked up the paper and was incredulous to see his name on the list. If only she had been alive to share it with him, to remember how they joked for all those years about his name being omitted.

I said it was strange that I had lived in Palmerston North for almost ten years yet our paths had never crossed.

Ray said he had policed the Massey campus during the seventies, but didn't remember meeting me.

"I must have been keeping out of trouble," I said.

As Ray rambled on with anecdotes about his police days, I kept think-ing of the ways in which the stories we tell reshape the experiences we have had and often eclipse our memory of an actual event. Perhaps this explains why people who commit what they consider a justified crime protest their innocence with such conviction. The story of what occurred is gradually supplanted by the story told in mitigation.

When I asked Ray about this kind of misprision, he said he was all too familiar with it. "It's very typical of sex offenders," he said. "They often imagine that their victim was a willing party to the act and even derived pleasure from it."

Ray described how some years ago, when he was relieving at Woodville, a man came into the police station and asked to see Constable X, who was normally in charge there. "He's away for a month," Ray told him. The man asked Ray if he could speak to him in private. When they were alone, the man confessed to sex offenses he'd committed in 1948. He couldn't live with the memory of what he'd done. He had to own up. Ray wrote down the names of the two girls who had been molested. He told the man he would look into the matter. The police traced one of the girls. She was now a married woman with three children. She did not want to talk about what had happened all those years ago. She'd tried to forget. There was no question of taking action. Of prosecuting. It was past, and she wanted to bury it in the past.

"Do you think Joe Pawelka's family also wanted to forget the past?"

"Forget, perhaps. But whether they ever forgave him is another matter. You should talk to Jack Hansen about that."

Jack Hansen, I now learned, was Joe Pawelka's nephew.

Talking to Jack Hansen

In 1890 Cornelis J. Hansen owned a drapery shop on the Palmerston Square. A canny businessman, he traveled the Manawatu in a horse-drawn dray, selling haberdashery and bartering needles, thread, ribbons, and fabric for a side of lamb or other farm produce.

With its bracing air and invigorating climate, Kimbolton was the one place where he found respite from his asthma. He moved there in 1891 and established premises on the main street. A couple of years later, his son William took over the business and opened a general store. The Pawelkas were among his first customers.

When I went up to Kimbolton to meet Jack Hansen, the store looked much the same as it did in photos taken a hundred years ago: clapboard exterior, verandah roofed with corrugated iron, seven verandah posts with wrought iron capitals . . . though HANSEN'S STORE on the fascia had been temporarily painted out.

Jack Hansen was the third generation Hansen to have run the store. He was born there, lived there all his life, and never married. The floor of the shop was covered with worn, brown body carpet. I took in the ubiquitous Tip Top ice cream signs, racks of chocolate bars and potato chips, shelves of tinned food and cornflakes. In the corner was the inevitable collection of Sylvester Stallone and Chuck Norris videos.

I explained to the man behind the counter that I was looking for Jack Hansen. Jack had a flat out the back, I was told. If I walked through the shop, I'd see his door. "Just knock and go on in. He's always there."

Jack was sitting in a fireside chair. He levered himself up and stood shakily for a moment as I introduced myself. I mentioned Ray Carter, and explained that I had come from the United States to do some research on Joe Pawelka.

We shook hands, and Jack gestured for me to sit down.

PLATE 4. MICHAEL JACKSON

"I hope the weather stays good," he said. "You never know what it's going to do at this time of year."

To broach the subject of Jack's uncle I referred to the stories my grandfather told me when I was a boy and my grandfather's opinion that Joe had got a raw deal. I also told Jack that I had lived in the Manawatu for many years and had always wanted to know what happened to Joe and where he ended up.

Jack's wry look unsettled me. I had a strong sense that I was broaching matters that were none of my business. I was presuming too much and would be told nothing.

"Well, he must have been a superman to have committed all those crimes," Jack said drily.

I mentioned the photo that Ray had described to me.

Jack remembered the photo. He had no idea what had become of it. It was actually a photo Joe's mother clipped from a newspaper—of a group of American or Canadian soldiers in France. Louisa was convinced that one of the soldiers in the photo was Joe. "She was absolutely sure it was he. I—I don't know. I suppose it could've looked like somebody . . . but then, would a mother know her own child?"

"Perhaps it was wishful thinking. Something for her to hang on to."

"Yeah. I think that's one of the reasons. She'd made up her mind it was him. That would give her some peace of mind. He promised to write. But he never did. I'll never forgive him for that. Because he broke his promise to his mother."

I asked if Joe's family ever spoke of him.

"Seldom, if ever," Jack said. "It was only when I was in my twenties and asked outright that I was told anything. The family kept its own counsel. Partly it was fear of prosecution for having aided and abetted the fugitive. Partly it was shame—because of the ill repute Joe brought upon them. It was hard," Jack said. "It was always hard for the mother."

Jack reminded me that he was born in 1913, a couple of years after Joe's final gaol break, so much of his knowledge was hearsay. "The family never said much. But everyone felt sorry for him. He'd been so unfairly treated." Jack was sure that a warder or policeman must have had a hand in helping Joe escape from the Terrace Gaol in Wellington. Leaving a door open. Leaving the way clear.

"My grandfather thought so too," I said. "But from what I've read it was his prison cohorts who helped him get away. They saw him as a victim of injustice, even more so than themselves. A kind of hero."

"People helped him up here, too," Jack said.

Jack gave me the impression that the entire Kimbolton community closed ranks to keep Joe hidden during the six months between the spring of 1911 and the summer of 1912. Jack's father, who was married to Joe's sister Agnes, was actively involved. "Dad had a finger in the pie," Jack said, "if he wasn't the whole pie."

Opposite Lowe's Boarding House, on the corner of Grammar Street and Kimbolton Road, there used to be a general store and row of outbuildings that belonged to Jack and Hilton Fowler. The last building in the row was a grain store. It was here that Willie Hansen hid his brother-in-law, Joe Pawelka. Years later, the Kiwitea County Council bought the buildings and converted the old grain store into a garage. When the floorboards of the grain store were torn up in preparation for pouring a concrete slab, some musty old prison clothes were discovered. Supposing them to have belonged to Joe Pawelka, the council presented them to Willie Hansen as a souvenir.

"Do you think your father was sympathetic to Joe, or was he simply being loyal to your mother's family in helping him out?"

"I think possibly because Joe was his brother-in-law, and he wanted him out of the way—" Jack chuckled, "—out of his—"

Jack's laughter left the sentence hanging.

"Did your father ever tell you what happened to Joe? Did Joe's fate concern him?"

"I don't think it worried him."

"He didn't ever try to find out whether—"

"No. No," Jack said slowly, but with finality. "I don't think so."

"Just getting him out of the district was enough? He'd done his job?"

"He'd done his job, yeah."

"Yet everyone in Kimbolton knew what your father was up to?"

"Everyone knew. Joe's mum cooked meals for him. Willie conveyed them over the road to Joe. And Joe used to help his father down at the forest reserve. I think the local vicar walked in on them one day. But he never spilled the beans. Even the local constable turned a blind eye."

"It was hard to know how accurate this observation was. At the time of Joe's escape, the police assumed he would try to see Lizzie again. Believing they would "get this man through his wife," they kept a close watch on the Wilson house in Ashhurst. It was also thought likely that Joe would return home.

On 11 October 1911, six weeks after Joe's escape, Sergeant Bowden went up to Kimbolton from Feilding to interview Willie Hansen. In his report, written the same day, Bowden noted: "Mr. Hansen says personally he has never seen Pawelka since he came out of the Palmerston North hospital that was before his trouble commenced." Willie Hansen assured Bowden that he "did not assist or succour Pawelka at any time, and he was quite sure his wife did not, as she had none of his money to do it with."

Hansen went on to say that if Joe was still in the country "his friends are keeping him safe, but if he had got out of the country and could keep away it will be a good job"—implying that Joe was so attached to his wife and child that he would go to any lengths to see them. When Bowden asked Hansen if he thought that Pawelka had left New Zealand, Hansen replied, "Oh, God knows where he is, but one thing is certain, sooner or later he will see his wife and child if they remain at Ashhurst."

At the end of the interview, Hansen and Bowden shook hands.

"Well, Sergeant," said Hansen, "Joe is a miracle to get away as he did. God knows where he has got to."

Bowden may have taken Willie Hansen's remarks with a grain of salt. Two weeks after talking to Hansen, he ordered Constable Fitzgibbon at Kimbolton to "carefully approach Mr. Hansen and ascertain if possible if he or any of the family has heard of the whereabouts of the escaped prisoner."

Fitzgibbon spoke to Hansen two days after Bowden interviewed him and filed his report on 28 October 1911.

Apparently, Willie Hansen volunteered the remark that he had given Bowden "the straight lip." Sooner or later, Pawelka was bound to visit Ashhurst. Fitzgibbon asked if this view was founded on facts.

> Hansen replied well to be candid with you, Yes. Hansen further stated, I have heard through his relatives that he was making for Ashhurst, and I expected he would turn up there long before now, but apparently he has been headed off, or some of his friends might have warned him that he was watched there. I have not seen Joe since he got out, and I don't know his whereabouts, but I know for a fact he has not left the country. I don't know what the police think of Joe, but it is my opinion the man is mad, in fact, he is a lunatic. He gets into mad fits at times. I don't know if it is through bad temper or not, but when he is in one of his mad fits he is dangerous, from what I have heard from Joe's relatives, and it is also my opinion that Joe will visit Ashurst [sic] to see his Child, and if he turns up there in one of his mad fits I am afraid he would murder his wife, that is, of course, providing she didn't receive him with open arms, but if she did things might be different, but as far as I am aware I don't think his wife has any time for him. Joe might change his mind and try to leave the Country, but this, in my opinion, is not a very easy matter to do. He must get impatient in time, and if the Police play a waiting game they are sure to catch him.

Fitzgibbon concluded his report: "I have carefully questioned Hansen but could obtain no further information from him. It is my opinion Hansen is not assisting the prisoner, but I do beleive [sic] he could give information as to prisoner's whereabouts, but this he would not disclose."

It is difficult to establish whether or not Fitzgibbon was part of a local conspiracy to shelter the fugitive. At the time he wrote his report he had been stationed in Kimbolton only fifteen months, though he would remain there for a further nine years. Whether loyalty to the community took precedence over loyalty to his office, one cannot judge. In Inglewood, my grandfather sometimes bent the rules or turned a blind eye on minor infractions of the law such as after-hours drinking, but helping an escaped prisoner evade justice was another matter. The story of Fitzgibbon's involvement is probably a reflection of our communitarian bias.

Indeed, it recalls a story Richard Hill tells about an Otira policeman whose best mate was allegedly Joe Pawelka. Given the absence of evidence that the policeman in question had any criminal mates, one may suppose that the anecdote is born of a collective desire to erase the differences between authority figures and underlings. Like the notion that prison officers rather than fellow prisoners helped Pawelka escape from the Terrace Gaol.

Then there was the vexing matter of Willie Hansen's vilification of his brother-in-law. Informing the police that Joe was most likely to head for Ashhurst could have been a clever ruse. Are we to suppose that calling Joe a lunatic was also a device to throw Fitzgibbon off the scent? Or was there more ambivalence in Joe Pawelka's hometown than legend would care to admit? I found it difficult to dismiss from my mind the derogatory way Willie Hansen had spoken about his brother-in-law when interviewed by a newspaperman at the height of the manhunt, particularly his assertion that Pawelka would "get no sympathy from his people."

I asked Jack if there had been bad blood between the Hansens and the Pawelkas. After all, Millar and Giorgi's drapery shop, which Joe allegedly burgled and burned to the ground on 5 April 1910, was, according to newspaper reports at the time, owned by Cornelis J. Hansen. Did Joe have a grudge against Hansen? If so, did this grudge have anything to do with the fact that Joe's sister, Agnes, had married a Hansen two years before?

Jack said my account was "not quite correct." C. J. Hansen's shop was next door to Millar and Giorgi's. Joe wouldn't have set fire to the draper's because his father-in-law's shop would have gone up in flames as well. "Anyway, Joe wouldn't have held a grudge against my father, because really my father protected Joe very much."

In fact, Millar and Giorgi's *was* leased from C. J. Hansen. Perhaps Pawelka hadn't known this, or hadn't cared. But I didn't want to press Jack on the matter. Not that I despaired at resolving it. Rather, I was more fascinated by people's stories of these long-ago events than setting the historical record straight. And there was also the question of discretion and tact— being sensitive to Jack's situation and his understanding of the past.

I asked Jack if he had read Des Swain's book, *Pawelka*.

"I've got a copy, yes."

"Was Des Swain correct in saying that Joe traveled to Auckland by overnight train and boarded a ship for Vancouver?"

Jack affirmed that this was true.

"Why Canada?"

"No idea."

Jack described how his father got a Masonic brother and close friend, a local farmer called Sam Hall, to buy the train and boat tickets. "They hatched the plan out on his farm." The Pawelkas, Hansens, and Willie Hansen's friend scraped up the money for the fare. It was decided that a young man called Ted Lawrence, who worked on the farm, would accompany Joe to Auckland. "They knew Lawrence could be trusted. That's how he came into the picture."

"Was Ted Lawrence a mate of Joe's?"

"No, no. Didn't know him. No, he just worked for this great friend of Dad's."

"Are there Lawrences still in the district?"

"No. No. Ted'd be dead many years, and I think his son, I think he's dead, too, now."

"Anyone I could contact?"

"No. At any rate, Lawrence wouldn't have dared mention it in case he was—"

"Accessory after the fact."

"Yeah. So his family wouldn't have known what their father got up to."

"So Ted took Joe up to Mangaweka?"

"No, Joe's father took him to Mangaweka, hidden under sacks in a dray."

"Then where did Ted board the train?"

"At Mangaweka, I think. I think they met at Mangaweka."

February. Midsummer. The overnight train pulled into Mangaweka in the evening. So it would have been daylight. It must have been a nerve-racking moment.

Next day in Auckland, Ted and Joe had only a short walk from the railway station to the new Queen Street Wharf where Joe was to board a ship bound for Canada.

Having got Joe onto the boat, Ted went ashore. He returned to say good-bye not long before the boat sailed, but couldn't find Joe anywhere. So there was no certainty that Joe actually sailed.

I wanted to press Jack further on this, but hesitated. I knew that Des Swain had interviewed Helen and had been unable to take Joe's story beyond the point I had reached with Jack. I had to assume that Agnes would have shared what she knew with her son. And I did not think Jack was prevaricating.

I glanced around the room. On either side of the fireplace were shelves of Agnes's old books. Frank Slaughter, Frances Parkinson Keyes, Frank L. Packard, A.J. Cronin. The same books my grandfather used to read. On the mantelpiece, a clock, vases of artificial flowers and family photos, includ-ing one of Jack's mother Agnes in her ninety-fourth year.

"You know, it's a pity you didn't get started on your research a bit sooner," Jack said, "when my mother was alive. And my Aunt Helen. She died only last July. She might have been able to help you, too."

I felt I had come to the end of the road.

"There's not a lot I can tell you," Jack went on. "Not a lot that's known. Like I said, it's mostly hearsay."

"It must be difficult, living with so many things unresolved," I said. "So much unfinished business." I didn't mean the rifts that might exist in the town. I meant the impossibility of ever knowing for certain what became of Joe after Ted Lawrence last saw him in Auckland.

Jack didn't seem to hear. He wanted to know what I planned to do with my research. What use I was going to make of it.

I said I was thinking of writing a book.

"A lot of nonsense has been written," Jack said, and promptly asked if I had seen the film about Pawelka that had been shown on TV a few years ago. "Rubbish!" he exclaimed. "It was all about the shooting of McGuire. All the scandal. Everything made so melodramatic."

Jack recalled a conversation with the producer/director, Allan Lindsay. Lindsay had requested an interview, and Jack agreed to a meeting in Feilding.

"I didn't want Mum to be a part of it," Jack said. So while he met the filmmaker in the Catholic presbytery, Agnes went into the church and spent the time on her knees in prayer.

By the end of the interview, Jack felt very uneasy. "You got any family?" he asked the filmmaker.

"Yes."

"Let's hope it doesn't happen to them."

Jack meant the shame and exposure.

For as long as his mother lived he "vetted" the daily paper before she saw it, clipping out items that might rub salt into her wounds. He still had the clippings in an envelope somewhere.

"She kept her hurt and her thoughts to herself," Jack said. "But people kept wanting to drag it all out into the open again."

When the Centennial Exhibition opened in Wellington in 1940, it included a "Chamber of Horrors" with a tableau showing Joe Pawelka's recapture in the Ashhurst cow byre. There were empty beer bottles on the hay bales, and Pawelka had pistols drawn.

"It made me sick," Jack said. "I hadn't been bothered much up till then, but I felt hurt at what I saw."

"Shame?"

"It was the shock that upset me. Not shame. It was never spoken of in the house, you see. I was shocked and upset seeing what had been kept in the dark now so exposed, so public."

I said that these were the things I found least compelling. It was the way Joe Pawelka's life touched our lives even now that intrigued me.

Jack said nothing, and I judged it was time to go. We stood up together and shook hands. I told Jack I was grateful to him for talking to me. "It can't be easy, dealing with some stranger who turns up out of the blue, asking a lot of vexing questions."

Jack assured me that he had enjoyed our conversation. Like Ray Carter, Jack was only sorry he could not help me more.

* * *

The sunlight was blinding as I crossed the road to the Commercial Hotel where there were some photos I wanted to see.

The bar was deserted, but the proprietor came out from a back room and asked if there was anything he could get me. I said I wanted to see some of the old photos in the front bar. Could I walk through?

There was one photo, considerably enlarged, of Lowe's Family and Commercial Hotel in 1901 or 1902. Standing in front of the hotel were the proprietor and his wife, three maids in pinafores (possibly the proprietor's daughters), and a few locals. There were also two gigs and Sam Daw's mail coach from Feilding.

The proprietor watched me from the bar as I scrutinized the photo.

"That young man standing in the road, that's Joe Pawelka," he said.

I looked hard. Pawelka would have been thirteen or fourteen at the time.

"He was a hard case," the proprieter said, and began regaling me with stories about how Joe lived in barns and sheds, and locals smuggled food and clothing to him. According to some reports, he was hidden for a while in the big warehouse behind Hansen's shop, which was always kept locked. At one time he was hidden under the floorboards of the shed that used to stand on the corner opposite the hotel. Often he was brought into the hotel at night for a hot bath and a square meal. No one gave him away, although one day his eight-year-old sister Helen came home from school at lunch-time, accompanied by a friend, to fetch a book she had forgotten and found him sitting in the kitchen.

* * *

Driving to the Pohangina Valley that afternoon, where I was staying with old friends, I kept thinking of the effect Joe's disappearance must have had on his family. For the police and for the newspapers, his disappearance was a mystery to be solved, a case to be closed. For historians, it was a matter of sorting out fact from fiction. But for the family it was a matter of surviving a loss whose repercussions might never be completely known. Of trying to find the fugitive shape of an ending for Joe's story in the story of *its* life over several generations. I was reminded of things I had read about Butch Cassidy who, like Joe Pawelka, grew up in a poor rural family, was a first-born son, got into crime, and became the focus of popular sympathy and the stuff of legend. What did his family think and feel during the years Butch was in South America, before he came back to the States to begin a new life under an assumed name?

When in her nineties Lula Parker-Betenson related the story of her brother, Robert Parker (Butch Cassidy), to a ghost writer, struggling to explain why he had become an outlaw. "Did he see too few roses and too many thorns?" she asked. "Too few rainbows and too many dark clouds?" She felt her brother had been "a victim of his early choices . . . trapped by his reputation; he could not escape it." But for Lula the real tragedy was not his, but his family's. "He didn't realize that when he went to prison, a whole family was sentenced with him, especially Mother and Dad. Even though he escaped retribution so many times by evading the law, we felt the full impact of his crimes. No amount of rationalizing that he was Robin Hood—taking from the rich and giving to the poor—could relieve our parents of the terrible load they carried every day of their lives because of him. . . . Mother's heart was broken over this wayward son. Her prayers remained unanswered. Even though we were a fun-loving lot, always there was the undercurrent of shame and humiliation. . . . Mother was fifty-eight when she died, and I have always felt she literally died of a broken heart."

I was also reminded of Robyn Jensen's story that had recently been reviewed in an Auckland paper.

Robyn Jensen's daughter Kirsa disappeared in the spring of 1983 when she was fourteen. Kirsa was probably murdered. The prime suspect killed himself in 1992. Kirsa's body was never found. For months, then years, Robyn Jensen had to endure not knowing what had happened to her daughter. "We were in a vacuum," she said. "Our grief was stationary. We were not able to move to the next step because there was no next step." One of the worst things for Robyn Jensen was the way the media appropriated the tragedy. Writing a book in which she wrested back control of Kirsa's story brought a kind of freedom, helping her reclaim what had been taken from her. But it provided no real ending. "There is no conclusion, no resolution," she said, "until Kirsa is returned to me."

* * *

Late that afternoon, Henry, Karen, and I went down to the river with a hamper of cold meats, home-baked bread, black olives, and a spinach salad.

As Karen shared out the food and Henry uncorked a bottle of his feijoa wine, I spoke of my conversation with Jack Hansen and of the fear in which the Pawelka family lived after aiding and abetting Joe's escape from New Zealand. "The worst of it must have been the distress of never knowing for certain what had happened to him, the impossibility of ever drawing the story of his life to a close."

"Why not write your own ending?" Henry suggested. "Isn't that what writers are licensed to do?"

"I wouldn't want to do that," I said. "The truth might not always be stranger than fiction, but it's usually a lot more compelling."

"What you were saying reminds me of my uncle," Karen said. He's now in his late seventies. He was adopted when he was a baby. His parents kept the truth from him until he was grown up, and then it was too late for him to trace his birth parents. Now it obsesses him. He says his life has been a travesty. The only thing that matters to him now is to know who his mother and father really were. To know their names. How they came to have him. Why they gave him away."

I said: "It's like those times when someone calls you and you're not at home, but instead of leaving a message on your answering machine the caller leaves nothing but a long silence."

"Or when the phone rings," Karen said, "and you don't get to it in time, and you're left wondering who on earth it was who called."

Henry read the sky. He pointed out the hogsbacks and mare's tails over the Ruahines, and said we were in for a change.

"I think I'll head south tomorrow," I said.

"Must you go so soon?" Karen asked.

"There's someone I have to see in Wellington," I said, "someone who's a vital part of the story."

That night it rained. I lay awake listening to the rain's soft flow and patter on the iron roof.

In my journal I wrote, "One writes to close an account. To make good a loss. Creating ghost dialogues in one's own mind in order to reach an understanding that was never quite reached in life. One writes to fill a gap that life has left in one's soul. In the artifice of closure is the hope of renewal. Which is why storytelling is akin to the healing arts. A way of making things whole."

In the darkness, Henry's pig dogs yelped at their chains.

Passing Strange

Driving south through the rain-rinsed landscape, macrocarpas massed against the morning as though they had soaked up the night and were hoarding it. Was my search for Joe Pawelka a wild goose chase, to use one of my father's favorite phrases? An attempt to recapture or work through my own troubled past?

At the turn off to the Ohariu Valley Road near Johnsonville, the road signs were silhouetted riders. Anne Harris's house was tucked into an armpit of the hill, a corner of the switchback road. There were ceramic pots and urns in the yard. Blue agapanthus, sweetpeas, and daisies.

Anne came out to greet me. Had I had any trouble following her directions? She invited me into a sunlit living room. Beyond the north-facing windows, the hills were cusped like molars.

"I'm just making a pot of tea," Anne said. "Or would you prefer coffee?"

There was a tape recorder on the coffee table, and a shallow bowl filled with sprigs of rosemary and slices of lemon.

"To help the memory," Anne said. "I'm so interested in finding out everything I can, but half the time I don't make a proper record of what I do find out, so today I'm prepared."

It took me aback that Anne should think I might enlighten her. But I was glad there'd be a record of our conversation. I wouldn't have to take notes. We'd be free to talk.

After pouring the tea, Anne switched on the tape recorder, and I began telling her how I had become interested in her grandfather through my own grandfather's stories.

Anne said she had learned of the identity of her grandfather only ten years ago. Joe's younger sister, Florence Helen Pawelka, had married Duncan Bryce. It had been their son, John Bryce, who had contacted her in early 1984 when he was doing genealogical research on his own family. This was the first time in her life she'd had any inkling of who her mother's father really was.

"Why do you think your mother kept you in the dark?" I asked.

"She wanted to forget it. It had such a terrible impact on her life. They felt they couldn't talk about it. But it was all so unnecessary, that flagellation."

"How did you feel when you discovered the truth?"

"I was totally aghast that I'd never been told. And very hurt. Hurt that mother didn't feel I was a suitable person to tell. She told my brother, after all."

"It must have been painful for your mother. For her mother, too. Always wondering if Joe would turn up again. Never being able to get over the misfortune of her marriage."

"It was tough. Pretty tough. My grandmother brought my mother up on her own. She reverted to her maiden name. But, I guess, had I known the story, I probably would have seen—" Anne hesitated. "Lizzie died relatively young. She was born in 1881, and died in 1945."

Anne opened up a scrapbook in which she'd written details of her lineage.

The Wilsons had emigrated from England on the Edwin Fox in 1878. They hailed from Rosedale, Yorkshire. Joseph was a farm laborer. His wife, Hannah, had already given birth to seven children. They settled in Nelson for a while, then moved to Ashhurst. Lizzie was born there in 1881, her mother's last child. Joseph died there in 1900.

Anne said she was struck by a recurrent motif in her family history. Hannah had been sixty-three when her husband died. Her youngest daughter, Hannah Elizabeth, was only thirteen at the time. So little Hannah, or Lizzie as she was called, grew up without a father. More significantly, she was made to fill the emotional void that Joseph's death had left in Hannah's life. This deep bond between mother and daughter may have made it difficult for Hannah to let Lizzie have a life of her own. Even if Joe Pawelka had been a "suitable boy" in her eyes, he could not but be seen as a threat to her relationship with her last-born.

"How did the motif recur?"

Anne explained that Lizzie was also destined to raise her daughter Iris alone. So, generation after generation, the shaping influence in the lives of these women was their mothers. The fathers were absent.

I mentioned to Anne the unflattering portrait that had often been drawn of her grandmother. Like Rosina Pawelka, Hannah Wilson is seen as a domineering woman, meddling in her children's lives, trying to control their destinies.

"Old Granny Wilson was a very strong lady," Anne said. "She may have felt that her daughter had married beneath her."

"What of Lizzie?"

Anne felt that it was unfair to blame Lizzie for everything that went wrong in her brief marriage to Joe Pawelka. "She was a very gentle person. She played the piano. She never struck me as domineering."

Anne showed me a photo of herself with Lizzie. There was a pine tree, a paddock. Gorse. The old lady is holding something in her hand and smiling as her granddaughter, Anne, reaches up for it. Anne was one and a half when the photo was taken, but has no memory of the occasion.

"Where do you think Joe went wrong?"

"Was it just a bad break?" Anne asked. "He married a woman six years older than himself. That may have meant more in those days. And he was just a butcher. Didn't have much money. And I can imagine my grandmother, with her mother in the background, probably telling her, 'He's not good enough for you—'"

The sun streamed through the windows. The convoluted landscape was lost in the summer haze.

When Anne discovered that her grandfather was Joe Pawelka, she sought from Joe's youngest sister Helen some insight into the kind of person he had been. Though Helen had been only eight when her brother disappeared, she was now Anne's sole link to him, and she didn't want to lose it.

"We had an understanding," Anne said. If Helen died, it was agreed that she would try to get in touch with Anne from the other side. "When you go, you must contact me," Anne told her. "When I hear you've gone, I'll be waiting by the fireplace."

I glanced at the fireplace in the shadows of the room.

"Funnily enough, the night after she died, I woke suddenly at two in the morning. I was suddenly wide awake. I got out of bed and came down here, and wandered around, but I couldn't think of anything, so I went back to bed. Next morning, I did the same. By this time, I knew she had died. So I sat down here and tried to clear my mind of everything. Then I remembered that the night before I had been searching through some letters and I'd pulled out one particular envelope and put it on the breakfast table. I hadn't even looked at the name on it. It was the last letter Helen had written to me. I thought to myself, well there are ways . . . and I prefer to believe that she was trying, in her way, to communicate with me."

"It reminds me of Joe's promise to get in touch," I said, intrigued by the resourcefulness with which we will imagine a history when "real" history proves inaccessible.

"Well, maybe he did manage."

Anne told me how a spiritualist helped her communicate with Joe. The spirit medium had stood in the middle of the room with a divining rod. Almost at once, his divining rod swung toward the south wall. "Is there anything of your grandfather's in the house?" the spiritualist asked. Anne realized that a pokerwork tray that Joe had made, and that Helen had given her as a memento, was on top of a cabinet in that part of the room.

Anne fetched the tray to show me. There were some flowers and foliage in bas-relief on a pocked square of poker-burned plywood.

"Joe had an artistic side," Anne said.

With this tray, the diviner had been able to get in touch with "the other side." His finding was that Joe had got as far as Hawaii, only to die in an accident there. When Lizzie passed away in 1945, she and Joe were reunited.

"This is my theory," Anne said. "It's what I think happened."

I was struck by the fact that Anne thought Hawaii to have been Joe's last landfall, because she had stopped over in Honolulu herself a few years ago on her way to Canada for a holiday. She'd even checked the Honolulu telephone directory for Pawelkas. In her longing to find out what had happened to her grandfather, had she conflated her journey with his?

To blur the line between what we imagine happened and what actually did occur is perhaps the only way we can live with the past. For when the past is shut out of the present, it becomes alien and menacing. It must be brought in from the darkness, to be reconciled with the life we actually live.

* * *

So our conversation ended. Anne let me borrow the tape to copy or transcribe. I promised to send it back to her within a few days. I also said that I would get in touch if I came up with anything new. Then I went back to Wellington, where I had begun my research.

Unfortunately, Anne had used an old answering machine tape, and only a few snatches of our conversation were audible. Perhaps, I reflected, her failure to "make a proper record" was consistent with her emphasis on the story she had created to make the past more bearable.

Still, I transcribed what I could and jotted down other details of our conversation from memory.

The tape ran on.

It was an old message from Anne's answering machine. "Jeanette Strange again. We'll get to each other one day. Bye."

Then silence.

Still Life with Lading Lists

It was two in the morning. I could not sleep. My mind was in turmoil, over-taxed by the events of the day. I remembered yellow road signs of silhou-etted riders, the hills like molars in the haze. The grisly flotsam and jetsam of the police museum still floated on the surface of my mind.

It had been Ray Carter who'd told me about the disguises. Rumor was that when Pawelka escaped from the Lambton Quay lockup in March 1910 he'd used a disguise. A wig and greasepaint were now on display in the New Zealand Police Museum at the Royal New Zealand Police College in Porirua. So on my way back into Wellington from Anne's place I called there and asked if I could see the forensic collection.

A policewoman at the front desk said the museum wasn't open to the public.

What procedure should I follow, then, to get permission to do research in the museum?

Grudgingly, the policewoman phoned the curator.

"He'll come down and see you," she said.

While I waited, I studied the enlarged photo of Pawelka's wanted notice on display in the foyer.

The curator was most helpful. He'd heard of the Pawelka disguises. They were supposedly in the old museum at Trentham, though he'd never seen them or spoken to anyone who had. "In five years here, I've never found them. I don't really think they were ever here."

But he was prepared to search through some computer indexes and rummage around in the museum storeroom.

I followed him upstairs, where he unlocked the doors to the museum.

I walked into a veritable chamber of horrors. Glass cases filled with meat cleavers, saws, axes, and makeshift murder weapons. A color photo of a bombed house. Another of a flayed body, its entrails spilling out. The man had been dragged beside a car along a tar-sealed road. Then a series of macabre black and white photos documenting the notorious floating suit-case murder. A young man, bullied and browbeaten by his father, killed the old man and dismembered the body with a tenon saw. He then stuffed his father's remains into several suitcases and threw them into the sea from the interisland ferry. The suitcases did not sink. Here was the thuggish head, squashed, bruised, and sea-invaded. Here the limbless torso. I turned away, only to confront a "suicide machine." A young man had made it from packing cases. He wired the trigger of a rifle to a bank of switches and some kind of timing device, then lay down in the machine and waited. Here he was, photographed in his shorts, bloodstains around his head, rigid in his own deathtrap. The curator drew my attention to the precautions the young man had taken against staining his landlady's body carpet.

I left the museum having failed to find the disguises, reeling under the impact of what I had seen. The sun-drenched day was filled with menace. Beneath the placid surface of this suburban world, anything was possible. I thought of the Taranaki town in which I had been raised, the rumors of violent death: the adolescent boys who shot their parents as they slept, the lonely farmer who hanged himself in his woolshed, the woman who drowned her moronic son in a swollen creek . . . all suppressed by a common conspiracy of silence. Now the truth was out. What had once been kept behind four walls was standing in the outrageous light of day. No censor stood at the gate. Bandages unraveled from suppurating wounds. Grievances, long buried in the ghetto of the heart, were voiced without apology.

That night I confessed to Les and Mary that I'd taken a bit of a battering by trying to cram too much work into too little time. Driving hundreds of miles to follow up some lead. The stress of talking to strangers. The violence I glimpsed behind our pastoral facades.

The small-town rural New Zealand I had known as a boy had changed. It was far less insular. Less preoccupied with respectability. But while it had become more open to the world, it had lost many of the props that once supported its self-righteous sense of security. The news media purveyed consumerist fantasies—images of a glittering stage where everyone could expect his or her moment of glory. But the stage was overcrowded, and its wings filled with shadows. For the few that might be favored, thousands were humiliated and spurned. What then of the promise of wealth, of success, that had been held out to them only to be snatched away? Was it chimerical? Refusing to believe that they had been duped by some trick of the light, the losers tore from the hands of whoever stood near them the life that was meant for them alone.

Les heard me out, then gently brought me back to where I had begun.

"What do you think happened to him?" he asked.

I said I didn't know, but mentioned the photo that Joe Pawelka's mother had seen in a newspaper. The group of soldiers in the desert.

If the soldiers were wearing lemon squeezers, Les said, they could have been either New Zealanders or Americans. "Though the Yanks didn't come into the war until 1917, and they fought only on the Western Front, never in Egypt or the desert."

"If Pawelka didn't sail from New Zealand but slipped ashore and tried to lose himself, could he have enlisted in the army?" I asked.

"It would have been fairly straightforward," Les said. "Compulsory military training began in 1912. He could have enlisted under an assumed name. His lack of a lung would not necessarily have been picked up. He could have volunteered easily in 1 NZEF. Conscription did not get underway until 1916. He would have probably gone to Egypt, then to the Dardanelles."

Indeed, there is a surviving soldier's letter from Gallipoli that mentions Pawelka. The soldier, who knew Pawelka in the Manawatu, mentions seeing him in the trenches. However, this was probably Joe Pawelka's younger brother Jack who served with the ANZAC force at Gallipoli before being invalided to England.

As for the mysterious photo, Les said that photos from the front would not have been printed in the dailies. But the *Auckland Weekly News* subscribed to the World Service and ran a four- to eight-page insert in every issue. The photo might have appeared there.

Les went to his study and brought back several photo inserts to show me. They'd been pulled from 1916 issues of the *Auckland Weekly*. One photo was of a group of New Zealand soldiers in Cairo. It was captioned: MERRY NEW ZEALANDERS LEAVE CAIRO FOR A NEW FIGHTING FRONT: THE MEN, WITH THEIR HATS DECORATED WITH FLOWERS, ABOUT TO TAKE THEIR DEPARTURE FROM AN EGYPTIAN TOWN. On the facing page were forty-eight photos of New Zealand noncommissioned officers and men "wounded in the cause of liberty."

A sobering statistic: 120,000 New Zealand men enlisted in this war: 43 percent of men of military age. Of these, 18,500 died in or because of the war, and another 50,000 were wounded.

If Pawelka remained in New Zealand, this may have been his fate. Even if his mother was mistaken about the identity of the soldier in the photo, the fact that she became so preoccupied with it might suggest that Joe had discussed with her the possibility of enlisting. Before his troubles started, he seemed to be attracted to the idea of being in uniform and talked of joining the police. For a man desperate to prove himself, the army might have offered the prospect of demonstrating his manly prowess, even of redemption. Perhaps he imagined that by some act of heroism he might win back his wife's regard—and even earn himself a pardon from the Crown. He held off writing home, first wanting to make good. But then it was too late.

* * *

In the morning I trudged back to the National Archives. Jack Hansen had been adamant that Joe left Kimbolton on 15 February 1912, and Jack's father, Willie, "knew Joe was bound for Canada."

I was now determined to try and identify the name under which Joe Pawelka sailed. Figuring that his assumed name would contain some small clue as to his true identity, I began combing shipping lists.

Unluckily for me, there had been a genealogical conference in Wellington during the weekend, and many of the participants were now eager to test out their newly acquired research skills. They queued impatiently, with a nervous self-absorption that I found touching. Like me, they were fascinated by how we are adrift in the stream of time, and by the psychological traits rather than physical heirlooms we may have inherited from another time and place. But I felt cynical, too, as people who set great store by respectability grubbed about in the shadows of their family trees, assured that enough time had passed to allow some colonial miscreant to be reinvented as a romantic figure.

It was mid-morning when I finally got my hands on the shipping lists for the R.M.S. *Makura* (4920 tons).

The *Makura* sailed from the new Queen Street Wharf, Auckland, at five in the afternoon of 16 February 1912, bound for Vancouver via Suva and Honolulu. Arriving early that same morning from Sydney, the *Makura* loaded a large consignment of butter and hides for Vancouver as well as ten tons of general cargo for Suva and Honolulu. It carried 246 passengers, 149 of whom embarked in Sydney.

In Auckland that day the wind was fresh and from the south. The afternoon air temperature was 70°F.

My heart was pounding as I scanned the names. On the strength of what Jack had told me about people scraping together money for Joe's fare, I assumed he would not have had a saloon or second-class ticket, so gave my most careful attention to the steerage passengers, fifteen of whom had boarded in Auckland. In the lists, they were designated "labourers and domestics." Of the twelve men, one was traveling with his wife. The destination of another, Mr. Peterson, was Honolulu. The ten remaining names, written in longhand and difficult to decipher, were these:

Mr. H. Neven (?)	Mr. A. Collins
Mr. R. Russell	Mr. H. Gadd
Mr. H. Bowker	Mr. F. Irving
Mr. J. Edge	Mr. A. Basich
Mr. J. Perrigo	Mr. A. Laidlaw

Despite drawing a blank, I decided to photocopy the *Makura* passenger lists as well as lists for the *Morea* that sailed from Auckland for Sydney and London the same day. Unfortunately, there was, an archival assistant informed me, a "blanket restriction" on photocopying shipping lists.

I asked if I could speak with the archivist. I was told it would be a long wait.

With time to kill, I went back to the shipping indexes. When was the next sailing from Auckland?

The *Makura* sailed on Friday. The next sailing was on Monday 19 February. The S.S. *Wimmera* (1871 tons) crossed the Tasman twice a month.

After filing my request for the *Wimmera* passenger lists, I went for lunch.

During the afternoon I worked my way through the names of the steerage passengers on the *Wimmera*. Seventy-six were men. One was a Mr. J. Wilson.

I was sure I had tracked him down. He must, I told myself, have had recourse to his second name, John. The thought that he might assume Lizzie's maiden name had already occurred to me. But what really clinched the matter was my discovery next day, in the shipping advertisements of the *New Zealand Herald* for February 1912, that tickets purchased for sailings on Union Steam Ship Company boats were interchangeable with Huddart Parker—the company that owned the *Wimmera*.

Was it possible that Joe Pawelka had not sailed for Canada after all? Keeping his plans to himself, had he come to a decision to cover his tracks, cut off all ties with his past, and never look back? When he gave Ted Lawrence the slip in Auckland, was it his intention that no one, not even his family, would know where he was going? As an escaped and hunted criminal, there was no future for him in New Zealand. His wife had washed her hands of him. His family had been obliged to farewell him forever. Under these circumstances, did he choose to die to the life that was now dead to him? Did he turn against the world that he imagined had turned against him in an act of symbolic suicide? An act of spite as much as it was an act of survival. Many of the men who crossed the Tasman in steerage each summer were shearers. Joe Pawelka could have fallen in with them, disembarked in Sydney, gone inland. When war was declared, he may have enlisted. There was a real possibility that he numbered among the thousands of ANZAC casualties at Gallipoli.

But I had no interest in corroborating this scenario. I did not want to pursue J. Wilson any further. I had gone as far as I wanted to go.

With all its horrors, the police museum had been a point of no return. The forensic photos, mug shots, and instruments of death had brought home to me how lives get blurred by our clinical descriptions, our pathological labels, our selective fictions. Museums are like morgues or whorehouses. They deal in partial truths. They fetishize fragments of the whole. They hold out the false hope that a shard, a mask, a memento can spirit a human life back into existence or magically recover its original form.

Part Three

The Remaining Pieces

Back in the States, I worked through the fall and winter on my book and sent what I had written to Jack and Anne. But I told them there were pieces missing from the mosaic, and that these pieces belonged not to the past but to the present.

Jack proposed that when I was next in New Zealand we have "a round-table conference." Together with Anne and Helen's children, we would try to "solve the remaining pieces of the puzzle."

"Everything," Jack assured me, "would sort itself out."

* * *

From Auckland I drove south to Mangaweka, then took the Ruahine road—the same road Joe Pawelka had traveled eighty-three years before.

The road went down toward the river. The water was turquoise. Exposed papa clay bluffs glistened with sweat. Crossing the Rangitikei, the bridge boards clonked and rumbled under the car.

The road was like wire from a caisson—curled. It twisted and turned through small valleys. Stones knocked against the floor of the car. My tires slipped on the loose metal. Dust churned up behind me.

Every now and then I glimpsed the Ruahines, cloud shadows moving slowly over the range.

I passed sheep sheds with roofs of faded red oxide. Sheep pens and holding paddocks. Hillsides were overrun with rushes or dead thistles.

In Kimbolton, I found Jack sitting in his high-backed armchair by a blazing fire, as imperturbable as ever. He was happy to see me and to have another chance to talk. But first a beer.

"What'll you have, Michael?" he asked. "I've got Tui or DB."

"I'll take a Tui, Jack. For old times' sake."

Jack shuffled out to the kitchen, and I followed him. As he took the cans of beer from the fridge, I noticed several bottles of champagne there as well.

We returned to the sitting room, filled our glasses, and drank to each other's health. Bright sunlight filled the window behind Jack's head, blurring the shapes of the furniture in the room.

Jack thanked me for sending him my manuscript. It had helped him understand what I was doing. When I visited him the first time and opened my notebook and started asking questions, he didn't quite know what to make of me.

"You gave a pretty good impression of not being mystified!"

"Ah, well, that's water under the bridge."

I asked about Anne and the others. Did they still intend to come? When would they arrive? Where would they stay? I was concerned that they might want to watch the final race of the America's Cup, which was scheduled for early Sunday morning, and not turn up.

Everything was under control, Jack said. They'd all be here, today or tomorrow. Then he added, "It's strange that after all these years everything is coming together. It's taken up to the third generation for everyone to get their backsides into gear and do something."

I asked Jack if he'd mind if I asked him a few questions and record our conversation on tape.

"You go right ahead," Jack said. "Ask away."

I began by asking about Joe's personal effects. Had anything survived?

Jack confessed he had found nothing among his mother's things; Helen's children had inherited Joe's few belongings.

What of the letters Joe had written home when he was a boy? Des Swain had seen them when he was researching his book. Had the letters been in Agnes's possession?

"Not Mum," Jack said quickly. "Not Mum. No, no, Swain never met Mum."

"Oh, really."

"No, it would have been Helen. Mum was dead before Swain came into it. And I doubt whether Swain would have got past the door if Mum had been alive. She was upset. Too much. I mean, I couldn't go on living with her tears day after day and that sort of thing, you know. I had to vet every blimmin' newspaper before it came into the house, just in case—"

"It's sad that she never overcame the—"

"No, no, never. Well, as she'd say, 'the shame of it.' And yet people just thought the world of her." Jack sighed.

I asked Jack to tell me something about himself. Had he always lived in the shop, with his mother?

"Oh, yeah, I was a spoiled bugger."

"And you never married?"

"Came close to it."

"I can't believe you didn't have your chances."

"Well, I don't think I'll die wondering. Put it that way."

"And you never felt like leaving Kimbolton?"

"I was away in the war, you know."

"After the war?"

"No, I've never regretted the eighty-two years I've spent here."

"Never felt isolated—"

"No. I had my friends. My music."

"What kind of music?"

"Piano."

"Did you play and teach?"

"Just played. Oh, yes, I enjoyed entertaining. It gave me great pleasure and happiness. I had my own orchestra."

"What did you call yourselves?"

"H and P."

"For what?"

"Hansen and Prince."

"Who was Prince?"

"He was a lad from Apiti who played the saxophone. And the drummer boy, he came from Palmerston. If we wanted a fourth one, the double bass came from Palmerston."

"Did you just play Saturday nights, or—"

"Played for dances, that sort of thing."

I waited for Jack to go on.

"Then I got very interested in Palmerston Operatic. I played the lead there about four times."

"Where did you get your musical gifts?"

"Mother."

Jack pointed to the array of photographs on the mantelpiece. "There's two of the photos of operatic days there," he said. "I think Mum's father was quite musical too. Mum said he used to play the cornet."

"What instrument did your mother play?"

"Piano. It was she that got me cracking at playing, too."

"Taught you?"

"Good lord!" Jack exclaimed, examining the back of his hand, "what have I done to—"

"What is it?"

"I don't know. Must have bumped myself with some wood. Skin's very thin."

Jack got up and walked stiffly and slowly to the big dining table at the other end of the room. He said he'd dug out some photos I might like to see. But first, how about another beer?

I said I would get it.

When we'd refilled our glasses, we went over to the table. I stood beside Jack as he showed me the photos.

In the first, taken around the turn of the century, the Pawelka family is outside its cottage in Edwards Street. Joseph sits straight in his chair. One hand is open, the other draws Jack to his side. Agnes stands in the middle of the group, one arm set awkwardly on her father's shoulder. She is holding a wicker basket of fresh flowers. Louisa sits beside her. Joe stands to his mother's right, wearing a bulky serge suit with wide white collar. His arms hang at his sides, his hands loosely cupped.

In poignant contrast, the second photo shows a much older Joseph and Louisa sitting together on deck chairs in their back garden.

Behind them is a corrugated iron water tank and a rank flax bush which has gone to seed. The year is probably around 1920. They are dressed in dark, formal suits. Joseph's beard is gray. His gnarled hands are clasped.

PLATE 5. JACK HANSEN

Louisa's resolute expression leads one to suspect that she is the stronger of the two, the mainstay of the family, the one who has endured.

This impression is even stronger in another photo of the Hansens and Pawelkas together in the orchard at Edwards Street one Christmas Day in the early 1920s. It is near the end of Joseph's life. He stands alone, face grim, eyes in shadow, his knobbled hands with nothing to do. He seems distanced from the others by the stalwart figure of Jack's father, Willie, who faces the camera square on. Willie wears a small bow tie and panama hat. He has a fob watch and chain. His hands are thrust deep into his trouser pockets. He is a picture of confidence, a no-nonsense businessman. To his right, shoulder to shoulder, diffidently smiling at the camera, are Agnes, Helen, Jack Pawelka and their mother, as well as Jack Hansen and his half-brother Ken. Ken has his arms around Jack, and Agnes, kneeling, gazes fondly at him.

How old were you that Christmas?" I asked Jack.

"I'd guess eight or nine," Jack said.

"And that was the orchard at Edwards Street?"

PLATE 6. JACK HANSEN

"Louisa loved gardening," Jack said, and he suggested I look at the photo of the house hanging in the passage near his kitchen door.

The photo showed wisteria or clematis clinging to the verandah posts, camellia bushes, and a profusion of European flowers and border plants. No lawns.

Louisa had tended this garden with the same devotion she gave her children. I wondered if she ever thought, pulling weeds, of the biblical parable of the tares.

* * *

When I left Jack's place at the end of the afternoon, I drove to Edwards Street and found the open paddock where the Pawelka's cottage had stood. There were some flax bushes along the fence line where once a high hedge—shaped as an arch over the front gate—had grown. Three silver birch saplings, tied to stakes, had been planted in the paddock. But there was no vestige of Louisa's garden, neither of the flowers nor the weeds. Only an empty field with a windracked macrocarpa tree beyond it, fretworked against the sky, and the land falling away in great green steps toward the south. When Joseph died in 1923, Louisa and Helen let the cottage and moved to Christchurch. Far from home, Helen found rent collecting onerous, and it was impossible to maintain the house and garden. The story is told that she came back and burned the house down to collect the insurance money. Perhaps it was also a ritual gesture, reducing to ash the place that had brought her parents such grief. Within the family, the story is an ironic commentary on the kinship Helen felt with her long-lost brother. "Helen and Joe inherited their father's temperament," Jack said. Agnes and Jack took after their mother. He described Jack Pawelka as "a fine guy; tall, dark and handsome; women used to fall for him."

In England during the war he fell in love with a woman whose family regarded him as a poor prospect. Yet she followed Jack out to New Zealand after the war. "Jack promptly took off to Apia," Jack said, "and buried himself there. The Pawelka business stood between them."

"Did Jack ever marry?"

"Jack left his heart in England. He never married."

A day before Jack Pawelka died, Jack Hansen flew to Whangarei to see him. He had purchased a plot in the Kimbolton cemetery so that Jack would one day be brought home. But Jack Pawelka did not want to come home and had specified in his will that he be buried in Whangarei.

As for Helen, she had hardly got to know Joe before he disappeared. But in burning down the family home she symbolically joined herself to him forever.

Only the land remained, until it was taken over in November 1964 by the Ruahine Rabbit Board, which paid three hundred pounds in compensation to the Pawelka family.

Guilt and Shame

I lodged overnight at a bed-and-breakfast place outside Kimbolton and in the morning drove back to Jack's.

As I parked my car in Jack's yard, I could hear starlings lisping and cheeping on the roof of his woodshed. It was a cloudless day, and in the Oroua valley rows of poplars, stripped of their leaves, stood like bundles of faggots, furled.

Jack had the fire blazing and the TV turned on for the America's Cup. On the tea trolley were champagne glasses ready to be filled. But it was neither Team New Zealand nor the prospect of the America's Cup "coming home" that Jack wanted to celebrate, but the reunion of the family. As far as today was concerned, he said, the sun was already over the yardarm.

It wasn't long before Anne arrived, bustling in to the room with files and folders. Then John and Fay—Helen's children—turned up with their spouses. They, too, had brought boxes of photos, genealogies, and family memorabilia.

Jack introduced me and ordered another bottle of Marque Vue sparkling wine uncorked.

When our glasses were charged, Jack said: "This drink is to having the family together for the first time in a long, long while."

Though my research had been the catalyst for our meeting, Joe Pawelka did not dominate it. For Joe's nephews and niece, clearing up the mystery of his disappearance eighty-three years ago was far less urgent than the affirmation of their survival as a family. John, Fay, Jack, and Anne had met separately but never together. Now, as they began to share their photos and memorabilia, the talk was less of Joe than of Agnes and Helen, who had struggled to escape his shadow. It was a struggle John and Fay had also experienced.

At primary school in Kimbolton, Fay remembered how kids used to taunt her in the playground:

One, two, three, four
Joe Pawelka jumped the wall.

She recalled some of her mother's memories. Of when she was eight and came home from school one lunchtime with a friend to find Joe in the kitchen with Louisa. Of the police poking pitchforks into the haystack behind the house, but too afraid to go into the hay shed lest Joe was hiding there.

But mostly Helen said nothing of her brother.

"Any time I mentioned the name Pawelka, the walls came up," John said.

"She felt shame," John's wife, Maria, added. "It ruined her life. You can't imagine what it was like back then. Joe's brother Jack never married because he carried the Pawelka name. He didn't want his children to be stigmatized by having to carry it too."

"When Jack was working for the post office they wanted him to change his name," Jack said, "but he refused."

"We were never allowed to mention his name," Fay said. "Mum didn't keep some of the things she got from Louisa. She destroyed a lot of things that had to do with Joe. She was ashamed of the memory."

When she was eighty-seven, Agnes wrote her nephew about a television film that was being made about her brother. She said: "When Joe disgraced us, we lost touch with everyone, thinking they would not want to have anything more to do with us. I suppose we were too sensitive; and now it's all going to be dragged up again in a film. I wish God I was dead and out of it. There is no doubt about the innocent having to suffer for the guilty unto the third or fourth generation. People are so cruel."

Toward the end of 1936, the *Weekly News* commissioned an article on Joe Pawelka and prepared to publish an updated account of the events of 1910. Jack Pawelka was sent the proofs. He at once dispatched an angry letter to Sir Henry Horton, owner of the newspaper, insisting that the article not be published. Jack must have told his mother about the article too, because she wrote Horton with the same request.

John showed me the telegram that Sir Henry Horton sent Louisa on 23 January 1937:

SINCERELY REGRET HAVING CAUSED YOU ANY DISTRESS PUBLICATION WITHHELD IN DEFERENCE TO YOUR REQUEST

Twelve days later, the editor of the *Weekly News* wrote Jack Pawelka. The letter, addressed to Mr John Pawelka, Telegraph Office, Whangarei, and dated 4 February 1937, began:

Dear Sir,

Sir Henry Horton has passed over to me your letter relating to the proposed publication of a new account of the Pawelka case. Naturally we do not wish to do anyone

an injustice but I would ask you to consider this point of view as it appears to me.
None of Joseph Pawelka's relatives are accused of anything. They have nothing to
be ashamed of.

The editor misses the point. For the Pawelkas, the question of Joe's guilt is not the issue, but rather the family's shame. Joe was still a wanted man. Though Joseph Senior had died in 1923, Louisa and her children feared the legal repercussions of having helped Joe evade justice. Sheltering him in Kimbolton during the summer of 1911–1912 and siding with him against the state had implicated the family in his crimes. Underscoring this was the deeply held conviction that Joe was their flesh and blood. Louisa embraced the Catholic Moravian notion that the blood-bond between mother and child was like the bond between self and God. Whatever one did in one's life would bring not only divine retribution or reward, but curse or bless every member of one's family. A bad seed or black sheep could condemn his or her family to shame, and, reciprocally, abandonment by the family could spell a person's ruin. Joe's guilt thus became his family's remorse. If he was written off as a lunatic, they shared the stigma. And as they shrank from the world, driven in upon themselves and their own spiritual resources, Joe's tragic fate only intensified their already fierce sense of unity and loyalty. Just as a death or birth may transcend bitter differences between a parent and a child, so Joe's loss deepened the bond between Louisa, Joseph, and their errant son. And it is out of this intense and inescapable kinship that the sense of shame is born. The family had endured a wrong and suffered a loss that no absolution or pardon could make good. The Pawelkas bore this terrible sense of difference as a sense of being marked and stained. It was a loss of face. A humiliation. A disgrace. Nothing could ever heal the wounds. Lizzie might revert to her maiden name, but the child she bore would always be the embodiment of her union with the Pawelkas. The families into which the other Pawelka children married were just as profoundly affected; both the Hansens and Bryces bore the Pawelkas' loss in sympathy and solidarity. As for the Wilsons, they too suffered the same stigma. In a conversation with one descendant, I would be told, "The oldies tried to keep the shame of the relationship between Joe and Lizzie from the kids. And the children of that generation kept mum for years. As youngsters growing up, everything was hush-hush in the family. Mum, as a young girl of nine or ten, took a lot of flak because of her relationship to him. She had to run the gauntlet past the Catholic school. Kids would taunt her about being related to a murderer and thief."

For the Pawelkas, nothing could bring Joe back. Nothing could rewrite the past or rectify the tragic flaw. The family could only hope to dull its pain by distraction or forgetting. As Jack put it, Joe's father "took to the grog," while Louisa "took to the garden and her rosary beads."

Despite adversity, Louisa kept a faithful record of every rite of passage in the life of the family.

When Fay showed me Louisa's prayer book, it was like being given a glimpse into the family's soul.

The small, battered Catholic missal measured about three inches by five. The boards were covered in purple cloth. There was a tarnished metal cross on the front cover. The binding was broken. I had to turn the dog-eared, age-blotched, brittle pages with care.

In several pages in the front and back of the book, Louisa had, over the years, written details of births, deaths, and marriages. Here was the date of her arrival in New Zealand and of her marriage to Joe Senior when she still called herself Louise König. Here were the birthdays of her sons, Joseph John Thomas (Joe) and John Alfred (Jack) and of her daughters Agnes and Florence Helen. Here also were the dates on which her children left home.

One page arrested me. Though the right-hand edge of the page was tattered, making it impossible to decipher two of the dates, here at last was confirmation of the date of Joe's final leave-taking. His name, Joseph John Thomas, was reduced to initials, possibly to disguise a potentially incriminating fact.

J. J. T left home 15th
Feb 1912

A later entry reads:

Joe left home 15th
Feb 1912

"She wrote him out of her life," Jack said.

Louisa had also noted the date Joe's daughter, Iris, was born, as well as the year Lizzie died. It showed the depth of Louisa's belief in the integrity

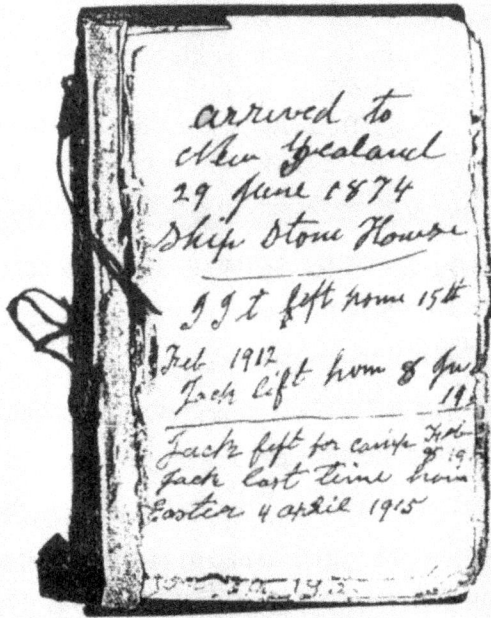

PLATE 7. MICHAEL JACKSON

and continuity of the family. Equally significant were the recycled names, such as Joseph and John, and evidence of Louisa's efforts to maintain the link with Joseph Senior's North Canterbury kin and all their in-laws.

I was especially interested in Louisa's contacts with the Wilsons.

"Did Louisa see anything of Lizzie and Iris?" I asked Jack.

"Oh yes, after the initial meeting, the two grandmothers were more or less friendly. They kept in touch with each other."

Iris's birth had begun the healing process. In July 1910, Lizzie's mother, Hannah, sent a picture postcard from Ashhurst to Louisa in Kimbolton. On one side of the card was a scene of the jetty at Day's Bay, Wellington. On the other:

Just a line to tell you that Lizzie (Mrs Pawelka) has a fine little girl born on the 23rd inst. Hope to see you down.

   H. A. Wilson

Perhaps Hannah Wilson was moved to console Louisa for the loss of her son. Perhaps the birth of Iris did transcend the tragedy that Joe had brought upon the two families.

On 3 October the following year, five weeks after Joe's escape from prison, Louisa telephoned Lizzie and asked if they could meet. A rendez-vous was arranged for the next day in a Palmerston North tearoom.

Inevitably, Lizzie was accompanied by her mother.

Louisa asked Lizzie if she could ever forgive Joe. She showed Lizzie a letter Joe had written in which he swore he had not killed McGuire and had not been solely responsible for stealing the furniture. Joe argued that because his accomplice was married and had children, he could not stop him. But he wanted to see his daughter and urged Lizzie to forgive him and go with him to another country where they could make a fresh start.

Lizzie was so distressed by the letter that Hannah took it from her and would not give it back.

Louisa then asked Lizzie if she would at least write to Joe.

But her appeals fell on deaf ears. Finally, Louisa asked if she could hold the baby and perhaps go out onto the street with her for a few minutes.

Lizzie said no. "She was terrified that the old lady was going to kidnap the babe," Jack said.

As Louisa got up to go, she implored the Wilsons not to tell anyone that they had met. But two days later, Lizzie gave a full report of the meeting to Constable Watts at Ashhurst, asking Watts to exercise discretion because she was afraid of what Joe might do if he got wind of what she had divulged.

When Sergeant Bowden interviewed Jack's father, Willie, a week after the meeting between Lizzie and Louisa in Palmerston North, Willie asserted that the Pawelkas "are now reconciled to Mrs Pawelka and child, and that the elder Mrs Pawelka has visited her daughter-in-law and grandchild at Ashhurst several times." He added, "The grandmother is anxious that her daughter-in-law let her have the child but she will not part with it, the friends of the family would also like Mrs Pawelka and child to leave Ashhurst."

Lizzie's fear was, in part, clearly a reaction to Louisa's suggestion that she give up her child to the Pawelkas.

"Did they ever meet again?"

"Oh, yes, regularly, I think, when Iris grew up."

Anne showed me a photo that had been taken by the fountain in the Palmerston North Square sometime in the early 1930s. Iris, Louisa, and

PLATE 8. ANNE HARRIS

Lizzie are sitting on the concrete edge of the fountain. Iris is flanked by her mother and mother-in-law. She is wearing a fashionable coat with fur trim, a hat, and gloves. Louisa's face communicates resolution and forbearance. In her dark suit, shirt, and striped tie, Lizzie looks as dour as the principal of a girls' church boarding school.

The room was filled with cigarette smoke. The blazing fire and sunlight pouring through the window made it almost unbearably hot. And we had been drinking sparkling wine steadily for three hours. My head spinning, I took in the empty glasses and bottles, the photographs and papers littered on the table, piano, tea trolley, and chair arms, and the Wedgewood saucers mounted on the maple-leaf wallpaper.

"Time for lunch," Maria declared.

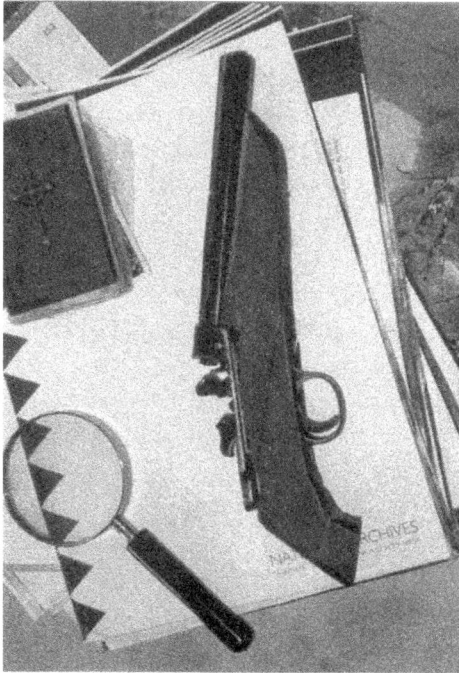

PLATE 9. MICHAEL JACKSON

She and Fay had made tomato and cheese sandwiches and prepared plates of sliced venison. Fay's husband, Wayne, refilled my glass.

Jack wanted me to be sure I saw everything. Fortunately, there was a photocopier in the shop. I had only to open the door behind my chair and it was two steps away. So I made copies of papers and photos at every opportunity and scribbled down as much of the conversation as discretion permitted. I took a photograph of Louisa's missal placed beside a magnifying glass and Joe's revolver. The revolver had been found in the family cottage in Edwards Street, Jack said. He kept it for many years, but when Agnes died Helen took it to Wanganui. Joe must have made the revolver himself, when he was a boy. It was a sawn-off .22 rifle. The beveled barrel bore the patent mark of H. Pieper's, Liege, Belgium. Joe had fashioned a wooden stock for it. It brought home to me that Joe had loved firearms from an early age and was a crack shot.

"Frankly," Jack said, "what are we going to do with it? Give it to Anne or to the Police Museum? What do you think, John?"

Jack had given other things to Anne. He wanted her to have something of the inheritance her mother had kept from her. He had sent her old photos, to help the bridge the gap between her and Joe.

But what of the photo of the soldiers—the one in which Louisa thought she had identified Joe?

Fay said that according to Helen, Joe had promised to send his mother a newspaper as a way of letting her know he was well. The photo did not come through the mail. Louisa saw it in a newspaper. "It was a picture of some Canadian servicemen," Fay said.

"The mother said, 'That looks like my son,'" Jack added.

"For a guy who loved his mother, he would have taken every opportunity to communicate," Anne said.

"I'll never forgive him for not getting in touch with his mother," Jack said.

"If he was dead, how could he have got in touch?" Anne rejoined.

Fay said she had consulted a Ouija board—not something she would ordinarily do—to find out what happened to Joe. The Ouija board gave her to understand that Joe had died at sea.

* * *

After lunch, I went up to the cemetery with Anne, John, Maria, and Fay. The day was warm and still. I sat on a gravestone, looking out over the Oroua valley to the blue range of the Ruahines, while John and Fay went around identifying the Bryce and Pawelka plots.

After returning to Jack's place, everyone began packing up and preparing to leave. For Jack, the reunion had been momentous. Calling me Mike and "young chap," he said, "It's been a great day. It won't happen again." Anne thanked me for bringing them all together.

But as I drove away from Kimbolton that afternoon, I felt bereft. I thought of staying another night, seeing Jack again, but then told myself that it would be better to see him in a week's time, when I had done what I wanted to do in the National Archives. So I headed south along the Kimbolton Road in dwindling light, thinking of the night Joe cycled furiously down the same road after escaping from the police ambush in Edwards Street.

At the bridge over the Kiwitea Stream on the outskirts of Feilding, I stopped to take photos of the shingle banks and scrub where Joe was seen next morning. I drove down Derby Street to East Street and on to Aorangi, taking the route he had taken to avoid the center of town.

At the corner of Aorangi and Cameron's Line there is a choice: to continue straight on toward Bunnythorpe and Ashhurst or turn west toward Awahuri. I wondered if Joe Pawelka had hesitated. These forking paths. His wife in Ashhurst. A friend in Awahuri perhaps, or beyond in Longburn, who might shelter him.

Should I drive to Ashhurst, take a look at the Wilson house at the corner of Salisbury and Wyndham Streets, or head toward Awahuri where Joe was arrested?

It was getting dark. I took the road he took.

Death's Secretary

The idea recurs: our lives are storied. Were it not for stories, our lives would be unintelligible; we could not make sense of the times we live. Stories make it possible for us to overcome our separateness, to find common ground and common cause.

To relate a story is to retrace one's steps, going over the ground of one's life again, reworking reality to render it more bearable. A story enables us to fuse the world without and the world within. In this way we gain some purchase over events that confounded us, humbled us, left us helpless. In telling a story we renew our faith that the world is within our grasp.

Any story is like a vessel shaped from wet clay under a potter's hands. In its roundedness, containedness, and completeness it provides the consoling illusion that life has meaning. And just as a clay vessel bears telltale traces of the potter's hands, so too, Walter Benjamin observes, every story carries the personal imprint of the storyteller.

Consider the stories occasioned by Joe Pawelka's life.

A psychotherapist might discern in the circumstances of Joe Pawelka's childhood, in his recorded remarks, and in his behavior under stress a picture of wounded narcissism. Convinced that fate has singled him out as a victim of injustice, this individual will do anything to draw attention to himself. To this end, heroism and notoriety, affection and contempt, are on a par. Deep down he remains a resentful child who thinks he deserves to be pandered, and when the going gets rough appeals to others for rescue and care. Thus the overweening and remorseless need for acceptance. The habits of feigned illness and sham dementia. The threats of suicide, the manipulative confabulations, the downright lies. Such aggressive narcissism is an attempt to bend the world to one's will. One's sole reality is one's own needs, one's own feelings, one's own state of mind. By contrast, the world of others is weightless and colorless; affectively it does not exist.

There may be grains of truth in this picture. But it is only a picture—underexposed and poorly developed.

What of the juridical story?

At Waikanae, I spoke to Stewart Lusk, a retired Q.C. who had become interested in the Pawelka case when researching his history of Kimbolton.

Stewart Lusk was convinced an injustice had been done: "The judge got it wrong, no doubt about that. Judges in those days had enormous power."

In the charge of murder, ballistic evidence was inconclusive. In the case of arson at the Palmerston Boys' High School, it is arguable that the techniques of fingerprinting which proved Pawelka's guilt were, in 1910, somewhat fallible. On other counts, the prosecution's evidence was circumstantial, and there is reasonable doubt in the cases of some of the crimes Pawelka was charged with. One has only to read police reports from the period when he was hiding at Kimbolton to see how things were stacked against him. In a report dated 9 September 1911, Sub-Inspector Norwood listed several "incidents" in his police district, including a breaking and entering at Tokomaru, a "mysterious fire" at Longburn, a suspicious camp site at Awapuni, the theft of food from a house in Palmerston, and an attempt to force an entry to Swallow's Booksellers' adjoining premises owned by Pawelka's "uncle" in Palmerston. Norwood drew this conclusion: "The depredations referred to may have been committed by any criminal, but the methods are, I am informed, similar to those adopted by Pawelka when he was last at large in this district." The irony was that even as Norwood wrote these lines, Joe Pawelka was positively identified near Mount Messenger in Taranaki!

Of all the stories that invoke fact, perhaps none are more tenacious than newspaper stories. Written in the confident if naive belief that "getting the facts right" will also settle the attendant moral, legal, and political issues, such stories quickly take on a life of their own.

When the *Weekly News* commissioned its article on Joe Pawelka in 1936, the rationale was that the facts be given precedence over personal sensibilities and possible slights. Thus, despite assuring Louisa that the story had been killed, the editor defended his right to publish it. Writing to Jack Pawelka, he argued: "I can understand your unwillingness to have the case needlessly re-opened to go over the facts as they have been published before, but I would point out to you that the author has had full access to police and other records and has gone to great trouble with his story with the object of doing your brother justice. Surely Joseph Pawelka has a right to have his name cleared. There is no shame for his family in this."

The editor went on to stress that the public was fascinated by the Pawelka story, and he urged Jack Pawelka to appreciate the need to have "the facts put straight" in "the interests of pure history."

But what of the interests of lived history?

The Pawelka family rejected the editor's argument, and fifty years later was still opposed to the idea of raking over dead coals.

In 1987, broadcaster and freelance journalist Des Swain began his research on Joe Pawelka and met with the same resistance.

In a letter to Iris McGaffin—Joe's and Lizzie's daughter—whom he had traced through a birth certificate, marriage records, and the electoral roles, Swain sought to mollify her by painting a flattering portrait of Joe and pointing out that he could not have killed McGuire and did not shoot to kill Pauline Kendall. Testifying to the "positive aspects of his character," Swain wrote: "I am satisfied that a large number of comments about Joe Pawelka had no basis in fact: that he was a much better man than people are led to believe."

Iris was elderly and ill when she received Swain's letter. Not wanting to confront the specter of the past, she did not reply. But her son Terry wrote John Bryce, suggesting he contact Swain. Terry made one stipulation: "Mum requests that you do not involve the newer generation, i.e., her children and grandchildren."

Des Swain dubbed his book a "historical novel." It reads more like a historical romance. Unabashedly sympathetic to his protagonist, Swain makes Joe Pawelka a tragic hero. At the end of his book, touching on Joe's disappearance, he writes: "I cannot for a moment imagine that Joe would not have let his family know when he was safe."

Not long after Des Swain began work on his "historical novel," Anne Harris learned of her kinship with Joe Pawelka. And the story she came to tell was also steeped in romanticism. "I'm a terrible romantic," Anne told me. "Lizzie and Joe must have been so in love." In Anne's view, Joe couldn't do enough for his young bride, but had very little money, "so when he had a chance to acquire some inexpensive furniture he jumped at it." Anne was aware that this was very likely not what happened. "It's my theory," she said. "It's based on the sort of thing I'd do."

For Joe's parents and siblings, invoking heroic nostalgia would have been as meaningless as the argument of the editor of the *Weekly News*: that proving Joe innocent of the violent crimes of which he was accused would alleviate his descendants' shame and stigma. The fact is that for Joe's immediate family there was no redemptive myth.

While Rosina may have told herself that Joe's tragic life was divine retribution for his parents' heedlessness, Louisa and Joseph could never bring their son's story to a close. It had a beginning, a middle, but no finality . . . though Louisa may have imagined some God-given resolution in the afterlife. Until their own deaths ended their self-questioning, they kept their silence and implored others to do the same. For the children's sake. In the hope that in forgetfulness and the fullness of time their pain might ease.

What then of the story I had written?

Alluding to Walter Benjamin's essay on the storyteller, John Berger observes that "any story drawn from life begins, for the storyteller, with its end." Most stories, he goes on to say, "begin with the death of the principal protagonist. It is in this sense that one can say that storytellers are Death's secretaries. It is Death who hands them the file."

At Jack's "roundtable" in Kimbolton I had been a ghostly eavesdropper, registering a story that at times brought tears, at other times laughter. But though I was privy to these unrehearsed recollections and shared memories, I was an outsider. Almost a voyeur.

What had brought us together? And why now?

Our meeting had little to do with vindicating Joe. If anything, it was a celebration of being free of his legacy. Greater than any sense of his presence was the sense of Helen's absence. If shame is a kind of perpetual grieving, then the family, working through their grief over Helen's death, had at last begun to unburden itself of the shame it had shared with her.

Helen had been the last of Joe's generation. "An afterthought," Fay said. Much younger than the others, she was the last to have known Joe in life. Though Jack liked to tell me that if Helen had been alive my research would have been easier, I knew that it would have been harder, because I, like the others, would have been bound by the same taboo against talking about the past—the sole defense Helen and the others had against further hurt. The generosity with which John and Fay showed me Helen's heirlooms, and confided to me what they remembered of her and Joe, expressed their freedom from an old constraint.

But this was only my guess. For Jack and the others, our meeting was a mystery. "It's strange that after all these years everything is coming together," he had told me, "like Barbara getting in touch at the same time that you got onto the story."

But as soon as we tried to clear up the mystery, we found ourselves again standing in Joe's long shadow.

Anne was convinced that Joe's spirit had brought us together. John's wife, Maria, agreed. Joe's spirit had presided over our meeting.

It was Joe who inspired Barbara Blyth (née Pavelka) to contact the others last year. And it had been Joe who had moved me to write my book.

Insofar as historicity encompasses phenomena that go beyond or lie outside our empirical grasp, I suppose it is inevitable that our experience of being-in-time will suggest the spiritual and the paranormal. And though I resisted such occult interpretations, it was clear to me in Kimbolton how powerfully present, perhaps even necessary, this way of thinking often is for those whose family histories have been scarred by shameful and traumatic events.

George Santayana once observed that those who cannot remember the past are condemned to repeat it. But what is the point of remembering the past unless it helps us get beyond the situation that has shaped the way we are?

Overshadowing the spadework of the scholar are the claims of the living. The limits placed on what we may know of Joe Pawelka are not fixed by the paucity of the evidence as to his character, his guilt, or his ultimate fate. They are set by the exigencies of the time and place in which we live.

Forays into the past are justified, I like to think, only when the past gives us some guidelines for how we can live less divisively and more generously in the here and now.

Stories Happen

After a final trip to Wellington, I went back to see Jack one more time. I told him that I had come to realize that there was a curious symmetry between Joe's story and my story about his story. Researching his life and times had brought me home. Not to the place I left thirteen years ago, but to a place where I wanted to make a new start. Ironically, in trying to make sense of Joe's disaffection, I had recovered a sense of my own belonging, my own *turangawaewae*. Joe's loss had become my gain.

"So everything's come full circle," Jack said.

* * *

The air was clear and cold. I heard only the sound of my feet on the road. Then, in the distance, on another road, a car changed gears, went on, and diminished into the hills.

When I heard the next car, I did not bother to turn. It sped by, scattering leaves, then stopped fifty yards ahead and waited.

I hurried toward it. I could see the driver observing me in his rearview mirror.

He was in his seventies. He shaded his eyes when he asked where I was going.

"Auckland," I said. Then, thinking I should explain why I was hitchhiking, I told him that my rental car had developed engine trouble and rather than rent another I had decided to hit the road and take my chances.

He said he could take me some of the way.

I opened the passenger door and threw in my grip. There was a Pekinese dog on the back seat. The dog got up on its front legs, sniffed the air, and settled back to sleep.

"You American?" I asked.

Ignoring my question, he asked if I could see smoke. "Or is that steam?"

"It looks like your radiator's boiling over."

"Can't be. It's a new car. Hasn't even done five thousand miles."

"My car was new, too."

When I suggested we take a look, he seemed reluctant. I had to ask him to unlock the hood. He stayed behind the wheel while I lifted and propped it.

Water and steam were sputtering from the uncapped radiator. I could see the cap. It was lodged against the crankcase. I reached down and got it between my fingers, and extracted it gingerly. Then I walked around to the driver's window and told him I would go and get some water to top up the radiator.

"Where are you going to get water out here?"

I said I'd take care of it, and set off back down the road to the house I'd walked past minutes before, at the end of a long drive, half hidden by a belt of macrocarpas.

A woman let me borrow a watering can. I unscrewed the rose and went to the water tank behind the house. There was a muddy depression and downtrodden grass where some kids had been puddling around. I straddled the mud hole and filled the can.

When I got back to the car, the American was smoking a cigarette and seemed unconcerned that he'd come close to blowing up his engine.

"OK," I said. "Start her up."

He switched on and slowly I filled the radiator. Then I secured the cap, slammed the hood and got back in the car.

"You wouldn't mind driving, would you?" he said.

"That's fine with me," I said.

"I'm not so used to driving on the wrong side of the road."

So we swapped places.

After returning the watering can, I accelerated onto the highway. It was a powerful car and easy to drive. I felt at peace with myself. I had hitched this highway for more than thirty years. Every stretch and bend in the road was part of an unfolding story, and every time I traveled the road another chapter was added. Yet the stories were as randomly connected as the lives of those who had given me lifts over the years or the makes of the vehicles they drove.

For several miles the American said little. Then, passing through Taihape, he said, out of the blue, that it looked like a lonely sort of place to have to spend one's life.

I had no idea what to say to this. I thought of telling him the story of Joe Pawelka, but he quickly followed up his remark by asking me if I was aware that the war had ended fifty years ago.

I had to admit that I hadn't really given it much thought.

"I guess it was before your time," he said.

He had enlisted in Brooklyn in 1941. Within a year he was with the Marines at Guadalcanal.

"You think thirteen's unlucky," he said. "Well, it was Friday the 13th. Our destroyer was thirteenth in the line. Our ship's number was 445 . . . that's thirteen if you add it up . . . and our Task Force number was 67 . . . thirteen again."

He was afraid. In the darkness off Guadalcanal, the sea was like glass. The destroyer's bow wave shimmered with phosphorescence, and the cloying air was filled with the hothouse fragrance of night blooming tropical flowers.

"To this day, I can't go into a florist's shop without it getting the better of me. In Wellington, I wanted to buy my daughter some flowers, but I couldn't. How about that? I had to take her a box of chocolates."

Then the night exploded with salvos from the destroyer's fiveinch guns and retaliative fire from the Japanese battle line. He was in the pilothouse. It filled with a reddish light, and a bolt of hot air concussed the ship. The destroyer ahead had blown up.

They ploughed through burning oil. He felt sick with horror at the thought of the men in the water they might be running through. He saw Japanese torpedoes pass beneath them. The sky was on fire. Star shells. Rocket clusters. Parachute flares. Oil was burning on the surface of the sea.

He remembers men cursing the bulky lifejackets that hampered their movements on the bridge. Then came the sound of an incoming shell, like a bedsheet being ripped down the middle.

He felt himself hurtling through the mouth of a furnace. There were screams. Screaming inside his head. Then he saw that he was on fire.

"When they got me out, I looked like a cheese melt on a piece of burned toast."

Suffering from burns and a leg shattered by shrapnel, he was flown to Australia. For weeks he lay immobilized in the base hospital at Townsville, oppressed by homesickness.

"I kept remembering Brooklyn. Brooklyn, Brooklyn, nothing but Brooklyn. Night and day. I guess I was lucky, though. Lucky thirteen, huh? At least I got out in one piece."

While convalescing, he had a fling with an Australian nurse. "I didn't know it at the time, but I put her in the family way." He went back to his unit, forgot the nurse, and presumed she had forgotten him. "She probably saw herself as a casualty of the war, like me, and left it at that."

"It's a strange thing, memory. I can never forget that smell of gardenias off Guadalcanal. Never forget my buddies. Things like this are more vivid to me than this morning's coffee. But I can't remember her."

Waiouru was behind us. To the west the mountains were in cloud. A soft rain was beginning to fall.

"I wouldn't want you to think I am a man completely without scruples," he said at last, "but memory's a strange thing. 'Specially in wartime.

"I've seen photos of her now. I still can't make the photos fit with anything I remember. I guess she didn't want to go crying over spilled milk. Never wanted to bother me. She had her child. A daughter. Raised her there in Townsville. Told her all about me. At least as much as she knew.

"The daughter never saw any point in going back into the past, either. It was her husband started looking for me. He convinced her she should know who her father was. You know, before it was too late."

"Is she in Australia?"

"No. Lives here. In Wellington. That's where I've been. Her husband's a Kiwi."

"How did they find you?"

"Talk about luck. I tell you. She knew my name, right, because her mother remembered it. She even remembered I was a Brooklyn boy. So the daughter and her husband place advertisements in the personals in the New York dailies. Then they get hold of New York telephone directories and start phoning up everyone with my name. Finally, they get through to a nephew of mine, and he tells them I'm living in LA. So we start exchanging letters. Before long, the whole thing gets too much for me. What the hell, I say to my wife. What have I got to lose? So I come out here to meet her."

He paused. "It didn't work out. We were strangers. What can you expect? Life's not in the business of happy endings. But I tell you, I was real excited for a while, coming all the way out here. I was going to reconnect with something I lost. Like getting in a time machine . . . She gave me the dog. She and her husband breed them. A memento, she said, to remind you of Mum. So I'm taking Memento back to the States next week. My wife likes dogs. I don't much care for them. And the quarantine's going to be hell for the poor little tyke. But my wife's got a soft spot for animals. She'll give it a home."

I was tired and famished. I needed a break from driving and from this relentless story. I regretted not stopping at Waiouru. Now, with the ashen landscape surrounding us, all tussock and hebe and mist, I knew it would be another half-hour before we got to Turangi.

But the Ancient Mariner wasn't perturbed. His daughter had packed some sandwiches for him. They were in the trunk of the car. Why not pull off the road somewhere. He wasn't hungry, but he could go for a cup of joe.

I stopped near Oturere Bridge. The beech trees were blackened with rain. But we were out of the wind, and the damp air smelled of moss and mountain water.

The American let his dog out for a run around. It scampered away into the flax and toetoe.

We sat at a picnic table and unpacked the sandwiches. He poured two cups of coffee from his Thermos flask. I wondered, now that his story was finished, whether he would want to take over the driving. Perhaps he'd want to be alone now with his thoughts. I considered leaving him there with his dog and catching another ride.

But he was not done.

He wanted to tell me about his Guardian Angel. He wanted to tell me the story of his three failed marriages. He wanted to show me photos of his house at Marina del Rey, to impress upon me how lucky he'd been to buy it before real estate went through the roof. He wanted to talk about his annual reunion in Brooklyn with his war buddies.

So we continued, with the lake coming into view under clearing skies.

He had talked for two hours without flagging. Now, as his monologue turned to trout fishing, I glanced in the rearview mirror at the weather closing in behind us. Then, for some reason, I tilted the mirror so I could see the dog on the back seat.

"Is your daughter's dog on the floor?" I asked.

He turned in a panic. The dog was neither on the seat nor the floor. The dog was still sniffing around the toetoe and flax by the Oturere Stream. We had forgotten to get it back into the car before driving off.

I stopped the car on the dirt track that ran beside the lake. "We'll go back for it," I said.

"I'll go back. You don't have to come."

"But if you hadn't picked me up, you wouldn't have forgotten your dog."

"It's not your fault, pal. I should've checked."

"You sure?"

"Sure, I'm sure. You go on. You've got a family waiting for you. You get back to them."

I got out of the car. Hadn't I told him my family was in America?

As I stood and watched, he turned back onto the highway and headed south into the murky weather over the volcanic plateau to look for his daughter's dog.

I went down to the lake. I wanted to record as much as I could of what he had said.

* * *

Later, when I got to thinking about it, I realized that the ending to Joe Pawelka's story could never be the ending I had originally sought.

Time was not a white line down the middle of a strip of bitumen, with a determinate point of departure and a final destination. Time warps and buckles and folds back upon itself, bringing the present into intimate contact with the distant past and making successive moments seem a lifetime apart.

If time is a river, it is a river that does not run its course straightforwardly to the sea. There are whirlpools, eddies, oxbows, falls, backwaters, and countercurrents. Periodically the river overflows its banks, obliterating the line between land and water, changing its course entirely.

Endings, like beginnings, are misnomers. Listen to the river. It fills the night. Listen to our lives as they replay the same piece of music in infinite variations.

Clouds were being tumbled across the sky. The lake water was breaking on the black shingle. As I wrote, the wind flicked the pages of my notebook against the back of my hand.

Time and Space

For Claude Lévi-Strauss, ethnography and history are "complementary perspectives." "Both history and ethnography are concerned with societies *other* than the one in which we live. Whether this otherness is due to remoteness in time (however slight) or to remoteness in space, or even to cultural heterogeneity, is of secondary importance compared to the basic similarity of perspective." To this observation one might add that space and time are not essentially different *realities*, but different ways of apprehending basic human experiences of relative nearness and remoteness, presence and absence. As Bergson observes, "Homogenous space and homogenous time are . . . neither properties of things nor essential conditions of our faculty of knowing them: they express, in an abstract form, the double work of solidification and division which we effect on the moving continuity of the real *in order to obtain there a fulcrum for our actions.*" Thus, in Northern Luzon, the Illongot map mythological events onto the landscape rather than the calendar. Though Bergson argues against the spatialization of temporality, arguing that duration is our most prescient sense of being-in-time, our consciousness of time passing is inextricably connected to our physical awareness of the *places* in which we dwell, between which we travel, and wherein we are actively and bodily engaged. Thus, "space" and "time" continually morph into each other. Nostalgia fuses a longing for another place *and* another time. Here and there readily become metaphors for now and then, and vice versa.

That time implicates space is particularly and poignantly true for the expatriate writer, since his or her earliest years are associated with another place, and often another language, which means that the past is *elsewhere;* not simply another time but another country.

This intimate connection between being displaced and traveling through time also informs ethnography and exploration, which is why journeys to the ends of the earth have so often been construed, in the social imaginaries of the West, as journeys to a more primordial or primitive point in time.

Even when going *elsewhere* is not construed as going back in *time,* displacement tends to unsettle one's sense of temporality.

On a late January evening in January 1971, I was sitting outside a guesthouse in the hills above Freetown, having arrived that morning from the UK to begin my second stint of fieldwork among the Kuranko. Watching the flimsy branches of the casuarinas stirring in the wind, I thought of Cambridge, despite having left there only a day ago, not as a distant place but as a remote time. Although my wife and daughter were probably sitting down to dinner at that very moment in our Cambridge flat, I did not think of this as happening *now* in another country, but as something that had occurred some time ago. And when I thought of my destination in Northern Sierra Leone, it was not as a place I was about to journey to but as a time still to come. Bergson observed that "time, conceived under the form of an unbounded and homogenous medium, is nothing but the ghost of space haunting the reflective consciousness." But surely the reverse is also true, which may explain why Kuranko tales are avowedly about events that are not of any time, and have not taken place anywhere, and always begin with the same stock phrases, *wo lai yan la* or *wo le yan be la* ("far-off and long ago").

Remote places and remote periods in history have something else in common: we cannot be sure that they are continuous with our world in the here and now, and unless we actually visit them we cannot discover whether their inhabitants are utterly alien or our coevals. Both knowledge and ignorance are relative to spatiotemporal distance.

For Hayden White, our objective knowledge of the historical past is limited by the fact that "past events, processes, institutions, persons, and things are no longer perceivable nor directly knowable in the way that present or still living entities are." Accordingly, historical writing is as conjectural as it is factual, and the past is constantly under revision as we selectively and creatively draw on it to explain or legitimate our actions in the present. The same may be said of culture. The literal and the literary are always entangled. Abstract generalities are anchored in empirical particularities. Personal preoccupations shape our historical or cultural explanations, and, as Hannah Arendt observes, the very possibility of history is grounded in the narrative form of an individual life: "That every individual life between birth and death can eventually be told as a story with beginning and end is the prepolitical and prehistorical condition of history, the great story without beginning and end."

At any given moment one cannot be sure whether one is blindly recapitulating a world one had no hand in making or actually creating a world one can really call one's own. Our lives waver continually between these two extremes, sometimes moved by fates and furies we can neither comprehend nor control, sometimes appearing to be within our power to determine.

Whereas some anthropologists have postulated radical differences between societies based on whether they privilege history or myth, whether they are cold or hot, changeless or changing, with or without history, a phenomenologically more faithful account of our being-in-time would be sensitive to the constant shifts that occur in consciousness *between* these different modalities of experience, and radically question our habit of defining entire societies in terms of one or the other of these traits.

My ethnographic research in West Africa and Central Australia persuaded me that people create the past to the same extent that they are creatures of it. In West Africa, one's fate is determined by prenatal choices that may, however, be resisted or revoked by what one subsequently does during one's life on earth. For Aboriginal people, the past is continually reappearing in people's dreams, hence the notion of the Dreaming. In the Warlpiri settlement of Lajamanu, a woman called Lorna Nakamarra saw ghosts in her dream, among them the ghost of her late husband. Her husband recounted a story from the Dreaming in which a certain man had abducted a woman from a distant country. The aggrieved husband tracked the malefactor across the desert. After ambushing him at a rock hole as he knelt to drink, they speared him to death. A few days after this dream was shared, the kinsmen of the dreamer initiated a ceremony in which the ancestral event was reenacted.

Traces (*kuruwarri*) of the past are not held in the unconscious mind; they permeate the earth itself, lying quiescent in the ground like grass seeds awaiting rain to germinate or sperm for an egg to fertilize. Should a woman pass through one of these potent tracts of country, its nascent life may enter her womb and quicken into new life, and the child she brings into the world will incarnate the personality of the forebear whose spirit lay dormant in the country she crossed. On a journey through the desert, Nugget Jangala told me of a man called Wagon Joe who had been conceived at the rain Dreaming site of PirtiPirti. In the Dreaming, a certain Jangala speared his brother there in a fight to abduct one of his wives. Today a pile of boulders is the petrified body of Jangala set atop the bodies of the two Nungarrayi wives. According to Nugget, Wagon Joe's crooked arm and pockmarked skin were scars from that primordial spear fight, physical manifestations of the *kuruwarri* of that place. A sensible connection between oneself and one's forebears is also felt in relation to other kinsmen. For example, a junior sibling is associated with the shoulder (*jija-warnu*—"shoulder-belong") perhaps because he or she is often carried on an elder sibling's shoulders. To feel a throbbing or twinge in the shoulder muscles may be interpreted as a telepathic sign that a junior sibling is nigh or that something untoward has happened to him. This sympathetic relationship between separated *bodies* is reminiscent of the phantom limb phenomenon in which one's body appears to mourn a lost member and may be compared with our metaphors of a marriage of *minds* or an elective affinity between ourselves and our precursors.

In this Aboriginal worldview, nothing dies. Lives pass out of sight and out of mind for a generation before reappearing, in the same way that one's ancestors in the Dreaming, their earth-shaping labor done, returned to whence they came, sinking wearily into the ground to become petrified forms that would, in time, be reanimated through the ritual labor of the living.

This sense that body painting, dance, and song quicken the ancestral dead into life, realizing the potentiality for the past to become present again, is not only ubiquitous in Aboriginal Australia. In societies through-out history and in the contemporary world, dreams provide evidence of the continuing presence of the dead and their power to intervene benevo-lently or malevolently in the lives of the living, depending on how they are summoned and how adequately they have been supplicated. Rebirth eschatologies are universal, and karmic ideas may be found in such disparate sources as Pythagorean and Vedic philosophy and tribal cosmologies. The Tlingit not only believe in the transmigration of souls and the possibility of the dead returning in another human or animal form; they consider every baby to be a maternal relative reincarnated. Since the dead are cremated, people might say of the time before their own birth, "Then ashes I was; not yet was I born." In West Africa, a dream or memory of a forebear is taken as evidence that he is still alive, albeit in another zone. A Mapuche thunder shaman assumes the form of a warrior mounted on her spirit horse and travels to other historical periods and places to gain the power and knowledge with which to combat her community's contemporary enemies, including forestry companies and settlers. In Cuba, a Kongo-inspired society of affliction known as Palo enables practitioners to viscerally experience, interact with, and work with "the ambient dead" in order "to transform the fates of the living." A person possessed by spirits in Mayotte is momentarily both himself *and* another. In the guise of avatars from previous epochs, people interact, debate community affairs, and hope to be healed from their personal afflictions. And in the mountain villages of east Naxos, Greece, dreams are as vital to the recovery of the past as papyri, bones, and stele are to the European archaeologist. In one dream, the Mother of God revealed contemporaries of Jesus of Nazareth, as well as the icons they carried and where these buried relics might now be found.

In all these instances the unconscious is without chronicity. Time collapses and is compressed so that, as Karl Jaspers notes, "historicity is the only way in which Being is accessible to me, as a being in time."

> What we call the beginning is often the end
> And to make an end is to make a beginning.
> The end is where we start from . . .
> We are born with the dead:
> See, they return, and bring us with them.
> The moment of the rose and the moment of the yew-tree
> Are of equal duration. A people without history
> Is not redeemed from time, for history is a pattern
> Of timeless moments.

Although we in the allegedly scientific West have come to think of our relations with the ancestral past largely in terms of genetics and epigenetics, alternative interpretations of the continuity of life over time persist in popular ideas of cell memory, reincarnation, hauntings, myths of eternal recurrence, and an endless fascination with facts and photos that corroborate ancestral links. What gives rise to these theories of history, whether designated scientific or phantasmagoric? What is it about our lives that engenders or prompts these reflections on our existential embeddedness in the past so that if these theories disappeared they would inevitably be reinvented from the raw experience of our being-in-time?

One answer to this question is that in order to think about our *immediate* experience of being-in-the-world we need to have recourse to images, concepts, and practices that appear to be *objective*—not completely *of* us yet not entirely unfamiliar *to* us. Such ambiguous forms, which participate in our subjectivity yet remain partly alien to it, include Gods and spirits, the dead, exotic places, distant times (either past or still to come), and other people (real or imagined). Through these various forms of otherness, our ownness becomes thinkable.

Consider the case of the great French writer Marguerite Yourcenar and her fascination with the Roman emperor Hadrian. The idea of ghostwriting Hadrian's memoirs first came to her during the period between 1924 and 1929. Then in her early twenties, she was aware that "a great part of my life was going to be spent in trying to define, and then to portray, that man existing alone and yet closely bound with all being." The project was begun and abandoned several times. At times, she felt too young to do justice to the work. Or she lost interest in it, feeling shame at ever having ventured upon the undertaking. She suffered that "lapse into despair of a writer who does not write." Then, around 1941, she discovered by chance, in an artist's supply shop in New York, four Piranesi engravings and bought them. One depicted Hadrian's Villa. Piranesi, she realized, had sensed "the tragic architecture of an inner world." For years, she gazed at this engraving every day as she drew inspiration from thirty years' experience of joy and sorrow, sickness and health, and "the perpetual testing of oneself upon the touchstone of fact." The memoirs were published in 1951 when Yourcenar was forty-eight. "We lose track of everything, and of everyone, even ourselves," she writes. Yet I imagine she might have grudgingly accepted the corollary of this: that though we disappear into our account of another, we also appear in it in a way we could not have foreseen or ordained. As she describes her habit of writing each night "in almost automatic fashion," before destroying the work each morning, she suggests an analogy with how, in each generation, we build our lives from the rubble of our parental or ancestral past, plundering and sundering what others have made in order to give birth to ourselves.

Marguerite Yourcenar's *Souvenirs Pieux* emphasizes the pregiven and the preexistent. Like any other memoir, her narrative begins with the birth of an individual subject. "The being I refer to as *me* came into the world on Monday, June 8, 1903, at about eight in the morning, in Brussels." But after her first perfunctory paragraph, the author moves back in time, recounting her paternal and maternal family histories in such depth and detail that she is herself quickly eclipsed, and the subject of the memoir becomes, in effect, her maternal lineage. Yourcenar's avoidance of self-centeredness is, of course, deliberate. By freeing the personal *voice* from the conventional autobiographical burden of tracing the development and career of a personal *identity,* she is better able to go "beyond the confines of individual history and even beyond History" and explore "the hopeless tangle of incidents and circumstances which to a greater or lesser extent shape us all." What makes Marguerite Yourcenar's memoir singularly moving is the fact that her mother died in giving birth to her. Her life was thus contingent upon the death of her mother. What I find arresting about the difference between most life stories and Yourcenar's is that while we are generally free to symbolically repudiate our parentage, she was not, because her mother died giving birth to her. As with children "given up" for adoption at birth, the biological parents' "abandonment" of the child robs the child of the freedom to symbolically abandon and outgrow them. Instead of playing out the oedipal drama of revolt and rejection in relation to the persons who gave the child her initial identity and name, the child is drawn back into the past in an endless quest for the person she can never reject or outlive because that person "rejected" her *and because this primal rejection has come to define her as someone who is fundamentally unworthy of life.* Moreover, while the child grows old, the parent remains forever young. Perhaps this explains why Marguerite Yourcenar's historical biographies and fictionalized autobiographies refer constantly to the past, not out of nostalgia for a golden age but because of the tragic connection between her own birth and her mother's death and her awareness that her own life cannot really begin until her mother's life has run its full course. When Marguerite Yourcenar recounts her mother's story, she (who is old enough now to be her mother's grandmother) symbolically inverts her relationship with Fernande and reverses the passage of time. Speaking of Fernande, Yourcenar observes that her memoir is an effort to "recapture and recount her history" and "fills me with a sympathy for her that I have not felt heretofore. She is much like those characters, imaginary or real, that I nourish with my own substance to try to make them live, or live once again." In recounting what befell her in the past, Yourcenar acts imaginatively on events she suffered in passivity, symbolically bringing her mother back to life in order that she, the author, can lay her ghost.

Perhaps this explains why expatriates feel compelled to revisit their natal countries, in reality or in memory. By going "home" they imagine themselves traveling through time, to complete something unfinished, redeem something lost, or realize a dream that was never fulfilled. As Joyce Johnson put it, "If time were like a passage of music, you could keep going back to it till you got it right."

The Enigma of Anteriority

Finally, after exteriority and superiority, one runs up against the enigma of anteriority: before the moral law, there is always a moral law, just as before Caesar, there is always another Caesar. . . . Here we find a sort of always-already-present, which causes any effort to discover a dated beginning to fail as it encounters the perspective of the origin. It is as though there were a dialectic of the origin and the beginning: the beginning should be able to be dated in a chronology, but the origin always slips away, at the same time as it surges up in the present under the enigma of the always-already-there.

—PAUL RICOEUR, *CRITIQUE AND CONVICTION*

First Things First

There are moments in life of which we later say, everything changed. Nothing was ever the same again. This is as true of our histories as of our lives. There is a before and an after; our world was turned upside down; we suffered the eclipse of all that we took to be tried and true. This eclipse may follow bereavement or falling in love. It can befall those who lose their homeland to an invader or a traveler in an antique land. And it often brings us to rethink the meaning of first things; to ask what hold our histories have over us and whether there is something about our first experiences in life that makes all that follows pale in comparison.

When I went back to my natal New Zealand in the fall of 2008, bent on pursuing these questions through conversations with old friends and visits to old haunts, I thought of my project as a Bildungsroman in reverse, for instead of moving toward a point where I came into my own, I was going back to the place from which I had started out. Yet my interest was not solely in my own roots, but in how our individual stories are interwoven with social and historical events that carry us beyond ourselves and pose questions for which we may have no answers.

In Joseph Conrad's *Youth*, a retired merchant seaman tells the story of his first voyage to the East. Marlowe is twenty years old at the time. In the middle of the Indian Ocean, the *Judea*'s cargo of coal catches fire. There is an explosion and the crew takes to the boats. Marlowe is in charge of the smallest boat. It is his first command. "I did not know how good a man I was till then. I remember the drawn faces, the dejected figures of my two men, and I remember my youth and the feeling that will never come back any more—the feeling that I could last forever, outlast the sea, the earth, and all men." Marlowe makes landfall somewhere on the coast of Java, and this moment will stay with him for as long as he lives: the feeling that his whole life stretches ahead of him, filled with boundless promise and possibility. "But age slowly wears us down," says the older Marlowe. "Our faces lined, wrinkled . . . marked by toil, deceptions, success, and love, even though our weary eyes continue to look anxiously for something out of life, that while it is expected is already gone—has passed unseen, in a sigh, in a flash—together with the youth, with the strength, with the romance of illusions."

Memory, like a good storyteller, is an artful liar. It reworks the past in ways that make it easier for us to live in the present. And while it may be consoling to think that one's life, or the history of one's nation, has a beginning, middle, and end, lived time does not evolve lineally or smoothly, or as a chain of cause and effect. In reality, our lives get bogged down and sidetracked; we go backward, stand still, get carried away, and lose the plot. Moreover, our lives are so tied up with the lives of others that it is impossible to disentangle a single strand and confidently identify it as "yours" or "mine." And though we sometimes evoke an original state from which our lives unfolded or fell away, making it fundamental to who we are and what we have become, the course of any life is so discontinuous that there often remains no "first spinning place" for us to return to except in the imagination.

But return I did, to New Zealand, driving a rental car around with an ad hoc itinerary and a handful of ideas that might never bear fruit.

This book is the result. Blending ethnography, history, and autobiography, it explores the presence of "firstness" in the ways we recount our stories, narrate our national histories, assign value, allocate blame, determine cause, and attempt to fathom the mysterious relation between individual origins and all that prefigures them.

Braided Rivers

Arriving in New Zealand by air, I am always struck by how exposed the landscape is to the elements. How buffeted by wind and rain. Crossing the South Westland coast, I caught glimpses of fretful sea, black rocks, and iron sand. And then, through scudding cloud, verdant hills, as if the greenness of the original forests, felled and burned to make way for English farms, had seeped into the denuded land like indelible ink, an ineradicable reminder of loss. Far below, the red roofs of farmhouses and shearing sheds appeared so random and solitary that I remembered my youth for its persistent sense of being in such a place on sufferance, of not belonging. At Christchurch Airport, I passed people who looked as if they had mislaid valued possessions or missed their flights. Weather-beaten, anxious faces, hair tousled by the wind. And a curious reticence, as if voicing one's thoughts could only make matters worse.

I rented a car and drove north through squalls of rain. Near Amberley, the weather cleared, and I pulled over to the side of the road to check my map. To the west were windbreaks of eucalyptus and pine, with wind-combed grasses glistening in the sudden sun. How ironic that so many foreign species have flourished here—pinus insignis and macrocarpa from Monterey in California; brushtail possums and bluegums from Australia—while so many New Zealanders have felt the need to go abroad to find their niche. Ironic, too, that we still drive on the left-hand side of the road as if, in the antipodes, history has produced a society in which many things are, from a northern vantage point, back to front. And who could have foreseen that within two years the city I had just left would be in ruins and that I would read a press release in which a survivor spoke of cars "falling into holes and everything was upside down"?

I was twenty-three when I saw the East for the first time, coming from the sea, like Marlowe, to a place of "danger and promise" where "a stealthy Nemesis lay in wait." I spent a day in Bombay, drifting around the city and getting lost in the labyrinthine red light district around Falkland Road, known locally as the Kamathipura. Street after street was lined with cages in which frail girls, like birds, sold into slavery for the price of a pair of shoes or a tin roof, whispered and fluttered. Pimps pursued me at every turn. "You want jiggajig, Sah?" "Sahib, Sahib, Sahib, you like leetle girl?" "Sah? Yes, Sahib, I can do, Sahib?" To escape the wheedling and pestering, I walked into a cinema and bought a ticket. Ushered into an upstairs seat, I found myself watching a film of the great Persian epic Sohrab and Rustam. I had never before seen an Indian film. Although I couldn't understand Hindi or read the Urdu or Malayalam subtitles, I was captivated by the music, and for months after leaving India I tried to recall one song in particular, a lifeline to a place to which I fantasized returning. Forty-five years later, having long forgotten the tune, I typed into YouTube the words "Sohrab and Rustam Hindi film" on the off chance that the miracle of digital technology might help me retrieve what my mind had been unable to retain. I discovered that the vocal music for the movie had been prerecorded by Lata Mangeshkar, perhaps the most famous playback singer in the history of Bollywood, and that the song that haunted me throughout the winter of 1963–1964, when I worked among the homeless in London, was called "Yeh Kaisi Ajab." The song is banal, yet, watching the beautiful actress Suraiya lip-synch Lata Mangeshkar's shrill and quavering vocals, I saw how this music and its setting could have enchanted me at twenty-three, much as Conrad's Marlowe was enthralled when he first set eyes on the East. Music, more than any medium I know, has this power to carry one across space and time, reviving dormant memories, recovering lost connections. But memory is so notoriously mutable that it is never the past one returns to but a version or illusion of it, and this sense that time is irreversible and the past irretrievable in its original form may either liberate us to live more completely in the present or drive us to despair.

On the winding road through Weka Pass, I was thinking of my first wife. At age fourteen, she was taken by ambulance to Christchurch Hospital over this road. Suspected of having rheumatic fever, she was hospitalized and placed under observation in a ward filled with senile or dying women. When her mother visited her five days later, Pauline was distraught. "Take me out of here, Mum," she cried, "take me out of here!" Feverishly turning her head from side to side and throwing back the bed sheets, she begged her mother not to leave her. Noellie took her daughter home to Waiau for ten weeks' bed rest. But something had changed. Pauline appeared to have lost any desire to go out into the world. She had been a champion swimmer; now she would not go near the baths. The previous summer, she had learned to drive. She now declared she had no interest in driving a car. She only wanted to see her horse, Rosie. With Rosie she felt in control.

Ten years after our marriage, when we were living in Palmerston North, Pauline began writing a children's novel that allegorized her experiences before and after hospitalization. On the surface, *Back of Beyond* is the story of two children who become involved in unraveling the mystery of an attempted murder. But Pauline intended her novel to recount, albeit obliquely, far more personal experiences. She began writing two years after undergoing radiotherapy and chemotherapy for Hodgkin's disease. This devastating experience was a replay of the trauma she had suffered as a fourteen-year-old girl in Christchurch Hospital. Though in remission, she lived without certainty, as if at any moment the ground might give way beneath her feet. And this contrast between what it is like to take life for granted, as though one had all the time in the world, and what it is like to live as if every day might be one's last, finds expression in the two very different protagonists of the story—a gauche and timid English boy and a rough, high-spirited New Zealand girl, brought together one summer on a high country station. In the solution of the crime lies the resolution of an existential mystery—how we may live with a sense of our vulnerability while drawing on our strengths, neither succumbing to our fear that the world is too much for us nor retrospectively seeing ourselves as heroic and virtuous simply because we survive.

Beyond Waikari, the serrated and snow-streaked peaks of the Inland Kaikoura range became visible, and over the last few miles between Rotherham and Waiau, every bend in the road, every stand of pines, every farmhouse or fence line was so familiar that by the time I approached 50 Leslie Street, where Pauline spent her childhood, I was beginning to imagine that she and her parents would be waiting for me there and wondering where in the world I had been for so long. I did not stop, but drove slowly past the timber mill that Pauline's father had once owned and on toward the Mason River Bridge where I parked under some willows, scrambled down the embankment and picked my way across the graywacke stones of the riverbed until I located the spot near the wooden foundations of the old bridge where my daughter and I had scattered Pauline's ashes in the ice-cold water twenty-six years ago. I sat there with the sun on my face, inhaling the sweet smell of broom and the sour odor of dung in the cold air, the silence broken only by the trilling and lisping of a bird and an occasional passing car. Time hung fire. I was on my way back to Leslie Street after a long walk and would return in time for lunch. Jack would be picking broad beans and digging spuds from his garden. Noellie would be slicing ham, setting the table, and pouring herself a home-brewed beer with lemonade. Pauline would be reading in her room . . .

Memories are like rain clouds. Just as a mountain range is needed for clouds to fall as rain, so the mind needs a familiar landscape, a piece of music, the smell of fennel, the taste of a petite madeleine, if its hidden depths are to be revealed. So uncanny and surprising is this confluence of inner and outer worlds that we often have the impression that a landscape or valued object actually holds our past life in its hands, as insects are held in amber, or that past events remain perfectly preserved in our minds. But this flowing together of the debris of the past and what is now at hand is, like the confluence of two rivers, under constant revision. One day, it may seem as though the past is all we are and that we merely echo events that have already occurred. Another day, it is as though there were nothing outside the present moment. Our entire existence, all that matters, is contained in the here and now.

I was watching the water, growing dizzy as it slipped by, the color of bottle glass, whorls where there were submerged boulders, an uprooted willow snagging the current. This image of a river took hold. I thought of the other rivers that flow into the Waiau—the Mason, the Doubtful, the Hope—and I recalled the Māori tradition according to which there were once two Waiau Rivers, their adjacent headwaters in the Spencer Mountains. One was female (the Waiau-uha), the other male (Waiau-toa), and they were lovers before they were rivers. When they were parted, they became turbulent water, forever clouded by tears.

A human life is like the course of a river—in this case, its snow-fed chalky water braided by shingle banks as it works its way toward the sea. But can one map a life as one maps a river? Can we identify sources or trace origins as easily? Can we liken the influences that shape our lives to tributary streams? Do we wind up in a place that can be compared with an ocean? One might sketch such a map and outline a few contours, but the detail, the scale, is beyond the range of any cartographer. We cannot encompass all that makes us who we are any more than we can fathom the extent of our freedom to refashion the raw material we begin with.

It must have been in 1933 or 1934, not long after he had gone into exile, that Walter Benjamin momentarily lost his immunity to involuntary memory. Sitting alone in Les Deux Magots in Paris, he suddenly glimpsed, "with the force of an illumination," the fateful links between his life and the lives of friends, comrades, chance acquaintances, and lovers, as well as books and places. On a sheet of paper, Benjamin sketched a series of family trees or a labyrinth, bestowing a semblance of order on the "primal acquaintances" that had revealed to him, over many years, new pathways and possibilities. Two or three years after his Paris epiphany, and having lost the scrap of paper on which he seemed to have found, like Theseus, a way through the labyrinth of his life, Benjamin was struck not only by the impact of others on his own life, but by the variousness of their destinies, and he wondered whether it would be possible to divine in such a disparate group any common thread or family resemblance.

Who has not, at some stage, contemplated the possibility of piecing together the story of his or her life, summing it up, as we say, as if, despite its twists and turns, its braided course, its oxbows and ancillary streams, a life can be recounted as a story? It is significant, I think, that Walter Benjamin lost the paper on which he drew a coherent diagram of his life, for this enabled him thereafter to indulge the illusion that everything that had befallen him could be connected, like the dots in a child's puzzle book, disclosing a hitherto hidden form. I prefer a different image—suggested by the arcane term *paralipomena*. Strictly speaking, the Greek word *paraleipómena* designates things we leave behind, shelve or dismiss from mind, that yet accumulate as a kind of supplement or backlog to the stories we tell. Despite being unfinished and fragmentary, such deleted scenes, outtakes and afterthoughts capture moments when we see our-selves differently, as through the eyes of another. When we experience our past as if it were a previous incarnation. When we are visited by strange dreams and imagine other lives—a road not taken, a rendezvous missed, a letter not answered, a stone left unturned. When we nurture the view that we have been thrown into this life by a quirk of fate and that our true destiny will come later, or elsewhere, or with someone else. When we wait, harboring these unspoken thoughts, lost in a wilderness of vain conjecture and second guessing, asking ourselves over and over what would have hap-pened had we gone down another road, if we had, to borrow Robert Frost's compelling line, taken the road less traveled by.

Against the Grain

On the road to Parnassus, I encountered only one car. The setting sun glinted momentarily on its windscreen as it sped by, eclipsing the driver's face. And then I had the wilderness to myself again, tussock, gorse, and empty hills.

It was evening when I reached Kaikoura, the town buffeted by a stiff wind off the sea and squalls of rain. Yet despite the dusk and drizzle I felt the adversarial presence of the mountain range and the ocean—the town-ship cast between them like a handful of poker dice. That night, in a hostel, I began rereading *Erewhon*, a book associated in my mind with Pauline's *Back of Beyond*. Just as her hidden valley was modeled on high country sheep stations she had known as a child, like Molesworth and Cloudy Range, Samuel Butler's preindustrial paradise was born of his reveries at the Rangitata Forks where he bought a sheep run in 1860. These are the kinds of places where a hunted man can hide, where a youngster can test his mettle, and a troubled mind find sanctuary. As his title suggests, But-ler's Erewhon turns the conventional world upside down. In this antipo-dean world, churches are banks, money is God, invalids are criminals, and universities are Colleges of Unreason. Houses are built facing north for the sun, not south. East and west are reversed. Moreover, people are drawn through life backward, their faces turned toward the past rather than the future. These reversals were anticipated by Butler's decision to migrate to the margins of the Empire, exchanging the gentility of bourgeois England for the wilds of New Zealand. The contradictory colony gave the young adventurer a great deal of narcissistic satisfaction. Animals, vegetables, and minerals called familiar identifications into question. In Canterbury, he could not decide whether the rocks were sandstone or slate, whether masters enjoyed a greater social advantage than their servants, or vice versa, and whether farmers were creatures of routines determined by the sheep they farmed. Butler's images of reversal suggest not only a contrarian disposition; they are evidence of his personal disorientation as he struggled to find his feet down under and to come to terms with a society in which the familiar and the foreign were juxtaposed as incongruously as the coinages that would pepper his fiction—Arowhena Nosnibor, for instance, and Kahabuka, also known as Chowbok—words spelled back to front, combinations of Māori and English phonemes, peculiar anagrams. Though the twenty-four-year-old Butler was exhilarated by the harsh light, the open horizons, and the prospect of living "beyond the pale of civilization," he experienced moments of desolation, when he longed to see "some signs of human care in the midst of the loneliness," some glimpse of Europe. Even more onerous was his intellectual isolation. New Zealand seemed "far better adapted to develop and maintain in health the physical than the intellectual nature. The fact is," Butler wrote, "people here are busy making money; that is the inducement which led them to come in the first instance, and they show their sense by devoting their energies to the work." While admiring the shrewd, hardheaded intelligence of the settlers, and their freedom from the pretensions of the old country, he missed his Handel and Bach and grew weary of conversations about sheep, horses, dogs, cattle, English grasses, paddocks, and bush. Isolated in his cob cottage at the Rangitata Forks, he found that the solitude was greater than he could bear. "I felt increasing upon me that dreadful doubt as to my own identity—as to the continuity of my past and present existence—which is the first sign of that distraction which comes on those who have lost themselves in the bush. I had fought against this feeling hitherto, and had conquered it; but the intense silence and gloom of this rocky wilderness were too much for me, and I felt that my power of collecting myself was beginning to be impaired." Eager to embrace the egalitarian ethos of the colony, Butler nonetheless felt "totally debarred from the intellectual society of clever men," and this unresolved tension between the raw physicality and practicality of the settlers and the intellectual and artistic traditions of Europe would become a recurring motif in New Zealand art and literature.

When I finally closed *Erewhon* and set it down on my bedside table, I hesitated to turn off the light, for Butler's images had brought back to me the mixed emotions of ecstasy and emptiness one often feels in remote New Zealand.

* * *

After waking at first light, I packed my bag, paid my bill, and drove to a café on the foreshore. My waitress presumed I was American, and gave me a tourist brochure to read while I waited for my muesli, toast, and coffee.

According to the brochure, the Kaikoura coast was "a Mecca for marine mammals." Fur seals and dolphins abounded in the inshore waters, and one could observe sperm whales further out, where nutrient-rich waters welled up from the Hikurangi Trench and sustained the groper, shark, and squid on which the whales fed. "It is hard to imagine how full of life the oceans once were. Let's hope we don't find that due to our stupidity, imagination is all that we have left."

When I'd finished my breakfast, I strolled along the seafront, sun on my face and a fresh breeze off the ocean. Someone had stapled flyers on the trunks of the big araucarias along the promenade. They advertised whale watching, fresh crayfish, pony treks, and other healthy outdoor pursuits. But I was seeing the insubstantial and curiously childlike buildings of the township through Samuel Butler's eyes, as though I had just disembarked from *The Roman Emperor* in January 1860, four months after leaving Gravesend. Perhaps, too, I was still under the influence of a recent trip to Mexico where I visited the great pyramids of the sun and moon at Teotihuacán. The pyramid builders had sited and designed them to echo the slopes of the distant hills, in keeping with a cosmovision that sought, in every aspect of everyday life, to bring human, divine, and natural worlds into alignment, so ensuring that the life force of one flowed into the others in a cycle of life-sustaining exchange. By contrast, one sometimes gets the impression in New Zealand that the invasive culture of Europe has found great difficulty in adjusting itself either to indigenous values or the physical environment. Everywhere there is evidence of how awkwardly it relates

to both. Paddocks come up against remnant stands of native bush, weatherboard houses are painted white and trimmed with colors that clash rather
than harmonize with the surrounding land. Leaving Kaikoura, I passed a
series of motels whose banal names—Norfolk Pine, Kaikoura Cottage,
Clearwater, Blue Seas, Seaview, Anchor, Panorama, Kaikoura Gateway—
suggested a reticence to come to terms with our history or to reimagine our
sense of place.

Rising sheer from the sea—or so it seemed—the snow-clad Seaward
Kaikouras took my breath away, setting me to wonder how one might adequately describe a scene that half the postcards on sale in the hostel had
reduced to a photogenic backdrop for a sperm whale surfacing or the name
of a motel. *Erewhon* gives us an inkling of how the new settlers would conjure a sense of being in control of the landscapes that filled them with
dread. They would fell and fire the forests and recreate the hills of home.
And in replicating England's green and pleasant land, or cultivating their
respectable enclaves, they would fool themselves into believing they could
master the homesickness that oppressed them within and the intractable
wildness of the world without.

I remembered the Matukituki Valley, hard under Mount Aspiring, the
summer Pauline and I stayed with our friends Bryn and Isabelle Jones in
the old Aspinall homestead. We heard stories of how difficult it had been,
a hundred years ago, living in a sod hut and raising a family, with the
unceasing sound of cataracts and glaciers drowning one's voice, depressing one's spirits. Not far from the homestead was a small stream. We used
to bathe in a pool that had been carved over the centuries by a waterfall
plunging from the cirque high above. With snowmelt in the spring, the
stream became a torrent. On such a day in 1899, Hugh McPherson was
crossing the swollen stream on stepping-stones, his daughter behind him.
The little girl slipped and fell into the swift water. Her mother, standing
fifty yards away, saw what had happened and called out, but the roaring
water drowned out her cries and by the time the father realized his daughter was being swept away he could do nothing to save her. In 1905, McPherson lost his own life. Returning from Wanaka with supplies, his dray struck
a submerged shingle bank and overturned, trapping him beneath the water.
The Duncan Macphersons, who built their homestead on the west branch
of the river, fared no better. Though she dreaded the noise of the river,
Mrs. Macpherson traveled to Wanaka with her daughter to vote in the

1919 General Election. During the day, the river rose, and as she started across, the spring-cart overturned. Her thirteen-year-old daughter managed to cling to the harness, but Mrs. Macpherson was unable to save herself. A year later, the surviving family left the valley for good.

* * *

Just north of Māori Creek, at the beginning of Mangamaunu Bay, I stopped the car and got out. After crossing the rust-stained ballast of the narrow gauge railway line, I found a track through lupin, toetoe, and wet marram grass that led to the beach. The snow-covered range was now on my right. On the river terraces and foothills, wind-stunted mānuka, karaka, and ngaio had been laid low by the calloused hand of the wind.

At my feet, the sea scrabbled and seethed, grinding the graywacke stones and leaving its spittle on the sand. Though nothing now remains of the site of the old Flat Settlement, it was here that the Australian poet Henry Lawson spent several months teaching in a Native school in 1897. One might have expected his poems and journal entries from this time to be inspired by the coast, but whenever he got away from Mangamaunu he seems always to have headed into Kaikoura, seeking the comradeship of the pub. His most notable piece of writing from the time is an embittered story called *A Daughter of Māoriland*, in which an open-minded new teacher at a Māori school shows compassion to a lonely and ill-treated pupil only to have her family repay him with gossip and exploitation. His experience at Mangamaunu led Lawson to conclude that it was "sentimental rot" and a sheer waste of time to extend human kindness to people who lacked the moral sophistication that would enable them to recognize and return it.

Lawson appears completely insensitive to the colonial context of his relationship with Māori. Like other Pākehā in positions of privilege and power, he assumed that Māori should be grateful for the religious enlightenment and secular education they stood to receive from their civilized betters and not bite the hand that fed them. But in the years since Samuel Butler arrived in Christchurch, the indigenous Ngāi Tahu had sold most of their land for derisory sums, usually with little understanding of what such "sales" entailed under British law. Although Kaikoura Māori had managed to retain a coastal strip twelve miles long and a mile deep and had fish, shellfish, crayfish, karaka berries, and birds aplenty, hunting and gathering alone could not provide for their needs, and many Māori men worked on whaleboats or in the Kaikoura try-works, or spent their summers shearing. Understandably, few felt much gratitude to the Pākehā who had, in a single generation, occupied their lands, visited upon them typhus, measles, tuberculosis, bronchitis, and syphilis, and now refused to settle outstanding compensation claims for the lands and livelihoods Ngāi Tahu had lost.

Lawson accepted the paternalistic Victorian dogma that assimilation was the only way that "primitive" people could overcome their natural inferiority. Yet when he and his wife arrived at Mangamaunu with only light hand luggage and two cement casks containing a mattress, a kettle, some pots and pans, and a few groceries, they were warmly welcomed by local Māori and for several weeks were wholly dependent on the baskets of kumara, wild pork, rabbits, pigeon and kaka, paua, fish, and watercress that were brought to their door. The Lawsons reciprocated with what they had to give. Berthe, a trained nurse, attended sick women in the kainga, and Henry expressed solidarity with Māori against local sheep owners who regarded "the nigs" with "contempt or aggressive dislike." After all, this was the poet who had built his reputation on an ethic of mateship, espousing empathy for individuals battling the powers that be. Whether Lawson was capable of extending these principles to people of color was another matter. His Achilles heel was his sense of inferiority, born of a lonely and loveless childhood and minimal schooling. "I was slow at arithmetic," Lawson confessed, "but I stuck to it. I was, I think, going into compound fractions when I left school." At Mangamaunu, "I could scarcely add a column of figures. I had to practice nights and fake up sums with answers on the back of the board and bluff for all I was worth; for there was a Māori girl there, about twenty, as big as I am and further advanced in arithmetic, and she'd watch me like a cat watches a mouse until she caught me in a mistake."

The Māori girl who put her teacher on the spot, and became the bane of his life, was also the model for the ingrate in Lawson's story, *A Daughter of Māoriland*. Her name was Mere Jacob, and her father had murdered her mother after a violent argument when Mere was six or seven. According to Lawson, Mere formed an unwanted attachment to him and his wife, haunting the school, even during the holidays, and hanging around Berthe "like a stray dog." He described her as morose and brooding and became convinced that she had inherited her father's violent disposition. Even before the Lawsons' arrival in the settlement, Mere would take to the bush if punished at the school, allegedly sitting for hours and sometimes days in a tree, withdrawn into morbid silence. "Poor girl," said Lawson, already betraying his fear of Mere Jacob, "but I shouldn't care to punish her if there were knives handy."

Berthe finally agreed to take Mere in as a boarder on the understanding that Mere work for the Lawsons as an unpaid domestic servant. Reflecting years later on her vexed months in Mangamaunu, Berthe would claim that Mere had been happy with this arrangement, but had inexplicably begun to pilfer groceries and neglect her housework. Outraged at her ingratitude, Henry described her as a cow, a pig, and a dog, bringing "a native smell" into the house and allowing herself to grow fat, lazy, and dirty. Indeed, he felt so disappointed and aggrieved that it did not occur to him that Mere might have felt justified in taking from the Lawsons what they owed her. After all, Mere was being treated as an unpaid menial, expected to be at the Lawsons' beck and call at all times, and her relatives had given bountiful help to the Lawsons. Henry's view came close to paranoia. Mere was spreading slanderous reports about the Lawsons and plotting with her relatives to do them harm. Not only was the girl not to be trusted; she possessed her father's jealous temperament and it was only a matter of time before he and his wife would fall victim to her scheming. On September 28, 1897, after only four and a half months at Mangamaunu, Lawson tendered his resignation: "As the loneliness of this place is affecting Mrs. Lawson's health, I wish to resign my position at the end of October."

I find it ironic that the teacher who spoke patronizingly of "my Māoris," presuming to be their moral superior, and leaving Mangamaunu a disillusioned and "cruelly wronged" man, would be remembered by local Māori without rancor or resentment. Under conditions of radical inequalities of power and wealth, it is often the subalterns who preserve their humanity while those who lord it over them, and do terrible wrongs in the name of civilization and reason, lose their souls.

* * *

Having now walked the length of the beach, I decided to return along the railway line to my car.

Not far from where I had parked, I happened on a sign:

Mangamaunu Bay

Selling Now

Pure Living Inspired by Nature

Another irony! A corporation selling lifestyle blocks on the same bay where, only days before resigning his teaching post, Henry Lawson had written

> ... dark and lonely,
> A wronged and broken man,
> He crouched and sobbed as only
> The strong heartbroken can.

I sat in my car for some time, listening to the washboard sea on the shingle and pondering the manifold ways in which our first experiences of life cast their shadow over what comes after.

Lawson's penchant for self-pity may be traced back to his childhood in the "miserable little hell" of New Pipeclay. Bullied at school, ignored at home, and further isolated by partial deafness from the age of nine, he would describe himself as a "delicate, shabby, soul-starved and totally uneducated Bush Boy ... drought born and drought bred," who found camaraderie in the pub but little fulfillment in home life or marriage. In Bill Pearson's words, "Lawson was predisposed to see in Mangamaunu the 'localism' and the 'ignorance' to which he had been so hurtfully exposed as a boy in New Pipeclay."

But what of Bill Pearson himself, to whom we owe our most detailed account of Henry Lawson's months in Mangamaunu?

When I took English 101 at the University of Auckland in 1958, Bill presented a memorable series of lectures on George Eliot's *Middlemarch*. A small man with thinning hair, he gave the impression of having spent his entire life indoors, and I wondered what in the world he had in common with the great Victorian writer whom many contemporaries found, at first sight, "magnificently ugly," but quickly succumbed to as "a most powerful beauty, a calm and sensuous soul." Years later, when I learned that Bill had been born and raised in an isolated working-class town on the West Coast, a shy and sensitive boy who preferred academic study to sports, I began to see how George Eliot's critique of English provincialism, and her sympathy with a young woman struggling to come into her own in a world of narrow, repressive values, might speak to his own beginnings. I could also understand why a young man with homosexual yearnings might learn to keep his head down and acquire the nervous, lopsided expression that made it seem as if Bill were about to be accused of some heinous crime. In rereading *Middlemarch*, I still find echoes of Bill. "There is no creature whose inward being is so strong that it is not greatly determined by what lies outside it, though at the same time every limit is a beginning as well as an ending."

My cohorts and I habitually drank in the corner bar of the Central Hotel with Bill and his academic mates, as well as members of the University Māori Club with which Bill had been closely involved since 1956. But it wasn't until after his death in 2002 that I discovered with what anguish Bill had wrestled with the question of whether to come out of the closet or to use the safer strategy in a homophobic society of keeping his sexual fantasies to himself. This same preemptive and self-protective wariness is evident in the opening lines of his famous 1952 essay "Fretful Sleepers: A Sketch of New Zealand Behaviour and its Implications for the Artist," written in London when he was twenty-nine, for Bill Pearson was acutely aware that many of his compatriots were as defensive about their national identity as they were about their sexual orientation. Writing critically might easily be seen, in a parochial society, as traitorous. Though Bill was loath to risk vilification as a queer, he found another outsider role in associating with Māori whom he idealized for their "courtesy and considerateness to guests," yet also regarded as victims. "I sometimes wonder whether I [was] trying to make up for some deficiency or loss within myself," Bill observed toward the end of his life.

With the resurgence of Māori activism in the 1970s, Bill began to realize that his promotion of Māori writing and his interest in Māori culture had been "naive and unconsciously paternalistic." In sympathizing with people who have suffered social injustices, there is a danger that we see them one dimensionally as victims and cast ourselves in the role of protector or rescuer, thereby underplaying the capacity of the alleged victim to redress the injustices on his or own terms. Receiving no gratitude or recognition for his goodwill, and encountering angry Māori with little patience for liberal Pākehā, Bill experienced something of what Lawson experienced at Mangamaunu, which may explain why he was drawn to Lawson's story. "I pulled out of the Māori Club at that time, I just felt I wasn't needed any more. . . . And of course, they had an expression for . . . people that had shown an interest in Māori things and then dropped out; they would say, 'He's swum back into the Pākehā sea.' If anybody remembers me, that's how they would look on me now. Occasionally I run into people I haven't seen for a long time, and they greet me, but I'm no longer considered of any importance in the kind of world I used to mix in."

Bill's sorrowful sense of insignificance leads him to assume that the New Zealand he knew has passed away, rendering him and his work anachronistic. A student of local literature might take an interest in *Coal Flat* or *Fretful Sleepers*, but these works have largely been forgotten. It may be true that history is a series of radical ruptures and discontinuities, but it is also true that every new generation puts the past behind it and imagines that it may bring a new world into being. Our current rage for demolishing old buildings and raising glass towers in their stead may be a symptom of our collective embarrassment with the past, comparable to the way that adolescents are embarrassed to be seen in public with their parents.

And so, with a vague memory of the "mud-brown" painting by Colin McCahon on the dust jacket of Bill Pearson's *Coal Flat*, I left Mangamaunu and drove on toward Nelson.

No Direction Home

I reached Nelson late in the day, joining my brother Miles and my sister-in-law Margaret as they prepared to leave for the restaurant where they played guitar and violin every Sunday night. The chef was Italian, his wife from Germany, and the risotto and Rhenish wine I was served that night were as satisfying as the music. Driving home, I congratulated Miles and Margaret for having achieved the kind of maturity and mastery that comes only after a lifetime of dedicated practice. I was also filled with admiration for the sanctuary, Escondida, they'd created among the regenerating bush.

Miles found it hard to imagine why one would choose any other life, and could not understand why I lived in a crowded and polluted city, devoting my energies to arcane intellectual pursuits and periodic forays into the third world. When he asked me what had brought me back to New Zealand, I was therefore hesitant to speak of my interest in first-ness, and described instead something of Henry Lawson's experiences at Mangamaunu.

"I'm mystified why Lawson was so uninspired by the Inland Kaikoura range or the wild coast that runs parallel to it."

"Actually," Miles said, "I'd find it depressing to live in the shadow of the range, the sun disappearing in mid-afternoon, the coast so wind-racked and the sea so vicious. Besides, Kaikoura is a dump."

I was unable to think of a response to this judgment, so I told him about my reading of Samuel Butler, how I'd been trying to get a sense of how the South Island appeared to the first European settlers. "It seems that our Kiwi vernacular has been with us from the beginning. Some of the idioms that Butler noted in 1860 I heard yesterday in Kaikoura: 'stuck up' for snobbish and 'skiting' for showing off. I find it compelling that the vocabulary and preoccupations of mid-nineteenth-century working-class migrants from Ireland, Scotland, and England have persisted here, despite our increasing affluence and education."

"That reminds me," Miles said, "I've got something to show you—something that will interest you very much. But for the time being I'll keep it a secret."

* * *

In the morning, Miles took me on a tour of Escondida. He particularly wanted to show me where his friend Larry had been planting bamboo. Each clump was surrounded by sacking in an attempt to stifle the old man's beard. After feeding kitchen scraps to the hens, Miles pointed out some of the native trees he had planted among the gorse. The unwanted gorse provided perfect protection, albeit at great cost to itself, for as soon as the natives outgrew it, the gorse died for want of sunlight. Whether Miles intended me to draw a moral from this, I did not know. I followed him down the road and uphill, past clay cuttings and stands of mānuka, before turning down a bush track that led to an ancient rimu—one of the few that had survived the fires with which the early settlers cleared the land. We then doubled back toward the house whose tiled roof brought home to me Miles's predilection for all things Spanish.

Over coffee on the terrace, where thyme flourished between the flag-stones, Margaret told me that only last week a flamenco group from Jerez de la Frontera in Spain had performed at the Nelson Arts Festival. After the group's final performance, Miles and Margaret invited the six visitors to a banquet of Spanish food at Escondida. Despite this hospitality, the gypsy singers and dancers appeared bored and impatient to leave. Perhaps they felt uncomfortable in a gadje (non-Gypsy) household. Perhaps they had been on the road too long, wearied by obligatory meetings with local musicians and interminable small talk in stilted English. When they had eaten, Miles encouraged the visiting guitarist, Jesus Alvarez, to play. Soon, Ana de los Reyes began singing with exhilarating passion, while the others clapped and chorused. Moved by the *soniquete,* Margaret decided to take a risk. Even though Jesus was playing in a difficult key, she found it and joined the voice of her violin to the voices of the gypsies. "The rapport was immediate," Margaret said. "They played and sang with even greater enthu-siasm, smiling in appreciation of my playing. Instead of returning to their hotel, they stayed for several hours. They told me that I possessed *instinto flamenco.* They even invited me to join their tour."

"But it was the vibrancy of the music," Miles said, "that stirred me most. Its power to cross language barriers, age and gender lines, reaching beyond Andalusia, creating a conversation in which even Margaret and I could take part. It's like falling in love."

"It was literally that for Francine," Margaret said, quickly adding, "Not your Francine, though she has the same love of life."

Auckland-born Francine Sweet was one of the flamenco dancers who had organized the New Zealand tour, and Margaret and Miles took it in turns to recount her story, which in some respects echoed theirs. Although Francine Sweet took dancing lessons from age five, it was an encounter with flamenco when she was twenty-three that defined the subsequent course of her life. After participating in a flamenco workshop in Christ-church, she eloped to Canada with the touring group's guitarist. Three years later she moved to Spain and trained under gypsy masters in Jerez. But remaking herself was an ordeal, and for many nights after her first performance she cried herself to sleep. "It was hard, very hard," Francine would tell a *Listener* interviewer. "It was in a *tablao* [a restaurant with a flamenco show]. I had to do it without any rehearsal, without knowing the common language or protocol of pure flamenco—nothing." Petite and dark, Francine translated her surname into her stage name, La Dulce. But the name was as misleading as her dulcet voice. "A will of iron is needed to learn gypsy flamenco, and the fire to dance it. I am increasingly passionate. I have to keep myself in the fire, close to the source of the art form."

* * *

It sometimes occurs to me that a careless demiurge repeatedly scatters the souls of the unborn across the face of the earth without a second thought for where they might thrive or feel at home, so that many of us are fated to spend a good part of our lives looking for where we properly belong. Strictly speaking, Francine Sweet's first life was her New Zealand life; she was born in Auckland, and many years passed before she left the country of her birth. And yet Andalusia is where she has always belonged, as if her struggle was not to break free of her family or birthplace but to realize her kinship with ancestors to whom no genealogical connections could be traced. This paradox—that one's life's journey is sometimes toward rather than away from one's true home—is nicely captured by Bob Dylan who, in an interview with Martin Scorsese, spoke of his own sense of having been born far from home. "I had ambitions to set out, like an Odyssey, going home somewhere. So I set out to find this home I'd left a while back, and I couldn't remember exactly where it was, but I was on my way there and encountering what I encountered on the way was how I envisioned it all."

I have given up trying to finalize my own views in this matter. But since arriving in Christchurch I had felt such a deep familiarity with the places I passed through that I took this as evidence of an irrevocable tie, both to the country and to my parentage, that transcended any ambivalence I might feel toward either. And yet, in writing emails to my wife and children on the other side of the world, I would be instantly transported *there*. Despite this disorienting oscillation from place to place, person to person, and period to period, or the strangeness that clung like a mist to the most familiar things, I was constantly aware of a primordial attachment to the first places on which I had opened my eyes, the first people I had known, and I felt that these first experiences were foundational. How does one interpret this contradictory sense of being in a place that is both familiar and foreign? Is it a result of seeing the place simultaneously through the eyes of a younger self who once lived there and an older self whose life is now located somewhere else? As I pondered these confusions, I was reminded of the idea of "originals" among the Mehinaku of the Upper Xingu in Amazonia.

For everything that exists, according to the Mehinaku, there is an archetypal, "true" version of it that was created before the first dawn broke upon the world. However, what we actually see are replicas of these first things. We therefore live in a world of masks or second skins that obscure an original reality that we may glimpse but never completely grasp.

Toward noon, Miles drove me into Nelson, where I had arranged to have lunch with Brigid Lowry. I once worked for Brigid's father, Bob, as a letterpress machinist, and Brigid, then nine, would often visit us at the press. Brigid's first published work was two poems that Bob printed for her, and one day, perhaps in appreciation of my support for her father, she presented me with a hat she had fashioned from a strip of cartridge paper stapled into a band. With Bob's red mark-up pencil she had written on the hat, "I am a Mike in this My Kingdom," eight words that were enough to convince me that she would one day become a successful writer.

Brigid answered my knock on her door, and rather than go inside we loitered on the path where I asked Brigid if she had cemented the shards of ceramic tile and crockery into the face of the steps that led up to the street. "One of my small labors of love," Brigid said. "I like to collect broken and discarded things and find a place for them. I'm glad you like my handiwork."

"Isn't this why we write," I said. "To mend the broken things in our lives?"

Over lunch, I shared with Brigid a little about my research, alluding to my brother's affinity for Spain, Margaret's fascination with gypsies, and the strange affinity we sometimes feel for places and people far from the country in which we have been raised.

"Asia has always been my other place," Brigid said. "I don't know why. Or whether my Buddhism came first, or my attraction to East Asia. I think it's karmic. We've been elsewhere in a previous life. The echoes and repetitions are so real."

Twenty years ago I might have rejected the notion of karma out of hand. Now I was more tolerant of the images we use in accounting for the mysteries of our experience of being-in-time. What cannot be verified is not necessarily inadequate to the phenomena we are struggling to grasp.

Inevitably, we also talked about writing, and I asked Brigid how she had become a writer.

"I enjoyed writing at school, she said, "but a literary career was not an option, even though my parents loved books, and our house was famous for literary parties. My mother was a frustrated poet with very little money, a husband who drank too much, and four strapping daughters. But despite being too busy trying to make ends meet to write, she did all that she could to nourish our creativity."

Brigid's first job after leaving school was in a library. "Next I was a waitress and a bookshop assistant, before becoming a primary school teacher, for which I lacked the necessary patience. Life took some interesting twists and turns, and at the age of thirty-five I reevaluated what I wanted to do. I had spent seven years living in a Buddhist community and was now a mother and second-time-around wife. I knew I loved books and writing so I did a BA at Curtin University, majoring in creative writing. The atmosphere was stimulating and supportive, and soon I was writing and publishing short fiction and poetry, mainly autobiographical."

Like many writers, Brigid regarded the literary vocation as a curse and a blessing. "Sometimes it seems the most pleasurable job in the world, sometimes it seems the most difficult. At times the work comes easily, at times it is like reaching into the depths of nowhere and finding nothing. I often wish I worked in a café and produced easy things, like soup or cake. The lesson I am learning right now about writing is to take my time and to enjoy myself more. Writing from a tight place will not produce good work. You need discipline but you also need joy and ease and playfulness."

I agreed with Brigid. I had never acquired the knack of writing research proposals or conforming to academic protocols. I preferred to carry a theme into the field and allow adventitious events, encounters, and conversations flesh it out or transform it. "This time around," I told Brigid, "I have yielded even more radically to the road."

"I never had a formal plan for *Guitar Highway Rose*," Brigid said. "The first line reads, 'I can't get started,' and that was pretty much the truth of it. I just followed my instincts along a dreamy road, led by a girl named Rosie who wanted a nose ring, and a boy named Asher who was dealing with a parental breakup. The collage format happened organically as well. The book just seemed to unfold, to write itself in that way. It gave me the freedom to begin wherever I felt like each day and to weave the story back and forth between characters and events, like a quilt, like life itself, which is never linear. Writing organically is a mystery journey, a process of joy and terror, and it doesn't always lead to a novel with a satisfactory structure, but with *Guitar Highway Rose* I was lucky."

When Miles picked me up from Brigid's, he drove me to the Nelson waterfront where the names of the 1843 New Zealand Company ships, together with their passenger lists, were engraved on black marble uprights. This was the secret that he had wanted me to see, so I dutifully studied the graven images and names until I came across the *Phoebe*, which arrived in Nelson on the 29th of March 1843. Among the passengers was Benjamin Jackson, a shoemaker, with his wife Mary Ann and their nine children. The youngest, Samuel Wesley, then four, was our father's father's father. The trades of the older children were also listed—shoemakers, shoe binders, and one wheelwright.

"Beginnings are not the same as origins," writes Paul Ricoeur. We may trace and date the year our forebears first arrived in their country of adoption, or when we were born, without, however, touching upon the hidden genealogy that encompasses individuals, influences, and transitions that cannot be identified with any certainty. Such was the genealogy that surfaced when Francine Sweet first encountered flamenco or when Miles first visited Spain. This was the enigma of anteriority—when something came to light that one's known lineage could not explain.

Other things, of course, can be known. Like the strongly practical bent that Miles and I had inherited from our father. Though D'arcy worked as a bank clerk all his life, he once admitted, "I would much rather have gone in with my father as a carpenter-builder, but the Depression had started and the work wasn't there. But I started woodwork just after I married. My first job was to make a bench. The only tools I had were a saw and a hammer and a screwdriver. Then I took a subscription to the monthly magazine the *Woodworker*. In those twelve volumes it shows you how to make every joint and how to use every tool. That was my working book."

That afternoon, Miles showed me the old carpentry tools that had once belonged to our paternal grandfather, Lewis, the son of Benjamin the shoemaker. As Miles lovingly dusted off the wooden smoothing planes, the gouger with its embossed metal frame, the bradawls and saws, I reminded him of the one item from our father's workshop that I requested when he died. Not only was this try square a link to my father, it was a souvenir of my beginnings and a guide to the kind of writing I sought to achieve.

Lies on my office windowsill,
its rectangular hardwood handle
blotched with paint and bearing
my father's thumbprint;
brass inlay, three metal pins
secure the metal blade.

My father used it to inscribe
parallel lines where his tenon
saw would bite, or chisel
begin a mortice joint; it
played its part in making
our toys, our furniture.

Now, no day passes that I do not
measure my work against his,
asking whether the words
I use, the bright ideas,
the balanced sentences,
can equal what he built for us.

Each day I go home
to my own children
with unblemished hands,
no cut from the teeth of a tenon saw
or bruise from a claw hammer;
empty as he also felt

when away from his tools
serving time in a bank, balancing
ledgers, blotting the red
and black inked figures, attending

to customers. We both
have been at odds with ourselves,

wanting the touch of timber,
the satisfaction of building a letter box
or putting up a shelf
rather than bookish
things that don't add up,
in rooms without the smell

of rimu, linseed oil, and rain.
In a shuttered building
I keep in mind the things he made
in secrecy, without signature,
measuring my words
with my father's try square,
going against the grain.

Although New Zealand aspired in the late nineteenth century to be a class-less society, the self-deprecating habits of the English working class died hard. A suspicion remained that intellectual and artistic pursuits were indulgences, if not sins, that could not be compared with earning a modest income from an honest day's toil. So you hid your passion for these arcane pursuits, as if they implied a shameful betrayal of your class and kind. You disparaged your craft even as you burned the midnight oil to perfect it; you put yourself down as if you could not possibly excel at anything. If you failed, as you inevitably did with such a negative self-image, you saw it as punishment for presuming to place yourself above the crowd, to fly so high. I suspected that Miles, like me, had never been able to overcome this appalling lack of confidence that had inhibited our father, and which we appeared to preserve out of respect for our humble beginnings. "Earlier this year," I told Miles, "I was in Scotland, doing some writing workshops with anthropology doctoral students. When the course was over, I went to St. Andrews to spend a weekend with old friends. Nigel and Elizabeth took me on an excursion to a mansion at the Hill of Tarvit. The house was built by Frederick Bower Sharp, who had made a fortune in Dundee, manufacturing jute products, including the sackcloth used for sandbags in the Ameri-can Civil War. When Sharp's only surviving child died in 1948 at the age of thirty-nine, the estate passed into the hands of the National Trust of Scotland.

"After lunch in what was once the kitchen, Nigel and Elizabeth invited me to tour the upper rooms of the house with them. But I was neither inter-ested in Frederick Sharp's acquisitions nor inclined to pay the entry fee to the first floor. So while my friends toured the house, I wandered around the garden and discovered a laundry building that had been preserved, together with drying racks and cupboards, tubs and coppers, hand-cranked man-gles, ironing boards and charcoal irons from the Sharp era. A notice explained that the laundry maids worked six days on laundry duties, start-ing at six in the morning, with another half day cleaning the laundry room and its equipment.

"I thought it ironic," I said to Miles, "that I should shy away from explor-ing the mansion and find my way to where the underlings spent their work-ing lives, then rationalize my discomfort with Sharp's ostentatious house by telling myself that the wealth of the Dundee jute barons was gained through the exploitation of tens of thousands of Bengali men, women, and children who were paid a pittance because of the surplus of cheap labor in and around Calcutta in the first decades of the early twentieth century."

Later, I discovered that in 1911 almost 200,000 Bengalis were employed in the Calcutta jute mills; 23,007 were children and 35,263 were women. Since most of the individuals whose labor and lives went into the building of the British Empire were illiterate, little of their experience remains, yet it is not untypical of people in such degraded circumstances, including Britain's own poor and wretched citizenry who migrated to outposts of empire like New Zealand, to see themselves as lacking the capacity to become masters in their own right, even regarding themselves as accursed, like Cain, for some ancestral error.

When Miles began sweeping wood shavings and sawdust from around his workbench and lathe, I went outside. I was thinking of a Macedonian gypsy myth that had always encapsulated, for me, the ironies of self-depre-ciation. Instead of the defiant and fiery spirit of flamenco, or the avoidance of gadje that is so characteristic of Romany throughout Europe, the Mace-donian myth suggests a preemptive and self-protective strategy of putting yourself down before you can be denigrated by others.

When the Roman jailers were given the person of Yeshua ben Miriam, whom the world would later call Jesus, that they should crucify him, two soldiers were given eighty kreutzer with which to go and buy four stout nails, but they first tarried at an inn and spent half the coppers drinking the sweet-sour wine that the Greeks sold in Jerusalem. It was late in the afternoon when they remembered the nails again, and they had to be back in their barracks by nightfall, for early the following morning they were to crucify Yeshua ben Miriam, the Jew who had talked ill of the emperor of Rome. Every Jewish blacksmith who the soldiers asked to forge the nails was unwilling to have a hand in the judicial murder of one his own people, an innocent man at that, and pleaded that it was impossible to forge four stout nails with the forty kreutzer they were being offered. The Romans killed every blacksmith who refused them.

That evening, exasperated and drunk, the soldiers found a gypsy blacksmith outside the walls of the city who agreed to forge the nails. The ghosts of the murdered Jewish smiths pleaded with the gypsy blacksmith to no avail, and the soldiers, now frightened by the falling night and the ghostly whispers around them, returned to the city with only three nails. The gypsy, however, forged the fourth nail and poured water on it to hasten the cooling process. The water sizzled off the iron. He kept trying to cool it with water, but the nail remained hot and glowing as if it were a living, bleeding body. The light from the nail now lit up a wide stretch of the desert. Terrified and trembling, the gypsy packed his tent onto his donkey and fled the scene. At midnight, he pitched his tent again and tried to sleep, but the nail still glowed in the darkness. He threw sand over it. He doused it with water from a nearby well. But still it glowed. Crazed with fear, the gypsy traveled further and further into the desert. In an Arab village he patched a broken wheel hoop with the iron nail, but days later, in Damascus, a man brought him the hilt of a sword to repair, and when the gypsy lit his forge the hilt began to glow because it contained the iron of the nail. And that nail appears in the tents of the descendants of the man who forged the nails for the crucifixion of Yeshua ben Miriam. When the nail appears, the gypsies move. It is why they move from place to place. It is why Yeshua ben Miriam was crucified with only three nails, his two feet being drawn together and one nail piercing both. The fourth wanders from one end of the earth to the other.

I recounted this story that evening, over dinner, to Miles and Margaret and their friends Christie Carlson and Larry Rueter.

"Maybe we're under some kind of curse," Larry joked. "We've spent much of our lives traveling."

"I don't know about a curse," Christie said. "Coming to New Zealand was like a blessing. I grew up in a small Swedish American town in Illinois. I felt like a fish out of water there and in all the other places in the U.S. I moved to."

Christy met Larry in Hawaii, where he was working as a botanist. His passion was bamboo, and his search for new varieties had taken him to every corner of East Asia.

"He's the Johnny Appleseed of bamboo," Christie said. "Everywhere he goes, he likes to plant bamboo, to spread the bamboo gospel. When we met in Hawaii, I was making a living as an antique dealer and knew a lot about bamboo furniture."

"So we had that in common," Larry said.

"But what we didn't have in common was a place where we both wanted to live," Christie said.

They had watched television coverage of the first place in the world where the new millennium would dawn. The East Cape of New Zealand looked like the very place they had been seeking, and they went there.

"Gisborne was a disappointment. It was like landing in the Wild West," Christie said. "So we moved on until we found Nelson. I felt immediately at home here. I remember one morning, not long after we arrived, Larry roused me, wanting to show me something on the foreshore. I went along with him. I didn't give it a moment's thought. Hair undone, face unwashed, no makeup. It was only when I found myself among the crowd on the beach that I became conscious of myself, of how unprepared I was to meet the day. But suddenly, like an epiphany, I realized it didn't matter what I looked like or how I dressed. I had been a model for many years. In that business you are never really yourself. But here you can be. It's as simple as that."

Miles spoke of the deep fulfillment of putting down roots. Planting thousands of trees, building one's own house. He sang the praises of self-sufficiency, of his carpentry workshop, chicken run, compost, fruit trees, and home garden from which Margaret had gathered the salad greens we were now eating. In Miles's view, one was morally obliged to care for the land, to bring it back to what it had once been, creating something not to sell or profit by but to pass on to one's children.

"You have to seek your dream," Christie said.

"But sometimes," I said, "we have to shelve our idea of what we want in order to do the work that may, if we are lucky, bring that idea to fruition. Myself, I work slowly, intuitively, without much idea of where I am headed. The goal is something I set aside in order to meet the demands of the task at hand."

There was a long silence, as if I had broken a spell or spoiled the vision that everyone at the table shared except me. I had committed the indiscretion of seeming to devalue the worldview that Miles and Christie had given me to appreciate and possibly emulate.

* * *

Next morning, as I made to leave, I sensed a shadow that, for all our goodwill, we could not shuck off. Hugging my brother and sister-in-law, thanking them for their hospitality, and expressing the hope that it would not be long before we saw one another again, I felt that we had made our peace. But as I drove down the steep track and turned onto the main road, it crossed my mind that we had for too long assumed that blood is thicker than water and kin are of a kind. Family is foundational, to be sure, but the bonds of siblingship and filiation are fraught and do not always last. If we pay lip service to the idea that such ties are binding, it may be because we need to believe that some relationships are irrevocable, just as certain rights are nonnegotiable. Yet we continually come up against the paradox of human plurality: that we are at once similar and different. As Larry had pointed out to me, all bamboos may look similar to the untrained eye, but the clumping kind (sympodial) stays put, while the running kind (monopodial) abandons its original roots and puts down new ones wherever it moves.

Wasn't it Gertrude Stein who asked what good is it having roots if you can't take them with you?

Crossing Cook Strait

High winds and rain had been forecast for the lower North Island, so I wasted no time in getting to Picton, not wanting to miss the late morning ferry and be forced to cross the strait later in the day in the teeth of a gale.

Queen Charlotte Sound was calm enough, but as we left Tory Channel and plunged into the open sea the wind swung the bows of the *Awatere* around, leaving her, or so it seemed, temporarily disoriented. There was a strong sea running, tearing itself to shreds on the rocky heads. Smeared patches showed where the wind was veering. Elsewhere, white caps were flailed and flung aside as spume. From the taffrail, I looked back at the same coast James Cook sighted in January 1770, when he realized that a strait separated New Zealand into two islands. But social divisions in New Zealand ran as deep as geological faults, and I thought of James K. Baxter's poem "Crossing Cook Strait," in which the poet comes on deck on a clear "night to stretch his legs, find perhaps gossip, a girl in green slacks at the rail," only to encounter the figure of Janus, who reminds him of the "angry poor . . . policies made and broken behind locked doors" and poets burning "with a wormwood brilliance" but lacking empathy and love.

Battered, chilled, and half blinded by the rain, I stumbled indoors and found a seat in the Fo'c's'le Lounge. The host of a television show was marketing a range of "Māori products" and leading a panel discussion on everyday problems that viewers had phoned in: a woman was finding it impossible to relate to her sister-in-law; an office assistant had been asked by a friend to cover for her so she could cheat on her husband who was "really nice"; a group of siblings needed a tactful way to persuade their father to replace his moth-eaten hairpiece. I tried to write in my journal, but the TV was a distraction and the ship was heeling unpredictably, its plates shuddering as the sea pounded and bumped, refusing its new heading.

When Pencarrow Lighthouse hove in view, I was back in Wellington on the morning of April 10, 1968, waking to radio reports of the interisland ferry, *Wahine,* struggling to enter Wellington Harbor against wind gusts of almost one hundred miles an hour. Despite the fact that the trees around our apartment were being torn apart in the same cyclone, my wife and I drove our Citroën Light 15 through the rain-swept streets of the city and along the coast road toward Island Bay. It was already a disaster zone. An army truck had been thrown onto its back, and two cars flung onto the beach near Owhiro Bay. Sheets of corrugated iron scraped and spun across the asphalt among a litter of broken tree limbs and foliage. Our car radio reported worsening conditions. At the mercy of immense waves and unable to turn back to the relative safety of the strait, the *Wahine* foundered on

Barrett Reef. Despite attempts by harbor tugs to tow the stricken vessel from the rocks, the tide and winds swung her around. With the *Wahine* taking water, listing badly and rudderless, the captain gave the order to abandon ship. Pauline and I waited in our car near Seatoun, watched a lifeboat come ashore and heard of passengers carried away by the strong seas to the westerly shore of the harbor or drowned. In this worst recorded storm in New Zealand's history, fifty-three people lost their lives.

* * *

As I drove from the ferry terminal, it was as though a long-forgotten me had suddenly reappeared and taken the wheel. This person knew where he was going, even if I did not.

At Havelock Street, Brooklyn, I parked by the same flax bush where I parked in the past.

The door was open, and I walked in on Les and Mary Cleveland as they were finishing a late lunch. The room had not changed—Les's photographs of ghost towns in Arizona, abandoned diggings in Nevada and Westland, and derelict buildings whose original use could only be guessed at. Postcards from Las Vegas. The potbelly stove.

Les had an eclectic range of expertise. He was a self-taught builder, welder, motor mechanic, and electrician. A poet, songwriter and singer, journalist and political scientist. A mountaineer, master photographer, and self-styled literary blacksmith. As with the classical bricoleur, everything was grist to his mill, and the past was the raw material from which he hammered out prose that spoke to our present lives. His attitude toward our ancestry was compassionate. *I've always tended to look back, I've always been interested in leftovers and survivals.*

"It seems like no time has passed since I was last here," I said.

"None of us is getting any younger," Les said, ever the realist, and without a pause he went on to describe what had happened to him a couple of months ago.

"I was lugging an armful of logs from below the house, up that fifteen-foot flight of concrete steps. On the top step I failed to shift my weight forward, and began falling backward. Something in me took over, as it invariably does in a crisis, so that I somehow turned completely, before landing face down with one arm clutching at the wall for support. I did not do this; my instincts did. Unfortunately, it wasn't enough to save me from a skull fracture and broken wrist."

"I thought he was dead," Mary said. "That's what my instincts told me."

Les was hospitalized only to discharge himself two days later, preferring to take care of himself and recover at home.

"It was a reprieve," Les said. "We both thought, this is it. But there was no magic moment, my life replayed in a split second. No tunnel of light, any of that stuff. But in the days that followed, I kept thinking of a bizarre incident during the war when I almost lost my life."

"Well, before we get into that," Mary interrupted, "I suggest you two get yourselves comfortable while I put the kettle on."

Les and I sat at the kitchen table. A large rain-streaked window overlooked a sodden sports field and the distant Orongorongos.

"We were in Northern Italy," Les said. "Dug in around, as well as occupying, a large house. Under cover of darkness, the Germans brought up a fixed gun, and its first shell scored a direct hit on the house. I would normally have been with Podge Hoskins at a machine gun post at an upper-floor window, but I'd been detailed to the kitchen and was frying up tinned bacon and egg powder when the shell hit. There was an ear-splitting explosion, splinters of wood, debris, dust. But in the midst of this maelstrom and the screams from the front room, I covered the frying pan with a tea towel and placed it carefully under the table. Only then did I go to the aid of the men in the other room. I had to kick down the door to get in. Almost everyone had been torn apart. Some were dead, others dying. The scene was as gruesome as any I had witnessed. Podge upstairs had been killed instantly. Yet I survived. And afterward, what I could not get over was that moment with the frying pan. How I could go on as though nothing had happened. Was it denial of a reality I could not deal with? Was it my military training?"

As Les talked and the rain fell steadily outside, I felt somewhat like the main character in John Mulgan's *Man Alone* who encounters Johnson in a Breton fishing village and repairs with him to a local café where they eat prawns, drink cheap red wine, and get to talking about the war.

In his introduction to *The Iron Hand*, a compilation of New Zealand soldiers' poems from World War II, Les mentions a close friend, Ted Scherer, who died of shrapnel wounds during the last offensive of the Italian campaign. Scherer was only inches away from Les when he was hit.

Shrapnel-ripped and lifeless on the Santerno,
Helmet tilted back into the lacerated earth,
Face twisted up for one last
Regretful look at the murderous sky

"It was April the tenth, 1945," Les said. "That very morning, Scherer had looked north and commented, 'When it's over we'll celebrate—we'll climb the highest point in the Alps.' After recovering in hospital from my wounds, I went into training in the Dolomites by doing some rock climbing. But I could not persuade anyone in the battalion to accompany me on an expedition to Mont Blanc. By this time, we were in bivouacs at Lake Trasimeno, near Rome. I set out from there on a goods train which took me to Milan, and I traveled by a variety of means through the mountains to Courmayeur where I was able to persuade a young Italian refugee to join me in the ascent. It was late in the season and the climb was arduous, particularly as our equipment was improvised and we suffered a good deal from inadequate food as well as from cold, exposure, and exhaustion. Every step of the way, I was thinking of Scherer and all the mountains we might have climbed together, and of all the other friends of friends, shuffling, legions of them, in long, suffering lines across the mortuary of Europe. What good being alive, when those who meant the world to you were dead? I was grateful to this young refugee, who had found sympathy and courage enough to march in a dead man's steps. When he suddenly mumbled, 'Kaput, guerra kaput!' what answer could this survivor give? 'Jawohl,' I mumbled, 'Guerra kaput!'

"Six hours up an icefall on the south face, we encountered a line of fresh tracks that drew us across the mountain's shoulder to a high-altitude, unlined metal hut. Inside, we found a party of German-speaking Swiss, laughing and talking over their experiences on the tourist route from Chamonix. The amiable holidaymakers were casually helping themselves to food from their rucksacks, innocent of the terror gnawing at their frontiers. In broken German, I enlightened them.

We are climbers, British soldiers.
They look disbelievingly at our improvised gear—
Wehrmacht rucksacks, Alpini boots, Kaiapoi woolen
Jerseys, caps comforter, and old army socks for gloves.

What sort of army is this? Probably deserters
Or escaped prisoners; maybe dangerous too.
Offer them nothing.
So I pull the Luger on the fattest of the bunch—
No Alpine-fucking-club outing this,
Ich haben grossen hunger!
We grab a loaf of their bread and some fruit
And drain a bottle of wine.
Nobody speaks: only the autumn wind
Snickers and squirms in the doorway.
Before trying the peak I pick over their parkas
And trade the best one for my military gas cape,
Then we buckle on crampons, adjust the rope
And start up the summit ridge."

After the war, the Scherer family got in touch with Les. In fact, he had recently received a letter from Ted Scherer's daughter asking if he would write down for her everything he could remember of her father. "It's a bit of a struggle," Les said. "It isn't easy to write about war without including the gory details. The sort of things no one would want to hear about or read about if they were going to have a positive memory of their loved one."

I was thinking: Les is eighty-seven. He has been returning to the war for sixty-three years, mostly to the experiences of others, including his recent translation of the notebook of Helmut Metzner, an obscure soldier in Rommel's Afrika Korps, that contains occasional critiques of the Nazi regime and a crude poem in which he imagines himself having sex with Lili Marleen. When he mentioned this project to me, Les said, "I would very much like a chat with Helmut, but we know for certain he is very kaput, kaput, kaput! Still, he lives on in my files along with Charles Smith and others." It was this remark that made me wonder whether the vital difference between Les's forays into the past and the obsessive-compulsive replaying of harrowing experience that we call posttraumatic stress disorder was Les's ability to make his own experiences secondary to those of others, putting them first, sacrificing his story in order that theirs be told.

When I first got to know Les in 1964, I often wanted to press him for details of his war experiences. This was before I realized the oblique and very private way in which he had come to terms with that period in his life. "After the war," Les wrote, "I would make many more difficult and dangerous journeys in our own mountains, but never under such emotionally disturbed and isolated circumstances. The Mont Blanc affair was a therapeutic venture into self-recovery and a wild leap into a new world of changed personal relationships; it also meant that a sense of bereavement and brooding anxiety could be thrown off in the exuberance of physical achievement."

Nevertheless, Les had, by his own admission, been "neurotic" when he returned to Christchurch in 1945 and tried to settle back into civilian life. "Fourteenth platoon suffered 40 percent losses, almost as high as the Māori Battalion's, and every soldier felt the burden of this. In Christchurch I would obsessively stare at the shoes of people walking in front of me, waiting for a mine to detonate. Any loud percussive noise and I would immediately be looking for somewhere to take cover. I had to leave the city and work in the Westland bush, where the only sounds were tuis and falling water. It took me three years before I felt ready to return to city life."

I had always been impressed by Les's sense of proportion and practicality, and in talking with Sierra Leoneans in the aftermath of their war it was constantly brought home to me that recovery depends more on one's ability to throw oneself into the tasks of everyday life—caring for a child, making a farm, putting food on the table, sharing with those in greater need—than in one's success in seeking revenge or compensation, or wringing some meaning out of the arbitrary events that changed your life forever. Intellectual reflection has a place in our lives, to be sure, but unless it is connected to the exigencies of life in the here and now it risks becoming morbid and dissociated. David Brooks discovered something similar among the survivors of the earthquake that struck China's Sichuan Province in May 2008. From the villagers he met, Brooks concluded that the history of the province must have given these people "a stripped-down, pragmatic mentality. Move on or go crazy. Don't dwell. Look to the positive. Fix what needs fixing. Work together." Perhaps this was why Les had steadfastly refused to participate in the writing of official history or attend postwar ceremonies that extolled the heroic sacrifice of the fallen. Certainly, his healthy pragmatism underlay everything he had written on soldiers' songs, poems, and popular culture. "If I were to attempt an epic of our military experiences that tried faithfully to evoke the consciousness of the ordinary soldier, I would probably relegate the formal historical details to a chronology at the back of the work in order to concentrate on things that really matter, like a concern with food, cookhouses, liquor, sex, clothing, the weather, rates of pay, equipment, loot, amusements, recreation, morale, the techniques of deviancy, how to maintain one's precious individuality and, above all, how to avoid becoming a grim statistic on one of our grisly war memorials."

In Les's view, combat soldiers share with civilian workers in hazardous occupations a sense of powerlessness that can only be countermanded by organizing collectively, fostering a sense of solidarity, and having recourse to gallows humor and dark laughter. You may not be able to buck authority, disobey orders, go on strike, or escape the nightmare of knowing that an organized army is bent on killing you, but you can preserve a sense of connectedness to a world where your individuality has some value and your actions matter by writing letters home, keeping a diary, or joining forces with your mates in ridiculing the situation in which you find yourself. Mutiny or deserting are out of the question, but mocking the establishment, protesting one's lot, turning to sexual fantasy, and venting one's frustrations in obscene songs can sometimes help you feel that you are a protagonist and not a victim. To dwell on a tragedy is to risk drowning in it. To turn it into farce is to remain afloat, treading water as it were, even though you may be simply deferring the moment when, exhausted, you sink beneath the waves.

I was momentarily distracted by the rain, flung against the window like scattershot.

Les might have been reading my mind. "This was what happened to many men," he said. "The psychological casualties who returned home, haunted by what they had seen and done, hoping that silence, time, and compulsive routines would heal the hidden wounds. It simply isn't possible to come home as if nothing's happened and step back into the role of Mr. Normal from Ashburton. There remains a part of you that is continuously preoccupied with questions like, How can I stop thinking about the bloke that got killed instead of me? Where is tomorrow's food coming from? Such sinister, unrelenting calculations. I visited a bloke on a farm in Taumarunui once. He had about a year's supply of baked beans, tinned vegetable stew, and other stuff under the floorboards of his house, not to mention a vast quantity of wine. He'd been a prisoner of war and was determined he wasn't going to run out of food ever again. I looked on in amazement when he said, 'I'll just get a couple of bottles of wine,' and proceeded to pull up the floorboards. He had cases of the stuff down there. But he was still living inside that cocoon of deprivation and fear, and had to come to terms with it by doing things around the farm. He was always supplying stuff to someone or other. He had some troubles with the local hardware people. So he bought a sawmill and set it up on the property and milled his own timber. Instead of bringing in a contractor to root up tree stumps and do a bit of earthmoving, he bought two bulldozers and had them sitting there in the shed. He was prepared for a siege. That's an extreme example of the POW mentality, but I think he had successfully coped with his experiences, even if his behavior was a bit odd."

Of all the soldiers' poems Les has collected in the postwar years, perhaps the most moving is by Charles Smith, who was among the New Zealanders ordered to hold a pass near Katerini, northwest of Mount Olympus, in order to gain time for the rest of the Second NZ Expeditionary Force, retreating from the rapidly advancing Germans. Smith's poem first appeared in the *NZEF Times* in August 1942. It is simply called "Greece." It is about the bonds that were formed between the New Zealanders and Greek villagers during the tragic campaign of April-May 1941 in which the New Zealand force sustained 2,504 casualties before withdrawing to Crete where, in the course of its continuing retreat, 3,853 out of the remaining 7,702 were killed.

Out of the soil comes greatness of soul . . .

These, shaped by old knowledge of their jealous sod
Take on unswerving courage. They belong
To trees and fields, and mountains; so to God.

So first we saw: and never bread so sweet
Nor gift so free, nor welcome waking so;
Kindness so laughing, quick and garlanded,
Nor carnival of fortitude so gay
As heart of Greece in spring, on Freedom's day.

So near the shadow! Yet in dark retreat
Came dusty envy that they still could cry
"Kalimera, English!" and "Goodbye!"

Hold fleeting friendship past the threat of death,
Give food and shelter: even understand
Our last desertion. Do they know
How heart-remembered all their faces go?

These things are deathless, memory's cornerstone,
That rivulet that feeds the golden stream . . .
Is Ag Demetrios still a mountain dream?
Storks on the roof and cobbles on the street,
White from Olympus faerying the pines
Where bitter snow and spring of promise meet
Thyme and wild daphne.

Does Kathrina wear
A soldier's badge still braided in her hair?

Some years ago, Les read this poem in the course of a radio talk. He mentioned that, despite his best efforts, he had been unable to trace the author and presumed him dead. Within a week, Les received an indignant letter from Charles Smith saying he was not dead. He was a farmer near Whangarei with a family and very much alive.

So we are surprised by what survives from the past, and what does not. And how something we carry into the present can be so transformed that it ceases to possess what drew us to it in the first place, what persuaded us it was worth keeping.

When Les recounted his visit to the Taumaranui farmer who still hoarded as if the war had not ended, he went on to say that there were many such men who could not tolerate confinement or bear to be shut up in a small space. "Who get out on their farms and go for long walks and talk to dead companions or to God. Some carry a lot of grievances, but they keep these to themselves."

I could not help but think of Les's own retreat in South Westland, as remote from the madding crowd as one could wish for, and close to the mountains and bush that have been his very present help in trouble. But why do earth, stone, trees, and the sea have this power to bring us calm in troubled times?

In the *Tao Te Ching* (XVI), stillness is identified with one's roots, one's infancy, and with the nothingness from which the teeming and myriad forms of both life and thought emerge and to which in time they return. This original nature may be compared to a rough and unpolished stone. To contemplate it is to be returned to the prephenomenal ground of all being. But the manifold and changing forms of things are also worthy of contemplation, and I find it difficult to accept the fetishization of firstness or the idea that foundations are necessarily more real than anything we built on them. This is why stone implies, for me, not absolute constancy, but an image of constancy that helps one endure the vicissitudes of life, in which everything is sooner or later shattered, worn away, or reshaped by the elements with which we have to contend. From this observation arises the question of art and of what we make of life. While it is important to remember one's beginnings, to bear in mind from whence one came and to whom one owes one's life, one must also recognize the importance of new departures in which the original material is refashioned, as it were, in one's mind's eye or in one's own hands.

On the wooden terrace of his Wellington house, Les kept, for many years, numerous river stones and boulders that he had found on his excursions into the wilds of Westland. These stones had not only caught his eye; they had, in a sense, possessed him—some because of curious blemishes that he could not reconcile with processes of natural erosion, some, like greenstone, because of their geological rarity, and some because of their uncanny similarity to the contours of the human body. Les would lug these boulders down mountain gorges and through heavy bush, sometimes for days on end and often in a rucksack emptied of his personal supplies, before bringing his booty home to be burnished by rain, commented upon by friends, or made the occasion for a story. When I left Wellington to pursue my PhD studies at Cambridge, I would often think of Les's collection of stones, and it was with considerable dismay when I discovered, on my return to New Zealand after four years abroad, that in enlarging the living room of his house, Les had built, in the middle of it, a massive fireplace whose chimney consisted of these beautiful stones cemented together into something resembling a cairn.

But now, having known Les for forty-five years, and sat in front of his fireplace countless times, deep in conversation about our various travels or current projects, I no longer think that the stones properly belong to the contexts from whence they came. They belong where they are. And at Harvard I would discover in the course of long talks on early Chinese traditions with my friend Michael Puett that my thinking was not inconsistent with a Taoist view that sees the world as essentially (and demonically) chaotic, so that our human endeavors to create spaces of order are always transitory, and Les's river stones are destined to be once again a natural shambles on a hillside where no vestiges of his house or handiwork remain.

Metaphor of the Table

In Wellington, I stayed with old friends in Roseneath overlooking Evans Bay. Cedars and pōhutukawa framed a view of wind-abraded water and the hills beyond, scabrous with gorse and coprosma. Jennifer and I were sitting at a kauri table in the front room. Allan had bought the table many years ago at a garage sale for twenty-five dollars. "We've considered it metaphorical that its four legs are two unmatching pairs," Jennifer said, "though I'm not sure what that's a metaphor of."

I suggested that, in some cases, it would make a good metaphor for parentage. "I mean, it may be impossible to decide which were the original legs, or which pair serve the table better."

For some reason, I found myself describing to Jennifer a television documentary I had seen about the biggest Chinese restaurant in the world, where a staff of one thousand served five thousand tables. Although the proprietress was one of Changsha's self-made millionaires, her story emblematic of the new China, what stuck in my memory was the deep sense of unworthiness she carried from her early childhood, and a scene in which she invites her parents to a great banquet in the restaurant to witness her success, to show them that she was not the insignificant person they assumed and almost doomed her to be. "It was not clear," I said, "if her elderly parents gave her the recognition they withheld from her as a child."

"Even if they did," Jennifer said, "would it have fully compensated her for that sense of being a maggot in the rice?"

"It reminds me of those Westerns," I said, "where a small boy witnesses his parents' murder and vows revenge. Years later, having finally tracked down and killed the last surviving member of the gang that murdered his parents, our vengeful hero feels neither relief nor satisfaction but a terrible emptiness, for his sole raison d'être was his dream of getting even, his belief that in redressing an old injustice he would finally be restored to life and have a future. He ends up with the realization that the past was all he had, that having extinguished it he has nothing left to live for. Perhaps we all carry in our memory an incident from childhood in which we were wronged or hurt, a wound that never heals. Perhaps such incidents reveal our childhood sense of being at the mercy of powers we cannot control or comprehend that limit our freedom, preventing the full expression of our autonomy. Whether we were disparaged, bullied, tricked, or subtly persuaded, our early efforts at self-expression were rebuffed or denied. In my case, this sense of the unfairness of life reached its apotheosis in the figure of my English master at Stratford Technical High School, "Chill" Blain. He seemed to have it in for me, ignoring me when I raised my hand in response to a question in class, putting me down whenever I did speak up.

"I was fourteen and had developed a passion for literature and a desire to try my hand at original writing, so when Blain assigned an essay, 'Winter in Stratford,' I wrote an inspired if florid essay on winter in Inglewood, my hometown, from where I bussed to Stratford during my high school years. For ten days I waited for my essay to be returned and my hard work acknowledged. Blain handed it back without a word. It had not been marked. No comments appeared in the margins or at the end. My hand shot up. My heart was in my mouth. 'Please sir, my essay has not been marked.' 'Off the subject, Jackson. You did not write on the topic set.'

"Nineteen years later, after several years in West Africa and the UK, I returned to New Zealand to take up a lecturership at Massey University. My wife and I, with our three-year-old daughter Heidi, were staying in a Palmerston North motel while looking for a house to rent or buy. One evening we walked into the Mark Twain Café on the Square for dinner. As we waited for our order, I noticed an elderly couple at a table not far from ours. The man was conveying food to his mouth with a palsied hand and having difficulty eating. From time to time his wife leaned over to help him cut up his meat and to wipe his mouth with a paper napkin. It was Mr. Blain. The man I had fantasized confronting some day, who had loomed so large in my memory—his dark eyebrows, ferocious eyes, and tyrannical manner—was reduced in a split second to a slobbering and pathetic old man with hunched shoulders, spilling food on his cardigan. All the hatred and vengefulness I had carried within me was transformed instantly into compassion. I felt sorry for the poor bugger. Deeply sorry."

As Jennifer and I swapped stories about loss, it was as if we were trying to find an answer to the same question: whether a single traumatic event holds one in thrall forever or whether it is simply a thumbnail sketch of a possible future to which our assent is required if it is to be realized.

"You remind me of that story Barry Humphries tells in his memoir," Jennifer said. "*My Life as Me.*"

A child of parents with plebeian tastes, Barry Humphries managed to accumulate, by his early teens, a small and precious library that included Sunday School prizes (*Kidnapped, Bevis, Masterman Ready*) and a few rare, illustrated editions (*Arabian Nights* and *Mother Goose*). One day he returned from Camberwell Grammar to find that his books had disappeared from his room. On being asked by her breathless and distraught son what had become of his books, Barry's mother casually replied, "Oh, those. You'll be pleased to hear I gave them to the nice man from the Army. They'll go to poor Protestant children who haven't got any books."

"But they were my books," Barry protested, now in tears. His mother laughed. "But you've read them, Barry," she replied. And as she dried her son's eyes with the corner of her handkerchief, she added: "I hope you're not going to grow up to be a selfish little boy."

To this early traumatic incident Barry Humphries would "attribute the occasional savage bouts of bibliomania" that afflicted him all his life, making him scour out-of-the-way secondhand bookshops and, more recently, the internet, for exact replicas of "those volumes confiscated by the Salvation Army, with [his] mother's charitable contrivance."

It occurred to me to ask Jennifer a question that I had never been able to answer to my own satisfaction, perhaps because it was too general. "Do you think this endless search to reconnect with something or someone you have lost, and that you feel is absolutely vital to your existence, is also characteristic of people who were enslaved or colonized, who had their lands confiscated, their language and customs denigrated, their rights denied? And being treated like shit, or shunned as second-class citizens, are they then driven to recover their roots, find their original parents, and angrily insist on being given back what they are missing, even as they mourn it, even as they pass on their grief generation after generation, until it becomes a way of life?"

One answer lay in front of us: a book that Jennifer had recently published to mark the sixtieth anniversary of the forced resettlement of the entire population of Banaba or Ocean Island to Rabi Island in Fiji in 1945. Jennifer's book was largely made up of Banaban stories of their recollections of time-honored practices such as the catching and taming of frigate birds, of life under the colonial regime, and of the move to Rabi. Like Nauru to the west, the high atoll of Banaba consisted almost entirely of phosphate. No sooner had the British made this discovery in 1900 than they set local and indentured laborers to quarrying it for export as superphosphate. Despite the Banabans' attempts to have mining restricted to certain sections of the island, to have the phosphate replaced with soil and trees replanted, the island became, by 1945, almost uninhabitable. Having endured the horrors of Japanese military occupation, the Banabans lost their homeland.

"Banaba is our mother," said Nei Makin Corrie Tekenimatang. "She brought us up."

Tears well up in the eyes of the old people as they recall the devastated landscape of their natal island, the contaminated water, the once bountiful mango, papaya, and coconut trees. They speak in the same breath of the homeland lost and the "second land" they found. "We look on Rabi as synonymous with Banaba . . . it's becoming like that," said Taomati Teai. "A place we have come to call our own." Others speak less of the past than of the hardships of the present, explaining the loss of laughter and joy in terms of the struggle for a living wage, the difficulties of "putting food on the table every day," and problems such as getting access to markets and health services.

One story affected me more deeply than all the others. Kabunare Koura, who was eighty-three years old when interviewed in 1999, was the sole survivor of a Japanese massacre on 20 August 1945. On that day, some 150 Gilbert Islanders, who had been brought to the atoll to mine phosphate, were rounded up and taken to a cliff top high above the sea. Blindfolded and with their hands bound, they were then bayoneted and kicked from the cliff. Many died on the razor-sharp rocks below. Others were killed by the soldiers firing shots into the fallen bodies. Despite his wounds, Kabunare made his way to a sea cave and after 104 days in hiding presented himself to the Australians who now occupied the island. Fifty-four years later, he would explain how he could still cut toddy, but no longer from the highest coconut trees. "Life is good," he said, referring to his nine children, twenty grandchildren, and four great-grandchildren. "The past is gone."

* * *

In the winter of 2011, I returned to Wellington. Allan had died of leukemia ten months earlier, and Jennifer was still struggling with the anguish of bereavement, an empty house, and the tasks of archiving Allan's papers and planning her own future. I sat at the table with the anomalous legs, gazing at the wind-bashed broadleaves beyond the eighteen-paned window, and the driven waters of the bay, feeling the cold weight of Allan's absence.

Jennifer was upstairs, proofreading Allan's festschift, and where, three years ago, her book on Banaba lay on the table, a recently published history of New Zealand popular music now invited my attention.

I was soon engrossed by the story of Ruru Karaitiana, who composed "the first complete New Zealand pop song," "Blue Smoke," that became internationally known and "marked the real birth of New Zealand's indigenous recording industry."

I had known Ruru, though not intimately. Appearing lost, even wounded, he used to hover on the edge of our drinking circle in the Duke of Edinburgh in 1967–68. In those days the pub was not a place for conversation; rather, it was a place to avoid it. The uproar of the bar, which reached its crescendo as six o'clock closing approached, made coherent exchanges impossible. So I never heard Ruru's story from his own lips, and for many years knew only two snippets of information about him: that his wife had been my wife's swimming teacher and that he had written "Blue Smoke." Now, however, Chris Bourke's research fleshed out the story.

Ruru was born in March 1909 at the Tahoraiti marae near Dannevirke and raised by his maternal grandparents. Even as a child he was "extremely shy." though he quickly discovered a talent for music and played piano in several local dance bands. He enlisted soon after the outbreak of war, trained with the 28th Māori Battalion, and in May 1940 sailed on the *Aqui-tania* for Suez. In 1949 he recalled that one day, "halfway across the Indian Ocean," he was sunbathing on the deck when a sergeant came along, stopped beside him, and looked up. "Look at that b-smoke," he observed, pointing to the smoke trailing from the funnels. "It's going the right way—back to New Zealand—and we're steaming farther from home!"

"These things are simply a matter of luck," Karaitiana said later. "He put the song in my lap. It was a natural." Within half an hour he had written the lyrics in his head to a melody he had already composed, and two days later he sang it in a shipboard concert.

> Blue smoke goes drifting by
> into the deep blue sky,
> and when I think of home I sadly sigh . . .

It is possible, however, that the tune was in circulation in East Coast pubs in the late 1930s and Ruru may have unwittingly adapted the song or revised the lyrics. Certainly, it is rare that we create art, or our own lives, *ab nihilo*; rather, we take what is given to us, exploiting whatever is offered, and making it our own. I am not surprised, therefore, that the first verse of "Blue Smoke," found on a page of notepaper in the tunic pocket of Te Moananui-a-Kiwa Ngarimu, killed in action in Tunisia on March 27, 1943, and awarded a posthumous Victoria Cross for gallantry, differed from the lines penned by Ruru Karaitiana.

> Smoke is drifting away
> into a blue sky
> when I think of you
> I heave a sigh.
> I can see her standing there
> with tears in her eyes
> Mother—dear old mother
> please don't cry.
> We are off to our pals
> to give them a hand
> the greatest little band
> from our Māori land.

Smoke is drifting away
into the blue sky
Mother—dear old mother
please don't cry.

That a composition whose subject is as commonplace as it is deeply personal will affect thousands of others the composer will never meet, or would not perhaps recognize as kindred spirits, is one of the most compelling mysteries of art. Even more poignant, perhaps, is that a popular song will continue to circulate and be sung long after its composer has been forgotten. Those of us who saw Ruru in the pub night after night, and knew of his singular achievement, treated him with indifference, as if the song were the only reality and he a superfluous and spectral footnote to it. Yet, the words of "Blue Smoke" remind us not only of the devastating experience of seeing a loved one sail out to die; they reawaken us to Ruru's personal story. Wounded in battle and later discharged from the army as "unfit for service," he returned home to the life of a drifter. Traumatized and plagued by nightmares, he intermittently played in bands, worked as a shearer or in the freezing works, recorded more "slow sad waltzes," but shied away from the success "Blue Smoke" had brought him. When he died in 1970, Jack Kelleher, editor of the *Dominion,* wrote, "I don't know whether Ruru ever felt free to start [over]. He continued to drift about Wellington, always it seemed on his own, a short, stocky, hesitant figure, an island in a community with musical tastes which had no room either for his vintage of pop or for a Māori symphony."

Ruru said that the inspiration for "Blue Smoke" was "simply a matter of luck." But what of his life? Was it governed by contingency, so that he could only hope that fortune would favor rather than ignore him? The glimpses that Chris Bourke gives us into Ruru's childhood habit of self-abasement (*whakama*), his difficulty of adjusting to an aggressive Pākehā world, his self-education in psychology and poetry, his army record of disorderly conduct and gambling, and the battlefield traumas he could never excise from his memory, all suggest that luck was not on his side and leave us with the question as to what determines the difference between a person succumbing to or surviving tragedy. Can we make our own luck?

Certainly, our chances of overcoming adversity are greater when friends and family are there for us in our hour of need. But there is something more—something that is laid down in early life, that remains embedded at the heart of our very being like a stone, solid and inviolable, that comes from having been loved as a child, in an intimate world that was as safe and secure as the world around was not. When Ruru sang of being true to his loved ones while away at war, can we assume that they were awaiting him when he returned?

> Smoke drifts above me
> whispering I miss you
> taking my thoughts back to you
> across the sea.
> I know that when I sail home again
> I'll find you waiting for me.

Destruction and Hope

It seemed nothing short of a miracle when Keith Ridler met me at the door of his Thorndon cottage next day. When I had last seen Keith, eighteen months ago, his marriage was on the rocks, his father had recently died, his university job gave him little satisfaction, and he was drinking a quarter of a bottle of whiskey a day, as well as wine with meals, and smoking a lot of dope. I felt powerless to reach him, let alone help him get back on his feet, and I resigned myself to watching another dear friend dig himself an early grave. Now, looking his old self, Keith led me through the hallway and kitchen to a brick-paved backyard where he had laid out bowls of arugula salad, olives, pickled onions, avocados, capsicums, fresh French bread, and a saucer of New Zealand olive oil from Kapiti Island.

"I have an Italian red for you," he said, uncorking a wine called Menhir from Manduria. Keith, however, was on the wagon. "No alcohol, no meat, no joints. I've returned to Buddhism," he said. "I meditate every day and try to take care of myself." He then uncapped a bottle of nonalcoholic French beer called La Force C'est le Goût.

"Then may the force be with you," I said, drinking to my friend's good health, though not without a pang of disappointment that he and Judith were no longer together.

"There's a zen parable," Keith said, "about an adept who retires to a tower determined to find enlightenment. He makes himself indifferent to the outside world, sits in zazen for hours on end, deprives himself of sleep, eats only enough to keep himself alive, yet enlightenment evades him. He begins to sink into despair, convinced that his goal is unattainable. There seems nothing left to live for. Climbing the parapet, he is about to leap to his death when he sees clearly for the first time."

"So we have to sink to the bottom before we start to swim?" I asked, and for a split second I was recalling the winter afternoon when I was three . . . falling into a liquid manure sump on a Taranaki farm . . . sinking fourteen feet through acrid and cloying cow shit until I hit bottom . . . pushing instinctively with my feet . . . surfacing, flailing . . . finding the concrete edge of the pit and pulling myself out . . .

As we ate the good food, I asked Keith if he had any plans.

"I have come back to myself," Keith said. "I've returned to my guitar. To tramping in the Tararuas. To food. To books. To life."

It sometimes happens that when things fall apart we revert to an earlier time, imagining ourselves starting out again, though on a different path. Just as Keith seemed to have returned to his student years in Wellington, so, when Pauline died, I regressed to the time before we met. And it was Keith and Judith who helped me onto my new path. Although their relationship was new and they had only just moved into a house together, they invited me and my daughter to live with them. It was an extraordinary act of generosity and compassion. Their music, books, food, and appetite for life helped me see, in that dark time, that there were pleasures and possibilities yet in store; my world may have crumbled, but the world was without end.

After lunch, Keith suggested a walk in the nearby botanical gardens.

It was a windless day, and as we negotiated a narrow track above the playground I told Keith of my conversations with Les the day before. "Not long before the end of hostilities," I said, "when Les was still in Italy, the New Zealand troops were shown American film footage of the liberation of Buchenwald, bodies 'piled like logs,' as Les put it, 'bewildered, skeletal survivors.' The film changed him. He felt then, and still feels, that more should have been done to prevent the Holocaust. After seeing the film, none of the soldiers knew what to say or do. Les said they didn't have the vocabulary for such experiences."

Keith was prompted to tell me about his father, who fought with the Special Air Service Regiment in World War II.

On April 15, 1945, Duncan Ridler was driving along a sandy track through a dense pine forest northeast of Hannover when his unit came upon some figures dressed in strange orange-brown uniforms. They were lined up on either side of the road as far as the eye could see. Dunc asked them who they were and what they were doing. They were Hungarians. They said there had been an outbreak of typhus or typhoid in the camp, and their job was to prevent anyone leaving. The convoy drove on to a road junction in the forest. Dunc was impressed by the whitewashed concrete curbs, the raked gravel, the military signposts. But there was something else, a stench that was almost overpowering in its awfulness. Instead of finding a camp where they might liberate some British prisoners of war, they had come upon Belsen. It was deathly quiet, with shuttered huts and no sound from the watchtowers. At first, the few German guards seemed unperturbed by the British jeeps, but then Dunc spotted a pile of rotten potato peelings, about six feet high, with what looked like filthy, animated skeletons feasting on the putrid leftovers. At that moment, a German leant out of the cookhouse window and shot one of the emaciated figures.

Though hardened by combat, the SAS men gagged on what they saw. Creatures who were once human, starved, utterly filthy, eyes staring out of slate-gray faces, wounds vilely infected, the stench insufferable. Then the soldiers came upon the pit. One took photos so that the world would know what had happened there. Another stumbled away from the discarded, unburied corpses, grabbed the nearest guard and beat him to death. The SAS didn't stay long in Belsen, but Dunc remained as interpreter for the officer in command of the 63rd Anti-Tank Regiment, Royal Artillery, who took over the camp and accepted the formal surrender of Josef Kramer, Belsen's commandant.

I had recently read a biography of Martha Gellhorn, and remembered the shame and disenchantment that overcame her at Dachau and, soon after, at Belsen. "It is as if I walked into Dachau and there fell over a cliff," she wrote, "and suffered a lifelong concussion, without recognizing it." Twenty-five years after the war, she confessed that, "looking back, I know I have never again felt that lovely, easy, lively hope in life which I knew before, not in life, not in our species, not in our future on earth."

Perhaps Dunc felt something similar. "After the war," Keith said, "he was looking for a new beginning, though several years passed before he found it."

Keith was born in Italy. He was seven when his parents separated. Dunc, with his "staggeringly beautiful," twenty-year-old "housekeeper," Grec, migrated to New Zealand. Keith remembers the glaring light, caused by the high levels of ultraviolet radiation in the southern atmosphere, the treeless landscapes, the absence of substantial buildings, and the gorse-infested hill where Dunc rented a bungalow. Dunc and Grec were in love. No longer did they have to pretend they were married. It was Dunc's new lease of life. As for Keith, he was happy with his wild and windswept surroundings, though even at seven he still felt Italy was home.

As we trudged through a grove of pōhutukawa trees, looking for the great Mediterranean pines that surrounded the children's play area, Keith said that he retained, from his earliest years in Rome, an affinity for all things Italian. A love of food, books, wine, and adventure. "New Zealanders still strike me as strange," he said.

"Yet I've always thought of you as the consummate Kiwi," I retorted. "Climbing mountains, white-water rafting, striking out into the wilderness."

"I mean the Anglo heritage. The repressed and cautious side of us. The tendency to share resentments rather than show compassion. Point the finger rather than cultivate conviviality. Despite embracing ethnic food, espresso coffee, European fashions, we remain awkward in our skins, preoccupied by tidiness, boundaries, and security."

"This may be true," I said. "I also abhor that uptightness you speak of, but I feel at home here in a way I don't elsewhere. This is where I have a right to be, even if I don't always feel like exercising that right."

"I feel like that in Italy," Keith said.

"Not here?"

"My thoughts wander between the two. One minute I can be thinking ahead to a weekend trip to the Tararuas with Pablo, the next I am thinking of that other green valley, eight thousand miles away, at the foot of the Brenta massif."

Keith had been returning to the Trentino in northern Italy for twenty-five years, doing anthropological fieldwork in an alpine village. His descriptions of his friends in Caderzone, and their everyday lives, are among the most ethnographically luminous I know. Pier Paolo the salami maker, and the smell of his *salumeria*—a pungent mixture of salted meat, garlic, spilled wine, and the damp pine sawdust on the stone floor. Augusto, who owned the land where Keith stayed, and shared with the young ethnographer details of village history, the workings of the transhumant system and life in the high Alps. "His sense of continuity was powerful," Keith said, "rooted in his own daily work as a *contadino* (peasant), a word he used with pride. He told me once, as we were haymaking together, that he had used the same scythe for more than sixty summers: 'The blades have changed,' he said, 'but it's always been the same handle.'"

"Isn't this what every expatriate feels?" I asked Keith. "That the blades have changed, but not the handle?"

When I said goodbye to Keith that afternoon, I urged him to keep in touch and to publish more of his Caderzone material. To write about the *professore* who cut his own firewood with a chainsaw and had the same appreciation of practical know-how and traditional food as the locals. But perhaps the moment had passed, and Keith would find something very different to devote his energies to.

As I crossed the city to visit Judith, it occurred to me how remote now was the Pohangina Valley where she and Keith had lived, where their three children had come into the world, and where I had, so often, enjoyed the bounty of their table, long walks into the hills, and exhilarating conversations about books and writing. How distant, too, seemed the summer night when I brought Francine to meet Keith and Judith for the first time. After a lavish meal of seafood, washed down by chilled white wine, we walked arm in arm along a moonlit road with the dark furled poplars on either side, and I realized how misguided people had been to tell me that Francine looked exactly like Pauline, as though I had to be awoken from a spell that could only bring me disappointment.

* * *

It was evening by the time I got back to Roseneath, and Barack Obama was just beginning his acceptance speech in Chicago. With Jennifer and Allan and my cousin Louisa, we watched the event on TV as daylight faded outside and the hills across Evans Bay disappeared into the darkness of the eastern sky. Emotions overwhelmed me and millions of others around the world—Americans, Asians, Africans, Antipodeans—as we watched Obama declare that we had reached a defining moment in our history, that we could change the world.

It is a cliché, I know, but the thing about hope is that it does spring eternal. We are knocked to the ground, but clamber to our feet and go on. We cut our losses and start over. We persevere or do our best to. Observe us at play. We stake all on a game of chance, though the odds are stacked against us and we are, in the long run, bound to lose. Still, we return to the table as if every new deal is the first. Life may not give us a second chance, but a game can always be replayed. Moreover, writes Paul Myerscough, editor at the *London Review of Books*, "while you are at the table, the world falls away and the game is all that remains." Politics occupies a curious position between the reality of life and the irreality of games. Sometimes, the world of politics seems to be beyond us. Yet when we vote, protest, or petition, we believe for a moment that old habits can be broken, the old order overturned, years of injustice redeemed with the stroke of a pen. Isn't the mantra "Yes we can" the same one we silently cite as we roll the dice one more time, make our new year resolutions, or vow never again to hurt the ones we love? Yet none of this crossed my mind as I listened to Obama's speech and watched Jesse Jackson's tear-streaked face, Oprah Winfrey half lost in the crowd, or the wide-eyed youth placing their trust in the messiah. I was not thinking at all; I was choking on the nameless emotions that welled up from deep within me, filling my eyes with tears, the slate swept clean, a new day dawning, the past eclipsed.

Distance Looks Our Way

If anyone could identify with my theme of firstness, it was my cousin Louisa whom I had met for the first time earlier that year when she stayed with Francine and me in Boston, en route to South America. I warmed to her at once, and her ambivalence about where she belonged echoed my own. On Louisa's second night with us, I took her for a walk in the nearby woods. Our family dog Clover bounded ahead of us, following her nose deep into the woods, occasionally returning, then running off again.

"It's strange how life can be so fragmented," Louisa said. "Sometimes I feel as if I've lived the lives of about four different people and it's hard to reconcile them all together into this one person. Have you experienced that, with all your different life phases, and moving between so many different worlds?"

Of course I had, and I told her so, which prompted Louisa to declare, "I still can't imagine living permanently anywhere other than New Zealand. I feel a real sense of belonging there, even though the culture and politics can be incredibly frustrating and insular. The land feeds my soul in an indescribable way: the smell of the air, the sight of the sky, the blossom on the pōhutukawa trees, the sense of infinite space and potential."

Perhaps Louisa needed this Edenic vision as an antidote to the ecological disasters she would soon document in Ecuador, though her early life had also been something of a disaster zone.

"I don't usually feel rapport with family members," she confessed.

Yet I was already astonished at how much we seemed to have in common.

"I was always the strange, intense one," Louisa said. "For as long as I can remember, I felt like an outsider. I could not handle school. My questions were treated with derision, dismissed as cheeky or seen as challenges to the teacher's authority."

Rebuffed, she sealed herself off from those from whom she had expected support, understanding, and encouragement. Her mother, a social worker, seemed incapable of understanding that her daughter's self-destructive and dissatisfied behavior was a cry for help. Her father was a loner who never held a job for long, could not manage money, and showed his daughter little affection. Unhappy and rebellious, Louisa quit school at fifteen and left home. For several years she lived in seedy flats or on the street, drawing the dole, enrolling in various courses only to drop out, smoking methamphetamines. Following a run-in with the police, a woman lawyer offered Louisa a job in her legal office—a magnanimous gesture that inspired Louisa "to get back into control of my situation." In temporarily changing the spelling of her name to Luisa, she sought to separate herself from her father's mother, Betty Louisa, who had committed suicide, and in whose memory Louisa had been named. "I was determined to escape the Jackson curse," she said.

At twenty-three, she set out on a journey around the world, fetching up in July 2007 in the town of Besease, southern Ghana, where she worked as a volunteer in an orphanage.

It was only when I began reading Louisa's blogs that I fully appreciated the parallels between her life and mine, for at twenty-three I had also worked as a volunteer in Africa, teaching in an orphanage in the Congo. What I hesitated to tell Louisa, however, when we began exchanging emails, was that her grandmother, Betty Louisa, who was a trained nurse, revered Albert Schweitzer, whose philosophy anticipated the ecology movement that Louisa so passionate embraced. Schweitzer's dismay at the rapid deforestation along the Ogooué River by European timber companies may have entered into his thoughts as he prepared his Nobel acceptance speech in 1952, in which he noted that "the most flagrant violation of historical rights, and indeed of human rights, consists in depriving certain peoples of their right to the land on which they live, thus forcing them to move to other territories."

After travels in Burkino Faso, Benin, Togo, and Morocco, Louisa visited Israel, Nepal, and Bhutan before passing through Boston on her way to Ecuador, Bolivia, Peru, and Chile. If Bhutan represented the best in environmental protection policies, Ecuador's northern Oriente was the worst. In one of the most biodiverse regions of the Amazon, Texaco had extracted crude oil for fifty years with scant regard for the environment. Louisa found a toxic wasteland. By the time Texaco left the area in 1992, forty-five billion liters of poisonous waste had been dumped into the fragile ecosystem, seeping into streams that the thirty thousand local inhabitants used for drinking, washing, and fishing. Louisa would compare the devastation to Chernobyl and call the northern Oriente the largest environmental disaster in the world. In her blog, she wrote: "I watched, in anguish, a woman who stood waist deep in this river, scrubbing clothes on a rock, toxic water [presumably] being gently absorbed by her internal soft tissue as she labored for her family, and downstream her children played by the river's edge next to an old Texaco oil drum. Near the notoriously lawless oil town of Shushufindi, I visited a family whose house had been constructed directly next to an abandoned waste pit where, after some thirty years, vegetation had grown over the surface. The elderly campesino who lived there greeted me warmly and led me to the rear of his property where he had attempted to grow some fruit and coffee trees. He broke pieces of soil with his work-roughened hands: thick black crude literally oozed from the center and the smell of the oil was overpowering. The trees here don't produce any fruit, and the ground water is so contaminated that this man was losing his eyesight and his wife lay ill inside their house, dying of cancer." Although petroleum hydrocarbon contamination is thousands of times higher than legal limits in the U.S., people could neither move away nor prevail on their government to decontaminate their environment.

In September 2008, after two years away, Louisa returned to New Zealand to study environmental law and actively contribute to the protection of the country's biodiversity. "A society is defined not only by what it creates," she wrote, citing John Sawhill, "but by what it refuses to destroy." But Louisa's commitment to the environment was also born of a deep nostalgia for the place where she had grown up. In August, on a beach in Chile, with the Pacific at her feet, she wrote of the prospect of coming home. "Aotearoa New Zealand represents who I am. I want wild salty waves that crash against black rocks, whipping winds and white sea spray, I want sea animals with their round soft bodies and leathery skin, give me pelicans and albatrosses, crying seagulls and hardened sands that crunch underfoot. Give me trees, wild and green, their trunks warped by wild ocean winds, give me green mountains, and skies peppered with clouds . . . arouse in me emotions of home as I walk this final road."

Like a soldier coming home after a war, the traveler may find it difficult to share her experiences with those who have not been stretched to the limit or journeyed to the ends of the earth. In her hometown in the Bay of Plenty, Louisa found the preoccupations of her old friends juvenile and irrelevant. "I loved being home," Louisa told me in Wellington. "This is my home. But in some ways I am no longer at home here."

"It was the same for me," I said, "returning from the Congo in 1964. I withdrew. I wrote about Africa. But all the while I was aware that this could be a road to madness, this dwelling on memories, disconnected from the world around me. When a colleague circulated the rumor that I was a confidence trickster who had not been in the Congo at all, I realized how preposterous my stories must seem and how difficult it would be to find a publisher for them. Yet they were all I had. They were the soil in which my poetry had already begun to take root."

I think it helped Louisa to know that I had traveled the same road, though I was cautious not to give the impression that because I had encountered these difficulties before her I was an authority on how to deal with them.

We are born into a world we did not make, but in the course of our lives we bring into being a new world (*te ao hou*). The world we come to call our own departs from the world we encountered at birth, though it bears the imprint of that world. We may suffer the consequences of our parents' acts or feel the burden of our history as a dead weight. Yet what really matters is the distance we put between ourselves and the past: the small departures that prevent the passing on of an accursed inheritance or that open up new possibilities for those who will follow us. We all have to blaze our own trails through the wilderness of this world. And each generation will hopefully open its eyes on that quasi-mythical land of the long white cloud, apparently uninhabited, never before glimpsed, holding out the promise of a new beginning.

The Illusion of Corsica

It was a walk I had done countless times before, in happiness and in despair. After descending the steps from Roseneath to Balaena Bay, I set out along the foreshore road to Oriental Bay. Locating the steps beside the bus shelter, I climbed through a grove of pōhutukawa, found a clay track through the pines, and made my way to the heights of Mount Victoria. From time to time I stopped to catch my breath and scribble thumbnail descriptions of the sudden silence in the pines or the fragments of windswept sky and blue water visible beyond the cathedraled trees. The path was crisscrossed with roots and strewn with pine straw, the city a distant murmur. In the past, I would imagine myself back on the Saronic Gulf where the pines are tapped for retsina, or remember Ernest Shepard's drawings of the "Six Pine Trees in the Hundred Acre Wood," or bring to mind Cézanne's views of Mont Sainte Victoire, pine boughs creaking in the mistral. Today, however, I was thinking of the Mediterranean pines outside the railway station at Garavan in the south of France. Perhaps this was because I had been reading Gregory O'Brien's recently published memoir of his year in Menton—notes that "oscillate between France and New Zealand and comprise a kind of free-floating meditation on Europe and the Antipodes." Greg's work suggests that an interesting history might be read between the lines of the journals, poems, and fiction of New Zealand authors who, since 1970, have sojourned in Menton on writing fellowships, working within cooee of the villa where Katherine Mansfield lived in 1920, battling illness, her ambivalence toward her natal country unresolved. Such a history would reveal our

awkward relationship with Europe, O'Brien suggests, for despite our reading knowledge of French or German, our admiration for Old World traditions, and our indebtedness to certain European writers, this metropolitan
culture remains foreign to us, partly because we were not raised in it, partly
because we inherit a very different history, blighted by Europe's imperialist
designs and violent appropriations. In his memoir, Gregory O'Brien makes
this tension a leitmotif. Though entranced by the adopted country of Blaise
Cendrars and Le Corbusier, he nurses an unassuaged anger at France's 1985
bombing of Greenpeace's flagship, *Rainbow Warrior,* in Auckland harbor.

A few weeks later, after returning to the U.S., I would leaf through my
notebooks from my own year in Menton, wondering whether they might
also contain a "free-floating meditation on Europe and the Antipodes." To
my surprise, I discovered that my Menton preoccupations had been very
different. I worried about where I belonged and where I wanted to live. I
was oppressed by dreams of Sierra Leone, and hauled over the coals by
Kuranko friends for not being with them. I anguished over Pauline's
failing health. I doubted that fiction was my forte. As with all questions
couched in either-or terms, life admits no answer, unless we learn the art
of living in the here and now. So I find it salutary that the very pages in
which these impossible questions appear are filled with accounts of the
people Pauline and I befriended during our months in Menton, as if I
instinctively knew that absorption in the detail of everyday life would save
me from the excesses of thought.

Simone Mortureux de Faudoas took us under her wing when we first
arrived, helping us find an apartment, insisting we call her "Aunt Simone,"
introducing us to "suitable" people, and even suggesting what I should
write about. From the outset, I was struck by the odd mixture of hauteur
and worldliness in her. She gave the impression of having lived among aristocrats but fallen on hard times. Unable to afford the appurtenances of her
true class, she had had recourse to disdain as a way of reminding people of
her pedigree. As it turned out, my guesswork was wide of the mark.

On a rainy November afternoon, she took Pauline and me to meet an
English friend who lived in the Riviera Palace—a hotel built at the turn of
the century for royals and aristocrats. Simone explained that their entou-
rages would occupy several floors. Victoria stayed there, and the czar of
Russia, who booked all the rooms on the upper floors so that no one but
God would be above him.

The hotel, now downgraded to *résidence*, had seen better days. Its parquet floors were in poor repair, plaster was flaking from the walls, and the friezes of pastel-blue lilies and pink carnations were badly faded. We climbed the marble stairs with their Italian balustrades. In poorly lit corridors, the ugly red vinyl made a sickly squelching sound underfoot.

It took some time after Simone had rung the bell before her friend opened the door. Mrs. Johnson's artificially blond hair had the shape of a beehive. Her eyebrows were penciled lines, her cheeks savagely rouged. She spoke almost immediately of the desolation of being alone.

"It is something you never get used to," she told us. "And now this terrible tragedy of Grace's death."

"We passed a lot of people in the Avenue Verdun," I said, "watching the funeral on television sets in shop windows. The newspapers are issuing color supplements with banner headlines: 'Last Kiss Between Rainier and Grace.'"

"They are saying that her daughter was at the wheel, that the brakes failed, or that she was arguing with Stephanie and took her eyes off the road," Mrs. Johnson said.

"The newspapers are unforgiveable," Aunt Simone added. "The way they probe and probe. Always looking for the truth. Things should be allowed to rest. What matter how the Princess died?"

Mrs. Johnson did not respond. Perhaps it was her deafness or her concern to usher us into the living room. Crippled with arthritis, she inched forward with the aid of two walking sticks, clearly in pain. "A nurse and a maid come daily to the apartment," she explained, "but they are not companions. Not like Johnny. I lost my husband last year," she added, looking poignantly at me. "Dear Johnny, without him I don't know where I am."

Over tea, we discovered that Mrs. Johnson had once been a notable stage actress. Now confined to her apartment, she spent much of the day sorting through old letters and photographs or looking out the window at a sea of olives and the limestone bluffs beyond.

After our visit to Mrs. Johnson, who appeared to have no other life than the one she remembered, clung to, and talked about with indefatigable sadness, I became curious about Simone's past and why she volunteered not a scrap of information about where she came from, whom she had married, and whether she had children. When I did inquire, she told me that when you are very old you don't have a lot to look forward to, so your mind goes back to the past. "But I try to keep myself focused on what is in between," she said, "taking one day at a time, visiting friends, doing what I can to help. I would rather die than become like Mrs. Johnson."

Even when Simone did recount her story, it was with the proviso that I not regard her as someone who looks back, who has regrets.

"I do not hanker after things I cannot have. But you are a writer. You want to know the secrets of everyone you meet. I have no secrets. But I suppose I have a story, like everyone else. You are welcome to make of it what you will. I lay no claim to my own insignificant history. Others lived through the times I lived through and did not survive. Others had a much harder life than mine."

She was born in the Basque country, "where boys were adored and girls ignored." That's the way she put it. "Like in China." She was nothing to her mother, who didn't care if her daughter existed or not. But she was close to her father until he was killed in northern France during the Great War. No longer obliged to keep up even the pretense of liking her daughter, her mother sent her to live with her grandparents. Simone was seventeen.

Her grandmother happened to be the model for Pierre Loti's *Le Roman d'un enfant* because *her* mother had been a close friend of Loti's. Unfortunately, this made no difference to Simone's situation. Her grandmother took no more interest in her than her mother had. When, finally, she married—a poor army officer—her grandmother told her, "Your husband will run off with another woman in a year or two. When that happens, don't come here looking for money or sympathy." "In fact," Simone said, "I would rather have died than take anything from my grandparents, even though Pierre Loti once pressured them to buy me a piano."

At the outbreak of World War II, Simone and her husband were in Romania. He'd been seconded there from the French army as a weapons expert. No sooner had they returned to France in 1939 than he was sent to the front. Days before the fall of France, he was invalided back to Paris with shell shock.

Simone heard rumors that her husband and other French prisoners were to be transported to Germany. Fluent in German, she "more or less told the Bavarian brute of a doctor" in charge of the hospital to release her husband into her care. It took a week of badgering before the doctor relented. He'd never known a French woman to speak such excellent German, he told her, or to show such courage.

After installing her husband in a villa (he had to remain in Paris and report to the commissariat once a week), Simone went south to the Basses-Pyrénées. She did not see her sons for four years. Her eldest spent the war in a German labor camp; a younger son went into hiding. As for Simone, she lived alone in a village between Pau and Bayonne, growing and selling vegetables to make ends meet. With great delight, she recounted how she secretly got horse manure from the German officers billeted in the village by bribing them with baskets of cherries from her allotment.

After the war, her husband received a government pension, and on a forty-hectare lot bequeathed by her grandfather she and her husband grew grapes, cherries, and maize for fifteen years.

In all the time I knew her, Simone only once raised her voice in anger. It was to castigate the Americans for their casual attitude to war. "They don't know what it is," she said. "They read about it in the newspapers over breakfast but understand nothing. Such people are dangerous. These are the people who will make another war."

Simone's remark immediately brought to mind George Santayana's observation that those who cannot remember the past are condemned to repeat it. But Simone was making a somewhat different point: that life is a struggle not to be consumed by what happened in the past, and that we must at all costs live affirmatively in the here and now.

It was through Simone that I met Mlle. Picard, who lived in a small apartment on the seafront, a short walk from the Garavan Palace. I cannot remember how she became my French tutor, but every Wednesday afternoon, after completing my daily stint of writing, I would join her for tea and conversation.

Mlle. Picard had been an English teacher until her retirement, so it was a very English tea she served—with Staffordshire china, water biscuits, and Dundee shortcake. She was eighty-five, passionate and intelligent, though her body was frail. Once, I ventured to ask her why she had never married. "I was born old," she said, "as well as crippled. Who would be attracted to such a person?"

"I would," I said gallantly.

She smiled. "Tu est très gentile. But you must remember, I have not been without a family. My family is my students. They are my children. Even now they still write to me." And she showed me several unopened airmail letters that she had received that week, postmarked Canada, France, Germany, and Russia.

Of her childhood, she said nothing for many months. Then, one afternoon, with rain falling steadily in the courtyard outside, she shared her story with me.

Her mother had fallen down a flight of cellar steps in the sixth month of her pregnancy, and as a result gave birth to her daughter twelve weeks before term. The baby weighed less than a kilo. In 1897, such an infant would not be expected to live. Incredibly, she survived, though she was four before she took her first ungainly steps and fourteen before she could run. That she walked at all, Mlle. Picard said, was entirely due to the devotion of her parents. Her grandfather had read a newspaper article about a Belgian doctor who specialized in treating children crippled from the effects of premature birth, and though her parents were too poor to afford specialist care, they traveled by train to Brussels with their daughter and found the doctor's house. Like pilgrims, then, they stood on the sidewalk outside, not knowing what they might do, hoping for some kind of miracle. After keeping vigil for several hours, they were rewarded with a glimpse of their savior. The doctor, top-hatted, red-bearded, carrying a cane and black bag, descended the steps from his front door. The family watched in awe and shame as the doctor passed through the gate and onto the street. Then, to their surprise and mortification, the famous specialist came up to them and asked about the crippled child the father was holding in his arms. A few minutes later the doctor was pulling up the little girl's chemise to examine her. Outraged, she grabbed the doctor's long red beard and pulled it as hard as she could. "With that kind of spirit, and your parents' love," the doctor declared, "you will one day most certainly walk."

The cure was banal. Back in Paris, the father began a routine of waking at four in the morning and walking across the city to Les Halles to get salt from the fish trays that came in overnight from the Brittany coast. Every other day he made the rounds of the wine markets to get lees from the large jars of wine that were brought up from Burgundy and the Rhône for decanting into labeled bottles. It was in this improbable mixture of fish-tainted rock salt and red wine sediment that the child was bathed every morning. The routine went on for more than two years, until the day she walked.

* * *

There was something about Aunt Simone and Mlle. Picard that moved me profoundly and made them unforgettable. Maybe it had something to do with their being very old. Of having lived through so much history that biography had become transmuted into myth. It's not one's own story any more, but the story of something wider, more universal. I have pondered this often, this gap between our little lives and Life itself—the something greater that surrounds us, extends beyond us, yet does not, for all its force, diminish us. But the question remains whether the *story* of a life bears more than an incidental relationship to that life as it was actually lived and whether, in our eagerness to give coherence to our experience, we betray it. The people, places, books, and ideas to which I have felt most deeply connected exist—despite the seriousness and passion with which I have engaged with them—beyond my reach. Would Aunt Simone recognize herself in my account of her? Does it really matter? In our encounters with others we momentarily lose sight of ourselves. We are eclipsed. And it is from these encounters that we return to ourselves, changed. As Theseus found in the Cretan labyrinth, the thread we unwind transforms impasses into paths. But paths may be lost as quickly as they are found, just as a ship's wake marks a channel or sea route for only a few minutes before the ocean returns to its natural ambiguity and inscrutability. For Lawrence Durrell, stories bring a temporary semblance of order to what is in its very nature "a fractured and fragmented world." In his view, "The solace of such work lies in this—that only there, in the silences of the painter or the writer can reality be reordered, reworked and made to show its significant side." But I do not agree with Durrell when he speaks of art as a "joyous compromise" in which the imagination makes good the disappointments and defeats of our quotidian life, for stories must, despite our rage for order, retain a strong sense of the fiery furnace in which they are forged and avoid giving the impression that the patterns we hammer out in art reveal an order that lies within life itself. As Virginia Woolf reminds us, "Every day includes much more non-being than being."

That I turned my hand to writing a novel during my year in Menton had as much to do with the fact that fiction was my first love as with my belief that it was a superior art form. This made the writing hard going, postponing the day when I would wise up to the fact that fiction was not my strong suit. A biography of Norman Lewis finally helped me understand where my own talent lay. Lewis wrote fifteen novels, all now out of print, though his travel writing is still read and widely admired. But his failure to write great fiction worried Lewis throughout his career, and he appeared unable to fully admit that his powers of invention required "the pollinating gift of facts." Paradoxically, Lewis was never more of a novelist "than when faced with a road drenched in the mire of actuality or a room beset with real horrors faced by real human beings," and he was at his best when confronted by an actual place or person that pulsed "with the perfect reality of an invented thing."

Had I realized the personal relevance of these remarks in 1982, I could have saved myself a lot of trouble. Lines scribbled in the dead of night that would not survive the dawn. Screwed-up paper littering the floor. Long walks into the landscape to collect my thoughts.

How many mornings did I walk out of my studio, glance up at the limestone bluffs of Ormea, and take the old mule track that led from the coast to Baousset, the rain-cleansed air resinous with pines? When I looked back, Menton was far below—the cubist roofs of the old town clustered around St. Michel, the sea plowed by a stiff wind racing away to Italy, and the promontories of Cap Martin, Monaco, and Cabbé clearer than yesterday. If only my writing could do justice to what was so freely given!

Bypassing Castellar, I took a track through broom, brambles, stunted pines, and untended olives, hoping to reach Granges St. Paul and thence one of the old smugglers' paths along the border with Italy. The air was fragrant with juniper, lantana, and fermenting figs, and not for the first time I found myself contemplating the labor that had gone into building the drystone walls and the terraces crumbling now beneath olives and holm oaks. So many lives vanished from the earth. So many untold stories.

Above me, against a deep blue sky, were the crags of Berceau. After clambering up the scree below the col, I plunged into knee-deep snow and silent pinewoods, marveling at how instantaneously it was possible to pass, in effect, from one season to another, one's mind following suit with fresh sensations and images.

It was mid-afternoon by the time I got back to Menton, too late to do any writing, too early to return to our apartment. I bought an espresso at

Le Narval and sat at a sidewalk table, facing the boat harbor. A stiff wind was rattling the halyards of moored craft—a loud tinkling of metal against aluminum masts, like the chime and chatter of a Buddhist monastery.

Occasionally, on clear mid-winter mornings, Corsica would be visible on the horizon. Houses along the coast, dark smudges of forest. "Un trompe l'oeil," my friend Roland Ghersi called it, pointing out that the island was too far away to be directly visible. "Density and temperature differences in the lower layers of the atmosphere tend to bend the light rays from Corsica, creating the semblance of a mirage and sharpening the visibility of the island." When I explained this to my twelve-year-old daughter, dipping a pencil in a glass of water and showing her how it appeared bent, Heidi rejected the analogy of pencils in water and islands in the sea. She wanted the substantiality of images. Perhaps this is why it took me so long to realize that fiction is as unfaithful to life as an academic treatise and that memory is a misnomer—a shadow cast across the conscious mind, a hypnopompic delusion on the threshold of waking. We speak of memory as though there is something solid to which our minds return, something in store that is retrieved. But what if the past were merely an eddy or backwater in the stream of our present lives and not, as we sometimes believe, another country? We sometimes cling to the idea of firstness as a shipwrecked mariner might cling to a rock. Perhaps we need such points of anchorage to negotiate a changeable and uncertain world. But while some psychologists find evidence for the permanence of some memory traces, others cast doubt on the idea of immutable memory, reminding us that we undergo perpetual metamorphoses in the course of a lifetime, each decade overlaying what went before, much as a palimpsest of tidal debris collects on a beach.

And yet there are moments when I do not have the shadow of a doubt about the recurrence of long ago events—of rain gusting over a tin roof, of my grandfather's potting shed where he regaled me with stories about his youth and early adulthood in New Zealand, or that taste of bush humus and foliage in my throat as I dived into a river swimming hole. It is often from such evanescent phenomena that we construct our life stories, creating the artificial forms of closure and completeness without which our existence would appear meaningless. We writers take it upon ourselves to make good the deficiencies of life, says Henry James, "to see people not only as they are but as they might be. In truth," James says, "everyone, in life, is incomplete, and it is [in] the work of art that in reproducing them one feels the desire to fill them out, to justify them, as it were." Perhaps it isn't that art enables one to complete these mysterious others; rather that we round out *ourselves* in writing about them. In his author's note to *Victory*, Joseph Conrad recalls the origins of his four main characters. Axel Heyst was a mysterious Swede whose paths crossed Conrad's for only a few days. Though Heyst left no trace of his past or his purposes, he provided Conrad with an unforgettable image of resolute detachment. And Conrad met Lena, whose love for Heyst would stir him so fatefully, in a café in the South of France. In a room filled with tobacco smoke, the rattling of dominos, and the music of a traveling group of musicians, Lena moved silently and somnolently among the tables, collecting money. When Conrad plots to have Lena meet Heyst, he wants her to be "heroically equal to every demand of the risky and uncertain future." Indeed, he ensures that this is so, and in view of her triumphant end asks if he could have done any more for her rehabilitation and happiness. But Conrad does not broach the question as to whether, or to what extent, his stories of Lord Jim, Kurtz, Marlowe, and Axel Heyst were means whereby he sought to rehabilitate himself. Nor does he ask whether our narrative plots, our moral conclusions, and our belief in the power of first impressions might be dispensed with, the better to accept the largely fragmented yet intriguing nature of life as lived.

Return to the Manawatu

The morning headlines read "New Dawn." But as I drove toward Palmerston North, clouds were being bundled across a leaden sky, trees and ferns flailing, herds of cattle huddling under storm-assailed macrocarpas.

I parked near the art gallery. Having lived for many years in this wind-blown city, I knew my way around. But I was now a stranger, and walked the streets of a ghost town, anonymous and unremarked. In Bruce Mc-Kenzie's bookshop I asked the assistant if she had any books on settler life in the Manawatu. I was hoping to compare the experiences of early immigrants in the region with those of adopted children, so bringing together, as I had done in my novel *Rainshadow*, the historical loss of a homeland and the personal loss of one's parents. Though several books on Scandinavian immigration came to light, I was disappointed to find the raw experience of these early settlers reduced to bare names and dates, the books informed by a heroic view of history in which intrepid individuals overcome adversity, create something from nothing, and bequeath a worthy heritage to their descendants. Only occasionally could I glimpse the tragic ironies of nineteenth-century colonialism, whose aftereffects are still felt. For example, Danes, having lost 40 percent of their land to Prussia in the 1864 war, escaped the suppression of their language, culture, and nationality by migrating to a country where, albeit unwittingly, they occupied land alienated from local Māori.

In a letter home, Emilie Monrad seems blind to her invidious situation. "A cherry tree, full of red cherries that we looked forward to eating, has been picked clean by a Māori woman, not as a theft, but because, since her father planted the tree, she felt she had the right to it. That the land with everything on it had been sold didn't affect her. To make sure that the same thing did not happen to our apple tree, Johannes picked all the apples at once and decided to make an apple dessert. However, in spite of all his work, he could only manage a mediocre stew because the apples were not ripe, but 'the Colony' approved."

In truth, though the land had been sold, many Māori regarded such transactions as giving Pākehā usufruct rights, not ownership of natural resources or authority over the tenure and management of the land (*tino rangatiratanga*). These arguments over which rights were retained by Māori and which were transferred to the British Crown in the 1840 Treaty of Waitangi have to this day been only partially resolved.

After leaving the bookshop, I drove to Terrace End where Pauline and I lived between 1973 and 1981, and where our daughter, Heidi, spent her formative years. In a 1939 photograph, reprinted in one of the local histories I had just purchased, you can see the gravel pit that adjoined our house, with the flank of the Rimutaka Range in the distance.

On May 9, 1879, thirty-eight-year-old Laurits Hans Gulbrandsen, who had emigrated from Norway in 1869, narrowly escaped death in the gravel pit. "He and his companions had just resumed filling railway wagons with metal, after their lunch break, when the top of the pit-face collapsed; those struck by the metal were Laurits, Hans Petersen, and a Mr. Rowlands. Petersen was badly bruised and Rowlands received a serious leg injury. Laurits was struck from behind and crushed between the avalanche of metal and the ballast engine that, in turn, caused a 'frightful gash' on his head. His skull was forced open by the pressure of the metal against

THE ENIGMA OF ANTERIORITY 195

his body—and his brain was seen to protrude. Immediately after he was extracted, the locomotive driver got up steam and raced up out of the pit to get medical assistance. Once freed, Laurits was kept conscious by a 'strong stimulant' and was taken to his home by train. There, Doctor Akers sewed the wound and bandaged his head. Surprisingly, apart from a few bruises, he had no other injuries." Indeed, Laurits lived to the ripe old age of seventy-seven.

Laurits's story set me thinking about the arbitrariness of fate and led me to recall the retired couple who lived opposite us—their white stucco bungalow, standard roses, and immaculate lawns a studied riposte to our own unruly section, which was dominated by an immense phoenix palm and numerous native shrubs that I had planted without giving much thought to how high they might grow. One winter afternoon we were visited by one of my wife's old university friends. Possibly following some tactless remark of mine about our neighbors' garden or their extreme reticence, Carol told us that these people were her parents. Her birth parents, however, lived over the range in Woodville. Because Carol's mother already had several children when Carol was born, she gave the newborn infant to her childless sister. Throughout her childhood, Carol said, her adoptive parents would take her on Sunday and Christmas visits to Woodville. These were the happiest days of her life: playing with her 'cousins' on their small farm, swimming in the river hole by the Balance Bridge, exploring the bush. When she learned that she had been adopted, everything changed. She now knew that the family she secretly wished she had been born into was, in fact, her real family, and that the dour couple with whom she lived, and who forbade her from opening the china cabinet or disturbing the peace of the house in any way, were relative strangers. From that moment, whenever she was with her natal family, she would seek some sign of recognition. An especially warm hug. A kiss. A comment that acknowledged the true nature of the relationship between them, and that revoked, if such a thing were possible, her mother's decision to give her away. Her birth parents, not wishing to compromise Carol's relationship with her adoptive parents, were careful not to show the love their daughter desired, and their feigned indifference left Carol feeling more heartbroken than she felt in the face of her other parents' coldness.

For some reason, Carol's story weighed on my mind, and as I drove along Fitzherbert Avenue to take a last look at the street along which I once cycled to and from work, I began to see how Carol's unconsummated relationship with her birth parents dovetailed with our nation's search for a way of reconciling *tangata whenua* and *manuhiri*—the indigenous people of the land and those who had been welcomed as guests but stayed as usurpers—as well as with the struggle of the people of the four winds, who, having lost touch with their home marae, have to renegotiate a sense of what it means to be Māori.

I know many moving stories of children, adopted at birth, who have been subsequently reunited with their biological parents or siblings. There is often disappointment. No sense of connection. Or an outright repudiation of the idea of a common bond. But sometimes it is as if the adopted child has been lost and living in a wilderness and has now come home. My uncle Harold, whom we called Mick, was haunted by this dream of reunion. He felt that he could never be completely himself unless he was rejoined with the couple that had brought him into the world only to give him up for adoption. "He felt rejected," my cousin Helen once told me. "He felt he had never been really loved."

According to Helen, her parents had taken good care of Harold's elderly and incontinent father during his last years. Her mother had washed her father-in-law's soiled sheets every day, prepared his favorite food, waited on him hand and foot. Harold was forty-two when his father died, and he discovered that no provision had been made for him or for his family in his father's will. For all their pains, they received nothing. For Harold, it was the rejection that hurt most, the revelation that, in his father's eyes, he had always been the black sheep of the family, inferior to his siblings, and somehow responsible for his own illegitimate origins.

At first I thought Helen was implying that her father had never, until that moment, been told that he was adopted. But she made it clear that what he was never told, and now would never know (because he was suffering from Alzheimers), was that his sister Noel was his biological mother.

"I thought that was just a malicious rumor," I said.

"Not at all," Helen said. "All the evidence points to it being true." She went on to describe how Harold had always been emotionally distant. Preoccupied by his own narcissistic wounds, he seldom showed affection to his children and probably gave little support to his wife Betty in her hours of need.

Betty Louisa Woswo hailed from Rahotu. Her grandfather had emigrated from Schleswig-Holstein in the 1870s, settling on land that had been confiscated from Taranaki Māori following the infamous invasion of Parihaka. Betty's father installed the first herringbone milking shed in Taranaki. "But he was an ogre," Helen said, "and my mother's life was hell. Life on the farm was cows, cows, cows. My mother hated them, especially the milking. Before school and after school, and every day of the week. She was the only one of her nine siblings to complete high school, and she longed for a life beyond Rahotu and dairy farming. The only way out was nursing, which is what she did. When she married my father, she probably thought she would have a home of her own, a family, and be happy. But he was conscripted, and she spent the war years in New Plymouth, working as a nurse for a local doctor. I don't think she ever found what she was looking for. She loved the piano, loved music. She was smart as a tack. But look where she wound up. Worn out looking after my father. Cooking, cleaning house, all without enough money. Harold bought all kinds of electronic gadgets for himself, but Mum did not even have a washing machine! And on top of everything else, she was doing her charity work. Red Cross visiting, Plunket, National Council for Women, and taking care of Māori babies when their mothers were ill. I don't recall ever having my bedroom without an extra cot in it and a wee Māori baby to feed in the night."

Helen blamed her father for her mother's suffering. "Men snare women," she said. "They put them to work for them, keeping house, satisfying their desires, catering to their whims, caring for their kids, and every call for greater fairness is met with 'Who pays the bills? Who's the breadwinner here?'"

"My mother was ground down," Helen said. "Worn away to nothing."

Six years after Harold's father's death, on a weekend when Harold and his younger daughter were away (the older children had already left home), Betty went to the local pharmacy with Harold's prescription for a repeat of his medication, returned home and took a lethal overdose of his pills. No one had any inkling of her intentions, and she left no explanation.

Helen's grim narrative made me think back, for the first time in many years, to the holidays I spent in New Plymouth with my favorite aunt and uncle. If Helen found her father wanting, he was, in my eyes, an affable and eccentric hero. I adored his radio transmitters and vintage cars, our visits to the Speedway on Saturday nights, and our foraging at low tide for paua. In retrospect, however, I remembered how careworn my Auntie Betty often seemed. The cloth diapers laboriously hung out to dry in the blustery Taranaki wind and, in winter, strung over lines in the basement or draped over a drying rack in front of an electric radiator. Porridge boiling over on the stove. A crying child. The endless difficulty—as she put it—"of making ends meet." And though she must have been exasperated by my ceaseless questions—why this, why that?—she indulged and cared for me. "You were her favorite," Helen said. "She would have done anything for you."

"So what of Noel?" I asked Helen, mystified as to why she believed that her father's sister was also his mother.

"She left home at seventeen, eighteen, and went to Wellington," Helen said. "Trained for a while as a nurse, but hated it and dropped out. She went to Auckland and found work as a legal secretary to Sidney Fitzherbert, a senior partner in the family firm. The father was Sir William Fitzherbert, who came out to New Zealand from England and made his mark. That bridge across the Manawatu River in Palmerston North is named for him, as well as Fitzherbert Avenue. Anyway, Sidney Fitzherbert falls for Noel. He's married, but so what? He gets her pregnant, and she has the baby in the Fitzherberts' home at 4 Shelly Beach Road in Herne Bay. I know the address well; the Fitzherberts later bequeathed their home to the Justice Department who turned it into a home for Māori girls in trouble [guilty of petty larceny or pregnant out of wedlock]. Poetic justice, eh! The Fitzherberts looked after Noel for eighteen months, helping her with the baby, working out how best to deal with the situation. There's a photo of Harold from this time. He's decked out in a sailor suit. Everything immaculate. You can see how well looked after he is. Then Sidney Fitzherbert and Noel's dad, Lewis Jackson, come to an agreement. The Jacksons will adopt the baby, the Fitzherberts will make regular payments to cover its upkeep and education, but nothing of this will be made public. So the Jacksons' neighbors in New Plymouth now see Noel pushing a pram around the streets with an eighteen-month child that is supposed to have been born to Eva [Noel's mother, who is past child-bearing age]! Naturally, everyone jumps to the conclusion that Noel is the mother, though the finger of local suspicion also falls on Eileen [Noel's sister]. I think this is why Eileen bought a one-way ticket to the U.S. and left home. Eva died not long afterward. Even Noel got out as soon as she could, leaving the baby to be raised by who?—our grandfather and your father. She never let giving away her baby ruin her life, though it was probably always a stone in her gut. Anna [Noel's elder daughter from her first marriage] told me that Noel made the only reference to her true relationship with Harold on her deathbed. 'Poor Harold,' she said. 'The trouble with Harold is that his mother gave him away.'"

Helen was convinced that this early abandonment and lack of mothering explained why Harold had been unable to relate to his own children. She recalled being dragged or driven around the city with him. Sitting for hours in his car while he talked to a customer about a radio repair or, more likely, chewed the fat or talked stock cars. "Once," she said, "I deliberately wet my pants to get noticed. Not that it worked, not that it made any difference to him."

I was taken aback by Helen's remarks, for during my childhood visits to New Plymouth I had also gone the rounds of the New Plymouth shops with Harold, sitting for long periods in one of his old Riley, Wolseley, or Citroën cars, the sun making the seats too hot to sit on, and the interior filling with a smell of varnished wood, leather upholstery, solder, and my uncle's sweat. I considered it part of the adventure, this idiosyncratic way in which my uncle conducted his business. Even when I learned that he had alienated yet another business partner or gone bankrupt, I did not think to blame him, but only the small-minded world that failed to appreciate his soft-spoken manner, his sensitivity, his tall stories.

"How do you feel," I asked Helen, "about your aunt being your grandmother?"

"Doesn't bother me, doesn't make any difference."

Not long after my conversation with Helen, I consulted the government registry of births, deaths, and marriages. Harold's biological father was indeed Sidney Wyndam Fitzherbert, but his birth mother was Madeleine Young, who lived only five hundred meters from the Cargen Private Hotel in Eden Crescent where Sidney lived in 1918.

I also dug out some old photographs of the four siblings, Harold, Eileen, Noel, and my father D'arcy.

Eileen (sunglasses in hand) is on a return visit to New Zealand. She migrated to the U.S. at the age of twenty-one. Having trained as a dental technician, she worked in dentistry in California before marrying and settling in Los Gatos, where she became an American citizen. Eileen had two

PLATE 10. MICHAEL JACKSON

grown-up sons, and this is her first trip home in twenty-five years. She has linked arms with Harold and Noel, pulling them close, drawing them together. Noel seems to have mixed feelings about the camera and the occasion. She rests her hand in the crook of D'arcy's arm, as though she feels more secure with him. D'arcy's left arm juts out at an angle, as though offering support to an invisible other in the space beside him. Look closely and you will notice that everyone's hands are closed or clenched.

It is the summer of 1956, the lawn close-mown and rock hard. Harold, the youngest sibling, is thirty-eight. D'arcy is forty-five, Eileen fifty-three, and Noel, the first-born, is fifty-four. I am the family photographer. My camera is an Agfa Record that I purchased the year before with money earned working for a milk deliveryman and a local greengrocer. But at age sixteen I have yet to learn that nothing in life is as it appears. I am focused on reading my Weston light meter, holding it close to the faces of my subjects, calculating the correct shutter speed and aperture. I want everyone to smile for the dickey bird.

I look at another photo—of Harold and Betty. Only now do I see how awkward they are together. They stand side by side, dutiful and stiff; Harold's hands are behind his back, and he is scowling. Betty's arms are folded, and her smile, I suspect, is for me alone, or simply the brave face she puts on, hiding her unhappiness. She is wearing her English Horrocks frock and her Queen Mother shoes—her outfit for a special occasion.

While it is evident from Harold's physical appearance that he is a Jackson in name only, his sense of being marginal is not entirely explained by this, nor by his adoption or the circumstances of his upbringing. Perhaps no narrative can do justice to the complexity and mystery of a life. As Helen put it, "You never know what you're in for. If you knew what you were getting yourself in for you'd probably never do it."

Harold remained obsessed by his origins for as long as he lived, haunted by the rumor that his sister was his mother and by the way his adoptive parents had treated him as second best, as a disappointment, and passed him over in their last will and testament. Perhaps he also felt guilty about the love he had withheld from his own family.

Although our lives may not transcend our origins, we seem to need to believe that this is possible, as in the myth of Maui who sought to return to the womb and be born again. But is the past ever really preserved in the present, or is it simply an idea we invoke—the primordial, the primary, or the prior—in order to authorize what we decide in the here and now? Looking at my photographs, taken half a century ago, I realize how difficult it is to retrieve the lived experience we like to believe that film can capture. I am reminded of the discomfiture that Roland Barthes speaks about in *Camera Lucida*, "torn between two languages, one expressive, the other critical." While photography promises the possibility of recording life as lived, it proves to be simply another mode of reduction in which the plenitude of experience is rendered as *nature morte*. When we photograph a place or person, or render an account of an event in writing, we inadvertently create a screen that will prevent us ever recovering what Walter Benjamin calls "the unique existence" or "aura" of the original.

Ironically, therefore, our attempts to preserve "moments of being" or "traces of the first" hasten their loss. Even with photos and documents, details of our lives get weeded out or blurred, and the ambience of mood and emotion that made an event memorable is dulled. There is no such thing as perfect recall. And because we are social creatures, continually engaging with new people and new situations, we must jettison what is no longer relevant, revising our versions of the past to create a space for the present. It is not only our faltering steps or forgetfulness that make it difficult to return to where we have been; our brains draw a curtain on the past in order to prepare us for the road ahead. I have—or think I have—a vivid memory of reading Thomas Wolfe's novels when I was nineteen and sharing with my mother my passion for Wolfe's writing. But it was Thomas Wolfe who famously said, "You can't go home again. . . . You can't go back to your family, back home to your childhood, back home to romantic love, back home to a young man's dreams of glory and of fame." And it was Thomas Wolfe who, at the end of his life, turned this lamentable truth into a credo. "To lose the earth you know, for greater knowing; to lose the life you have, for greater life; to leave the friends you loved, for greater loving; to find a land more kind than home, more large than earth—Whereon the pillars of this earth are founded, toward which the conscience of the world is tending—the wind is rising, and the rivers flow."

Burned Places

North of Wanganui, a cloudburst made it difficult for me to see the road ahead, so I pulled over and waited for the squall to pass. As rain lashed and smeared the windows, I scribbled notes, asking myself why we should cleave to the view that the prior is necessarily primary. Why do we pay lip service to the seriality of the seven ages of man, the succession of BC and AD or cause and effect, attributing to the first term a generative or greater power? Why is it so difficult for us to make the present the *axis mundi,* the measure of all things, the place where past and future come into being, the sole reality we recognize?

My metaphysical ruminations were brought to a close by the rain easing and pale sunlight suddenly illuminating the drenched hills.

Descending the road into Patea, I glimpsed the sea. Sand hills around the river mouth. The derelict buildings of the old freezing works.

Seventy-five years ago, a thousand workers were employed here during the peak season, but when the meat processing industry collapsed in the early 1980s, the works were closed. All that remained were rain-stained concrete wharves along the river, splintered timber, broken windows, rust and decay. The site wasn't just ugly; it was toxic—riddled with asbestos cladding and insulation, heavy metals, chemicals, boiler ash dumps, and rusting fuel storage tanks. It was also a hangout for locals with nowhere to go and nothing much to do. Earlier in the year, arsonists had tried to destroy the buildings, perhaps in the hope that they would magically reverse the misfortunes that had befallen the town—a declining population, falling property values, and high unemployment.

Among the men who worked summers at the Patea Freezing Works in the 1940s was the writer Ronald Hugh Morrieson. Morrieson's biographer, Julia Millen, writes that "he and a friend Bill Webb would go across the bridge over the Patea River to the 'Eagle,' as the men called the network of roads and ramps and loading bays, workers' huts, storage sheds, stockyards, the wharf, cranes, freight wagons, and the great slaughterhouse itself with its towering chimney. Morrieson worked from four in the morning until midnight, trudging up and down slippery stairs from one of the freezing chambers to the cavernous cool rooms, standing all day with sacking known as 'sneakers' wrapped around his boots on cold wet concrete, stacking carcasses, tossing cartons of export meat on to conveyor belts, heaving and shoving the still-twitching carcasses along the chain."

In my own hometown forty miles away, and still a child, I would lie awake at night hearing the pitiful baying of bobby calves in packed cattle trucks or railway wagons, awaiting the last day of their lives, so that when I later learned that Morrieson felt revolted by hearing and watching lambs and calves going to their deaths I felt an affinity for him and, not for the first time, wondered whether I could ever settle in my hometown, drawing on my familiarity with its dark side to write fiction, rather than seek out remote villages on the other side of the world. Conservative and respectable though these Taranaki towns seemed, Morrieson knew, exploited, and celebrated their gothic underside—the lonely and unloved; the sly grog sellers, whores, bookies, drunks, crooks, delinquents, idiots, and perverts who haunted their margins. In doing so, he left a bitter legacy. Like Rabelais, Morrieson took a perverse delight in turning the world upside down, revealing its underbelly, mocking its pretensions. In medieval Europe, such antinomian excess could be tolerated on ritually prescribed occasions, but not every day. The same was true of Hawera where, in 1946, the local Savage Club staged a revue called "Topsy Turvey," in which Pākehā men performed Māori haka and "classique ballets." As opportunities for "a bit of hoo-ha," these role reversals were hardly invitations to cross-dressing, let alone racial integration, for by demonstrating the impossibility of men passing for women or Māori becoming Pākehā, they paradoxically served to entrench the very social divisions they momentarily and ineptly transgressed.

In the 1940s and 1950s, Māori lived in the small settlement of Taiporohenui on the outskirts of town. A few found employment in Hawera, but social and sporting contacts with Pākehā were rare. Undoubtedly, many knew of the destruction of the great meetinghouse, Taiporohenui, by British forces under the command of Major-General Trevor Chute in January 1866, and the occupation of the settlement by colonial troops in pursuit of the guerrilla fighter Titokowaru. And all nursed grievances over nineteenth-century land seizures, government duplicity, unequal opportunity, and racial prejudice. Many Pākehā, on the other hand, saw Māori in the same light as they saw Rodney Hugh Morrieson, or Patea saw its derelict freezing works—problems they prayed would quickly go away. In the postwar years, the steps of Hawera's National Bank, where Māori shoppers waited for their bus, were known as the Taiporohenui Grandstand. Pākehā complained about the Māori who ate fish and chips and drank soft drinks on the steps of the bank or loitered there after leaving the pub across the road. In his historical ethnography of Hawera, Allan Thomas cites one local who averred that "business people proceeding to transact business at the Bank have considerable difficulty in gaining access to the premises. The whole set-up presents an eyesore."

Morrieson died in 1972 at the age of fifty in the house in which he was born, depressed and destroyed by years of alcohol abuse and heart disease. His home became an aluminum factory. Twenty years later, 1 Regent Street came up for resale. When a multinational fast food chain showed an interest in the site, a fiery debate began over whether Morrieson's home should be preserved as a literary museum or demolished. Predictably, conservative voices prevailed, citing Morrieson's spiteful vision and dissolute life and arguing that the town's pastoral image had to be restored. Besides, if Hawera did not get the Kentucky Fried Chicken franchise, Patea would.

As I made my way along the main street I noticed many shop fronts boarded up, state houses going to rack and ruin, Māori kids in hoodies slouching to a local dairy that advertised lotto tickets and ice cream. *Te Hawera* means burned place in Māori. The Titahi of Whareroa insulted a Ngāti Okahu person of rank, who then sought *utu*. The avenging taua carried bundles of dried fern by night to the Titahi encampment. After killing the sentinels, they placed fern bundles around the enemy's sleeping house and set it on fire. Is it possible that such ancient associations still infiltrate the thoughts of the living, accounting for the fire that destroyed what remained of the Patea Freezing Works, not to mention the blaze at 1 Regent Street that Morrieson used in *The Scarecrow*, published in 1963, not long before I left New Zealand for the first time?

Revenant

Driving north, I was amazed at how quickly the Taranaki towns sped past, as though I was stationary and the landscape was fast-forwarding like a film. When I was a boy, time dragged. The bus from Inglewood to New Plymouth seemed to take the best part of a day to make its ten-mile journey. The daily commute to my high school in Stratford, with its detours and frequent stops, was a depressing prelude to the ordeal of getting through the day. My life itself was lived as a long wait for some indefinable transfiguration.

I spent fifteen years in Inglewood, longer than I have resided anywhere else in my life. Inglewood was the locus of my first memories, my first lessons in life, my first love. But it was the last place I would have chosen to spend my formative years had it been possible to preordain such matters. Nevertheless, the closer I came to my hometown, the more aware I became that one's sense of belonging to a place (or a person) is less the outcome of some natural compatibility than of having weathered the ups and downs of life there over many years. The resulting sense of fateful familiarity transcends considerations as to whether or not the relationship is fulfilling or even deeply felt. Milk may be a potent symbol of the primary bond, but milk is not some essence that makes this bond inevitable, or even viable. The bond is the breast, the landscape of the maternal body, the place that nurtures one's first dreams and one's earliest nightmares.

In a poem to another of Taranaki's sons, I once wrote that we shared "the breast-fed Taranaki sky," invoking the image of the mountain as a nurturing source. However, the place itself did not shape us, but rather our struggles in that place—to find ourselves, to give birth to what lay dormant within us. Were I to write that poem to Toss Woollaston today, it would be the quiescent volcano I invoked, not the milk of human kindness.

The closer I came to Inglewood, the sharper these connotations became. At the corner of Dudley Road, I stopped the car. During my boyhood, this was the local golf club. Players had to share the fairways with sheep, and the natural hazards were not sand traps and trees but a stony river, drainage ditches, barberry hedges, and sheep shit. There was now no trace of the clubhouse or the course, something that would not have surprised or bothered me were it not for a promise I had made myself four months earlier to play the same nine holes my father played year in and year out without significantly decreasing his handicap and, as far as I could tell, without finding much fulfillment in the game. Indeed, it may have been his losing struggle, not only to play well but to gain the respect of his peers, that kept me from taking up golf until the summer of 2008. I simply could not forget or forgive the local burghers who would rib my father for his dearth of scatological stories or his refusal to compromise his teetotalism. But when my seventeen-year-old son, Joshua, developed a passion for golf and encouraged me to play with him, I overcame my resistance.

Through dedicated practice, Joshua quickly outstripped me in skill and confidence. However, the pleasure of his company compensated for my ineptitude until, one afternoon, my game fell apart so badly that I did not play the final two holes, not wanting to drive the ball out of bounds again, duff another iron, or miss another easy putt. I felt sick in the stomach, enervated and furious at myself that I lacked even the skill to make contact with the ball, and I nursed this wounded feeling for the rest of the day. Firstness, I realized, was often synonymous with winning. To come first implies superiority. By contrast, secondness suggests failure. Being the runner-up.

The night after my aborted golf game, I could not sleep for replaying the round in my mind, retracing my steps, rehearsing every botched shot. "That's the bad part about golf, that memory bank," Johnny Miller observed as Retief Goosen prepared to hit a putt similar to one he had missed a few years before, almost losing the U.S. Open as a result. "If he loses he'll think about this one all night." This is what happened to me. It was as if some demon had taken over my mind, forcing me to revisit the scene of my failure as an infernal punishment. This unhappy experience bore such a resemblance to trauma that I wondered how I might shift the demon from my back, forget my bad round, and move on. At the same time, I was strongly reminded of how people often perform spontaneous postmortems on lost games and missed opportunities, as if their mistakes can be made good in memory. Then it occurred to me: why not, during my planned trip to New Zealand, play a round, however poorly, on the old Inglewood golf course? I would be with my father. In a sense I would become him. My limitations would affirm our kinship. And in retracing his steps over that accursed ground, my understanding of his struggles would be revived; by entering fully into the tribulations of another, I would, in effect, transcend my own.

* * *

The idea is as old as the hills: if memory can return us so vividly to the past, surely it is but a short step to actually travel backward in time. That we seldom pursue this idea with much seriousness is not because it is unrealistic, but because art provides the vehicle with which we cross this bridge from where we are to where we would like to be. Through music, stories, and ritual acts we replay events that have befallen us, reshaping them in a different image. In these simulations of what occurred some time ago, we make coherent that which was chaotic, make straight that which was crooked, and make right that which was wrong. The course of life, like true love, never runs smooth, but art makes it appear otherwise. In art we allow ourselves the last word on events that left us speechless. By interpreting events that baffled us, we give the impression that we understand the workings of the world. In reality, we are often at the mercy of events, ignorant of their import. But in the stories we tell we redeem ourselves, wise after the event, and appear to be the authors of our own lives.

* * *

In Inglewood, I left my car in a back street and wandered through the town like a revenant, confronting a ten-thousand-piece jigsaw puzzle with so many pieces missing that you could not be sure what the puzzle depicted. The old brick and stone post office had disappeared without a trace, the municipal chambers had been transformed into a library where I was pleased to see every section labeled in both English and Māori and many shelves devoted to Māori language readers. In a town that Māori had long avoided, there was now a marae.

Though I knew no one now, I nonetheless amused myself with the thought that if I stayed a few days I would encounter avatars of the individuals that inhabited my childhood world. And it was as a child that I retraced my steps along familiar streets, coming at last to the house where I grew up.

I am wearing sandals. The clay track bears traces of a hopscotch game. In the palm of my hand I can feel the sand-filled tobacco tin that I will throw into the numbered squares. It lands with a thud and skids on the clay. It is quarter past six in the evening, and Mr. Eva is lurching along the footpath, blind drunk and mouthing curses at the hedge. I cross the street to Ethel Hastie's house, my hand fumbling with the loop of number eight wire that holds her gate shut. The path along the sunless side of her house is covered with moss. At her back door I stand on the rumpled superphosphate sack that serves as a doormat. Mrs. Hastie emerges like a figure in a photographic darkroom, asking if I have come for eggs. From the doorway, I watch as she selects the eggs from a large ceramic bowl and places them in a brown paper bag. The shelves of her pantry are filled with preserved fruit in Agee jars. Marmalade simmers in a large pan on her coal range.

My errand done, I return to the street, now passing the Fabishes'cottage. The garden is filled with chrysanthemums that Mrs. Fabish will distribute among her Catholic neighbors on All-Soul's Eve. Her husband Mate is in his sixties yet as strong as an ox. Twice a year he trims our gnarled and unruly holly hedge with a long-handled slasher while I rake up the leaves and cart them in a wheelbarrow to my father's compost bin. A ramshackle and unpainted garage, housing an ancient Oldsmobile, separates the Fabishes' from the Potrozes' cottage where my childhood self hesitates, wondering if Eddie is home and whether he will allow me to read the latest issues of his American comics (which my mother prefers me not to read, arguing that English comics are more "wholesome"). With somnambulant slowness I move past the Barrys' house, a bungalow that for all its modesty is superior to the rundown cottages of the council workers and war widows, with their narrow hallways running from front to back, floorboards covered with broken linoleum, dingy bedrooms lined with sagging scrim and peeling wallpaper. Mr. Barry owns a shoe shop in town. He returns home for lunch every day, striding down the middle of the street, bristling with optimism and whistling the tune of "You Are My Sunshine."

> You are my sunshine,
> My only sunshine.
> You make me happy
> When skies are gray.
> You'll never know, dear,
> How much I love you;
> Please don't take my sunshine away.

As a child you see only appearances. You are unaware that Mr. Eva lost his wife to cancer and is trying to drown his sorrows. You do not connect Mrs. Hastie with Gordon Hastie, the idiot boy who lives with his slatternly mother in a former butcher shop and pushes a battered pram up and down Rata Street all day. Years will pass before you are told that Gordon was not an idiot at all; belatedly, he completed his schooling and went on to train as a teacher. Nor do you know that Eddie Potroz's father will abandon his mother, or that Eddie will never succeed in tracking him down. And how could you possibly know that Mr. Barry is singing of unrequited love?

> You told me once, dear,
> You really loved me
> And no one else could come between,
> But now you've left me
> And love another;
> You have shattered all my dreams.

What shattered dreams drove Stanley Reid Amies Wood to take refuge in Inglewood is anybody's guess. He lived behind barred windows and locked doors in a brick building opposite the school playgrounds, venturing forth only to borrow books from the local library or buy bread and meat. I would often pass him in the street, wary of his military bearing and swagger stick. Whatever the weather, he wore khaki shorts, a blue shirt, red necktie, sandshoes, and black stockings pulled over his knees. We knew him as Dicky Wood, and were taught to give him a wide berth. When he died in 1962, aged eighty-three, he left a curious inheritance that included a life interest in his estate to a young woman with whom he had been infatuated for several years. His will also specified that, on her death, money from his estate should be given to the Church of England for the purchase of carillon bells on which the girl's name would be engraved. Investigations showed that Rae Lowe, née Lamb, was only one in a string of goddess wives that Dicky Woods had married in his imagination, depositing gifts at their homes and sending them endearing letters. Little of his past came to light except that he was born in England, was estranged from his English kin, had worked in Burma for the telegraphic service until 1920, when he came to New Zealand. He also had considerable investments in the London stock market.

Sometimes we tell stories to make good the gaps in our knowledge, to put flesh on the bare bones that remain at the end of a life. Sometimes we tell stories to repair what was broken, to rectify the mistakes we made. Sometimes, however, we tell stories in order to marvel at the discontinuities and anachronisms that fill our lives—the gap between our lives as children and as adults, the private truths hidden behind public dramas, the traumatic events whose shadows are still discernible, in certain light, in our otherwise green and pleasant land.

Te Āti Awa

I stayed that night in a local motel, improbably called White Eagle, and left early next morning with the intention of driving to Waitara via back roads I thought I knew by heart. When I was in my teens, scarcely a weekend passed that I did not cycle into the hills, pushing myself to the limit in an effort to break out of the wilderness in which I felt confined. The asphalt was covered with red lichen. Wild hydrangeas and tree ferns sprouted from roadside embankments. And when I stopped to catch my breath, I would look back at Mount Taranaki, called Egmont at that time, as if it was the hub of a wheel from which I was finally spinning away.

At Pukerangiora Historic Reserve, punga, tī, tawa, and rangiora now grew in the space that had been covered, when I biked here as a boy, by bracken fern or overshadowed by pines that creaked in the wind and filled the collapsed fosses with broken branches, pine straw, and cones. But the shriek of a blackbird and the ghostly wind in the trees were disturbingly the same, as was the vertigo I felt standing at the cliff's edge, looking down at the Waitara River 330 feet below the ancient pā (fortified settlement). Though a picnic table offered support, nothing could calm my troubled thoughts of what transpired here in 1831, less than a generation after first contact between Māori and Pākehā in the far north.

By the early 1820s, Northland Māori had diversified their agriculture to include pig breeding, as well as growing imported crops such as turnips, parsnips, carrots, cabbages, and peas, and by 1830 most chiefs had Europeans living among them, mediating trade relations with the outside world. Profits from the sale of flax and other produce were used to acquire muskets, gunpowder, and iron tools. But in settling old scores, capturing slaves to grow flax, and collecting tattooed heads to trade with itinerant Europeans, the northerners wreaked havoc wherever they went. Throughout the 1820s and 1830s, musket warfare disrupted the fragile balance of power among iwi, and thousands of displaced people sought refuge in mountainous areas further south, safety in new alliances, and revenge for remembered wrongs. At the same time, epidemic illness decimated Māori. Not only was the tapu system of controlling food production and conserving resources undermined by the market economy, pigs ravaged gardens, and villagers often starved or worked themselves to exhaustion in an effort to produce goods for Europeans.

All these tragic repercussions were felt in Taranaki well before the arrival of the first Pākehā settlers.

In 1821, a war party (taua) of Waikato and Ngāti Maniapoto fell fowl of Te Āti Awa in northern Taranaki. Following this skirmish, many of the invaders took refuge at Pukerangiora pā, only to be besieged by Te Āti Awa, who erected a palisade around the southern end of the pā, penning the enemy in what became known as Raihe Poaka—the Pig Sty. When word of this degradation reached the Waikato chief Potatau Te Wherowhero, he led a taua south for revenge, but was defeated by Te Āti Awa and Ngāti Toa under Te Rauparaha at the northern Taranaki pā of Te Motunui, where Potatau lost several hundred men.

Ten years later, Potatau Te Wherowhero returned to Taranaki with a vengeance. After a surprise night attack on Pohokura pā on the north bank of the Urenui River, hundreds of Te Āti Awa fled to the overcrowded fighting *pā* at Pukerangiora. In their panic, none thought to gather the valuable food crops—maize, potatoes, kumara, taro, melons, pumpkins—from gardens on the river flats to the southeast. After a siege lasting three months, the morale of the starving defenders was broken, and during an attempt to evacuate the pā in broad daylight 1,200 people lost their lives, many throwing themselves from the clifftop to avoid capture. The invaders showed no mercy. Potatau himself killed 150 prisoners with his greenstone mere, Whakarewa.

I walked back to my car with an image in mind of the old earthworks thrown into relief by early morning shadows and the Waitara River catching the light—source of life, bourn of ancestral spirits, waterway to the sea.

It is all too easy to write history in European terms, as a noble battle between civilization and barbarism. Deploying such antinomies, we either see ourselves as bringing enlightenment to a primitive people or adopt the late twentieth-century view that we were tragically mistaken, and were ourselves the barbarians. In the nineteenth century, we wanted indigenous people to repent their savage and sinful customs by converting to our way of life; a hundred years later, it is our arrogance and greed that we must atone for. But colonialism is never a simple relationship between oppressors and oppressed, the first unequivocally evil (because they wield greater power), the second heroically good (since victims are always seen as virtuous). Between the abstract poles of dominance and subordination lies a gray zone where power finds expression as coercion or persuasion, and those without power collaborate or resist (violently or passively). The history of relations between Māori and Pākehā is replete with figures that both exemplify these strategies and blur the line between them.

But there may be little profit in judging who was right and who was wrong, since we are never the sole authors of our actions, and whatever we do—whether virtuous or vicious—will have ramifications we cannot foresee. The simple fact, Hannah Arendt observes, is that—practically or intellectually—we can grasp neither the manifold influences that bear upon us, nor the fateful implications of what we do. This is not to reduce human existence to contingency, for our lives would be unthinkable without at least the ideas of agency and design. Arendt wants to emphasize that human action always involves more than a singular subject; it occurs within fields of interaction that she calls the "subjective in-between." Accordingly, whatever anyone does or says is immediately outstripped by what others do or say in return. Every action calls out a reaction that "strikes out on its own and affects others." Obvious ethical questions are entailed by this view. If one can never know exactly the extent to which one's actions make a difference, or the extent to which one is responsible for what one does, it becomes difficult to decide, for example, where precisely to lay blame or praise.

While it may be impossible to understand every antecedent cause or contingent factor that bears upon our actions, Arendt does not take the view that we are thereby in thrall to the past. We may, through forgiveness, find release from the consequences of our past actions or the effect of the actions of others upon us. Through the promise we make to ourselves and others, we may find redemption from "the chaotic uncertainty of the future." These strategies, she says, reflect the fact of "natality"—the power of action to bring the new into being.

Forgiveness and the promise, like storytelling and redressive ritual, offer the perennial possibility of redemption, suggesting that we are responsible for our actions and can change our course and put the past behind us. However, Hannah Arendt avoids the question of whether such strategies are merely magical means of transforming our perception of the world or real means of changing the way things are. Perhaps this question is beside the point for, in Aotearoa New Zealand, we are obliged to continue addressing Māori grievances, recognizing indigenous rights to resources, and compensating iwi for confiscated land, lost mana, and stolen cultural property, even if this fails in the long term to create the bicultural society many of us see as our best possible future. We therefore struggle to live as creatively as we can with the destructive reality of our history, focusing on what is conducive to life rather than death.

Such a view finds compelling expression in Māori thought. Life is a constant struggle between progression and regression. In this tension between the processes of *tupu* (unfolding, growing, strengthening) and *mate* (weakening, dwindling, dying), an individual or a kin group will seek whatever will augment rather than diminish its being. Sometimes this will demand being welcoming and open to the outside world; sometimes it will demand closure and opposition. Hence the saying "Ko Tu ki te awatea, ko Tahu ki te po" ("Tu in the daytime, Tahu in the evening"). Tu is the god of war and his spirit Mauri Tu governs the space in front of a meeting house where visitors are met with aggressive displays; *tahu* (to light) symbolizes the "milder and quieter reception within the lighted house at night."

What matters, however, is life—life that produces life. As my friend Te Pakaka Tawhai put it, "ancient explanations and ancestral wisdom (*kōrero tahito*) are invaluable, not because they hold the key to understanding every epoch or every existential quandary that human beings face, but because they are flexible and adaptable, able to accommodate the capacity of the narrator to render them more relevant to the issues of the day."

We might agree with William Faulkner when he writes that the past is never dead, it is not even past, but it is surely *what we do with the past* in creating a just society here and now that is the burning issue. Writes Judith Binney, "For Māori, the past is seen as that which lies before one, *nga ra o mua* (the days in front)."

* * *

In Waitara, I was looking for a shop that sold pens and notebooks. Two Māori men in the main street, whose Taranaki accents were so pronounced I had difficulty understanding them, directed me to the New World Supermarket.

After buying what I needed, together with some fruit and muesli bars, I headed toward the bridge. Incredibly, many of the street names still honored men who played major roles in the alienation of Te Āti Awa land, including the chief crown purchasing agent Donald McLean, Land Purchase Commissioner Robert Parris, Governor Thomas Gore Browne, and military officers Charles Emilius Gold and Peter Cracroft. Indeed, I would later read, in submissions to the Waitangi Tribunal at Waitara, of how deeply offensive these names were to local Māori whose own leaders remained uncelebrated and whose grievances were still unresolved.

In 1860, the spurious and self-serving arguments for the alienation of Māori land assumed that it was lawful to confiscate the land of hostile tribes, including the land of those that gave them moral support; that it was reasonable to seize land and property to defray the costs of the war; that many Māori had signed away their land; that Māori had never made full use of the land; that Māori society was anarchic; that, in the case of Te Āti Awa, rights to the land had been lost when they migrated south to escape the predations of northern invaders.

In 1848, the Te Āti Awa chief, Wiremu Kingi, returned from exile at Waikanae. Almost six hundred men, women, and children accompanied him, some driving stock along the coast, some traveling on horseback, some in canoes. Governor George Gray had proposed preventing the migration, destroying the canoes, and persuading Kingi to give up his claims to land south of the Waitara River. But Kingi was resolute. "I will not agree to our bedroom being sold (I mean Waitara here), for this bed belongs to all of us; and do not you be in haste to give the money. If you give the money secretly, you will get no land for it. You may insist, but I will never agree to it. . . . All I have to say to you, O Governor, is that none of this land will be given to you, never, never, till I die."

Though lacking the authority to do so, some Māori did sell—for mercenary gain, to curry favor with the government, to redeem lost status— allowing the government to claim, in 1859, nearly all Te Āti Awa land south of the Waitara River. Consultation with tribal authorities like Wiremu Kingi or respect for Māori customary law were simply not in the Pākehā interest.

On the eve of the declaration of martial law in February 1860, Wiremu Kingi sought a peaceful resolution to the conflict. "Friend, Colonel Murray, salutation to you in the love of our Lord Jesus Christ. You say that we have been found guilty of rebellion against the Queen, but we consider we have not, because the Governor has said he will not entertain offers of land which are disputed. The Governor has also said that it is not right for one man to sell the land to the Europeans, but that all the people should consent. You are now disregarding the good law of the Governor, and adopting a bad law. This is my word to you. I have no desire for evil but, on the contrary, have great love for the Europeans and the Māori. Listen: my love is this, that you and Parris put a stop to your proceedings, that your love for the Europeans and the Māori may be true. I have heard that you are coming to Waitara with soldiers, and therefore I know that you are angry with me. Is this your love, to bring soldiers to Waitara? This is not love, it is anger. I do not wish for anger; all that I want is the land. All the Governors and the

Europeans have heard my word, which is that I will hold the land. That is all. Write to me. Peace be with you."

The European declaration of martial law effectively paved the way for a military assault against Te Āti Awa. In 1863, the army, now vastly outnumbering Māori and using heavy artillery, adopted a scorched earth policy, attacking undefended villages, destroying stores, stock, and crops, laying waste to buildings and cultivations, driving people from their land. "As the troops advanced, the Government built an expanding line of redoubts, behind which settlers built homes and developed farms. The effect was a creeping confiscation of almost a million acres of land, with little distinction between the land of loyal or rebel Māori owners."

It is not difficult to imagine the demoralization and panic of Māori, displaced from ancestral lands, their livelihoods destroyed. But I find it harder to come to terms with the self-righteousness and loathing that many of the destroyers felt. Consider the comments of Richard Brown, a New Plymouth merchant and land agent and captain of a Native contingent, jotted down after a raid on Warea, a Māori settlement that had prospered by supplying New Plymouth with potatoes, pig meat, and flour, but whose fighting men had joined Wiremu Kingi in defense of Waitara. "I hitch up my horse and pass to the front. The nigger's [sic] have taken to the scent on the other side of the river, and it is deemed prudent to follow them. Move on with Captn. Seymour to the mill the door of which he coolly kicks open, we enter and find it unoccupied but 3 sacks of wheat in it and a barrel of tar. Up comes the party and smash go the cog's and every breakable portion of the machinery. . . . Several sacks of wheat and 60 sacks of oats found in one of the houses are claimed by Mr Parris but doomed by the chief [Colonel Gold] to destruction and scattered about under the impression the sea is too rough to allow for their shipment. Orders are passed to pull down the houses, demolish the pā and destroy everything destroyable." It is not simply Brown's mindless violence that I find disturbing. Nor am I surprised by the evidence of plunder as a motive for sacking a defenseless town, for Māori had been successful, from the earliest years of contact, in transforming their economy along European lines. What troubles me is the depth of Pākehā ignorance of Māori, and the fear born of that ignorance, if not of an unacknowledged guilt—that Pākehā had no right to be in that place, that they were common thieves and trespassers, and that the place would overwhelm them and exact on them and their children a crippling tithe.

At Owae marae, overlooking the Waitara River and the lost lands, I paid my respects to Wiremu Kingi Te Rangitaake and Sir Maui Pomare. I had come here as a boy, photographed the statue of Sir Maui, and meditated on a history whose moral complexity I was then struggling to understand. Pomare's Sicilian marble statue was unveiled in June 1936 at the same hui that inaugurated the carved house Te Ikaroa a Maui. The tekoteko figure atop the painted bargeboards is Maui-tikitiki-a-Taranga, the trickster hero who fished up the North Island from the sea. Below him is the stylized head of Sir Maui, who pushed the government to set up a royal commission in 1927 to inquire into Māori grievances relating to the confiscation of Taranaki lands. Wiremu Kingi Te Rangitaake stands at the base of the pole.

Even before the end of the second Taranaki War in 1869, two prophetic Te Āti Awa leaders and close kin, Te Whiti-o-Rongomaia and Tohu Kakahi, had established a community at Parihaka and declared their intention of negotiating a peace with Pākehā based on the principal of coexistence. Europeans could remain on the land they now occupied, but there were to be no further encroachments on Māori land and no freehold titles, since chieftancy (*tino rangatiratanga*) of the land remained with the people of the land (*tangata whenua*) and was inalienable. In 1878, despite Māori petitions and protests, the government began surveying Central Taranaki, determined to open it up to European settlers. Te Whiti and Tohu, now leaders of the largest and most prosperous Māori settlement in New Zealand, led a campaign of passive resistance—fencing and plowing occupied farmland, pulling up survey pegs, and escorting surveyors from the land still under their control. Though hundreds of these plowmen and fencers were arrested and imprisoned, others took their place. Settlers feared that the resistance campaign was a prelude to renewed armed conflict, and under pressure from Native Minister John Bryce, whose hatred of Māori was no secret, the government ordered Parihaka to be shut down. At first light on 5 November 1881, sixteen hundred troops stormed the town, only to be met by two hundred skipping and singing children offering them bread. Maui Pomare was one of these children. He was five at the time, and lost his big toe after a trooper's horse stamped on it. The soldiers then rushed the singing children and seated women, calling them bloody black niggers and threatening to cut off their heads. Te Whiti and Tohu were arrested and jailed for sixteen months. Sixteen hundred Parihaka inhabitants were expelled and dispersed throughout Taranaki without food or shelter, and the remaining six hundred were issued with government passes to control their movement.

One hundred and fifteen years after the destruction of Parihaka, the Waitangi Tribunal noted that "it cannot be assumed that grievance dissipates with time. Witness after witness described the numerous respects in which they, in their view, have been marginalized as a people and how the burden of the war is still with them and their dispossession has preoccupied their thinking. When a grievance of this magnitude is left unaddressed, it compounds with time and expands, as do generations, in geometric progression."

There is a tragic irreversibility about colonial violence. While one welcomes gestures toward reconciliation—such as the 1999 Heads of Agreement, involving a public apology for land confiscations in Taranaki, recognition of cultural associations with sacred geographical landmarks and land areas, restoration of tribal access to traditional food gathering areas, monetary compensation totaling NZ $34 million, and commercial redress for economic loss due to land confiscation—some losses cannot be made good; some wounds cannot be healed. Moreover, every slight and injustice in the present will be referred back to the past, fuel for a fire that might otherwise die. Indeed, the hold of our history over us is so great that I sometimes think that, despite the need to redress old injustices and promote a bicultural future, we are deluded in believing that we can sink our differences and unite on equal terms. And for all the rhetoric of reconciliation, the apologies and payments, the status quo remains unaltered—the poor get poorer, Māori youth languish in prisons, Māori health and education statistics show little sign of improvement.

We all have our way of imagining how the weight of past generations can be borne. In his memoir, *Being Pākehā Now*, the historian Michael King argues that firstness does not confer primary rights. "The fact that one group has been here longer than others does not make its members more New Zealand than later arrivals. . . . As far as I am concerned, my own people, descendants in the main of displaced Irish, had as much moral and legal right to be here as Māori. Like the ancestors of the Māori, they came as immigrants; like Māori too, we became indigenous at the point where our focus of identity and commitment shifted to this country and away from our countries and cultures of origin." But pointing out that all New Zealanders are immigrants is not a helpful response to the claims of tangata whenua who regard the second comer as guest (*manuhiri*) or "angry friend" (*hoariri*), and it ignores the aspiration of many Māori to be Māori first and New Zealanders second. On my flight from Los Angeles, I had watched a documentary about James Cook in which the English explorer was depicted as a humanitarian, ahead of his time, whose commitment to communicating and cooperating with indigenous people proved ineffective against the expansionist interests of those who funded his voyages. But for the Ngāti Oneone of Poverty Bay, whose ancestors had been shot by Cook's men when their bellicose displays were misread as mortal threats, there was no forgiveness. In a wharenui, a descendant regaled a group of children with a narrative of the violent encounter, exhorting them never to forget it. There is, therefore, both authority and authenticity in firstness. To continually evoke an event that marked a tragic and irreversible moment in one's history or one's life is, in effect, to endow that event with such power that there can be no possibility of transcending it. But for the powerless, the invocation of firstness may be their only way of flagging their identity and finding their moorings. This is the allure of cultural fundamentalism—the notion that one shares with one's own people a unique essence that, when nurtured and shared, will fortify one against the depredations of a more numerous and more powerful other. It is absurd to argue against this trope of firstness on the grounds that it is epistemologically false when, for those who invoke it, there are few other options for laying claim to social justice or countering the sense that they have been historically reduced to the status of second-class citizens, denizens of the third world.

Can one draw strength and sustenance from one's history without being consumed by it? In Sydney, I would buy a copy of *The First Australians,* edited by Rachel Perkins and Marcia Langton. Although Rachel and Marcia recount the colonization of Australia from an Aboriginal perspective, they take great pains to contextualize both indigenous and settler worldviews and show that enlightenment is always compromised by prejudices and interests born of one's historical situation. Though no one, black or white, may have been in a position to alter the course of colonial history, everyone was free, to some extent, to resist its dehumanizing and demonizing excesses, to refuse the language of otherness that it deployed. In my novel *Rainshadow* I wrote as if I were part-Māori, a child of opposing worlds. Obliged to choose between them, I chose neither. In the real world, however, claiming to be a citizen of the world may be as unrealistic as living, like Diogenes, in a barrel. Nevertheless, I am convinced that even though racism underwrote the colonial violence whose scars we now bear as guilt or grievance, it is imperative that we deracialize our discourse about the past, ridding ourselves of the notion that any one race is intrinsically more or less human than another. Not only have those who proclaim to be autochthonous—born from the soil—been guilty of displacing others; all human beings tend to make the same kinds of arguments for strengthening their claims to the places they call their own. We would do well, therefore, to adopt the stoic dictum of Terence, that being human, nothing human is alien to us (*humani nil a me alienum puto*), which is to say that we accept the possibility that, under certain circumstances, each one of us is capable of evil as well as good, that no genealogy exists that does not include persecutors and victims, and that the price of harboring notions of ur-belonging is often the violent exclusion of those who allegedly do not belong.

From Waitara I drove through a darkening and seemingly deserted landscape, stopping only at the Te Rangi Hiroa Memorial near Urenui—a canoe prow thrusting from an overgrown hillside toward the sea. Born of an Irish father and Māori mother, Te Rangi Hiroa (Sir Peter Buck) remained attached to his roots, although his first language was English. His stepmother's mother was his tutor. She taught him his *whakapapa* (genealogy) and history. After Kapuakore's (Cloudless's) death in 1908, Te Rangi, now twenty-eight, went to her sleeping hut and found the canoe paddle the old woman had used when ferrying him across the Urenui River. The paddle remained in his possession for as long as he lived, mounted on the wall of his office at the Bernice Bishop Museum in Honolulu. "It hangs on the wall of my study as my most precious family heirloom. I have studied under learned professors in stately halls of learning. But as I look at that paddle, I know that the teacher who laid the foundation of my understanding of my own people, and the Polynesian stock to which we belong, was a dear old lady with a tattooed face in a humble hut walled with tree-fern slabs."

Looking toward the sea, which was now indistinguishable from the sky, I wondered why men like Maui Pomare and Te Rangi Hiroa had been my role models as a boy. Even though I loved my grandfather, I could never identify with the Methodist values he espoused, nor feel anything but claustrophobia for the cult of respectability to which, in deference to his wife, he paid lip service. Though my growing identification with Māori was misplaced and sentimental, it nonetheless gave me a way of protesting an ethos for which I felt no affinity, glimpsing a world in which one's humanity came first and one's particular citizenship, ethnicity, age, or gender was a secondary consideration.

Symbolic Landscape

It had been a long day. North of Mount Messenger, the landscape was emptier than I remembered—dark green hills descending to the sea in great terraces, and the horizon so low that the ocean appeared to have drained away. Not far from the Tongaporutu River mouth, I spotted a sign for a bed and breakfast. After climbing over a padlocked gate, I picked my way down a gravel driveway and knocked at the door of an unpainted house. The ocean was a stone's throw away, its torn crochet flung on the iron sand, flax bushes flayed by the wind. I could taste the spume.

No one answered my knocking. I peered through an uncurtained window into a room littered with children's toys before walking away, spooked by the isolation and the ransacking wind.

By the time I reached Mokau, dusk was falling. But I found a room in "the last motel for 75 kilometers" and had dinner at a nearby café that advertised fresh whitebait.

Mokau was "the whitebait capital of the North Island," but the inanga (*Galaxias maculatus*) I was served at the Whitebait Inn had been deep-fried in rancid oil, killing the subtle taste of the fish. I ate without appetite, the only diner in a shedlike space that was filled with tubular steel furniture, outdated fly-speckled calendars, Pepsi signs, and a rust-streaked freezer. In a brochure, I read that the Mokau estuary was one of the last viable spawning habitats for inanga. Many local pensioners supplemented their incomes by netting whitebait in the spring, and people made annual pilgrimages to their baches and jealously guarded stands along the riverbank, patiently taking their quota of the silvery galaxiids that had become scarcer every year as farms encroached on the forest, cattle trampled the riverbanks, and fertilizer polluted the streams.

"Did you enjoy your meal?" the girl asked when I paid at the counter.

"It was fine," I said, not wanting to give offense. But our brief exchange triggered memories of other encounters on the road, when I felt that people were asking for my assurance, as children sometimes do, endearingly assuming that the world is run by adults and that they are always at risk of being in the wrong. At Waitara, I had asked the checkout girl at the New World Supermarket if she knew of any motels on the road north. She was sorry, she didn't know of any, but would ask. Within a minute, three assistants were standing in front of me, racking their brains for an answer to my offhand question, and collectively apologizing for not being able to help. I was particularly touched, as I made to leave, when an older woman followed me to the door, a look of deep concern on her face.

"You be all right, de-ar?" she asked, as if I was venturing into the unknown. And because she was Māori, I wondered later if she was unconsciously expressing a sense of the historic tragedy that had unfolded along that littoral, and that the Southern Ocean had not yet erased from memory.

Not wanting to return immediately to my concrete-block motel, I went for a long walk along the estuary. The river flats were covered with rushes. Every few yards along the riverbank was a small corrugated iron shed and jetty. The gaunt inland hills were already lost to the night. Nearer the sea, I could hear waves battering the beach. The wind was filled with grit. A stench of decaying kelp filled my nostrils.

I had not planned to spend a night in Mokau. But as I trudged back to my motel, I thought it inevitable that I should return to the place where my uncle Harold sought refuge after Betty committed suicide in 1966, aged forty-seven. It was as far from New Plymouth as it was possible to go without leaving Taranaki. Here, in a ramshackle house behind the local tearooms, he muddled through the next forty-two years of his life until Alzheimers obliged him to move to a retirement home in New Plymouth. My cousin Helen described his house as a pigsty. When she helped sort through his possessions after he died, several truckloads of junk had to be carted away. When I asked Helen how her father had occupied himself at Mokau, she responded curtly: "He collected junk." In a kinder vein, my cousin Peter said Harold was a beachcomber and dog walker, a finder of objects that he thought could be repaired and one day given a new life.

"After Betty, there was no other woman in his life," Helen told me. "He kept her piano in his living room for as long as he lived at Mokau.

Everything else was rubbish. He collected useless gadgets. I don't think he had much use for people."

After showering, I lay on the counterpane of my motel bed writing up notes. The wind moaned and whined in the ill-fitting French windows as if my uncle's ghost was locked out in the cold, and I thought of his unhappy life, his doomed marriage, and his inability in find in his family the same satisfaction he found in a valve radio, an electrical device, a jet boat trip upriver, or the flotsam and jetsam blown ashore on that wild North Taranaki coast.

I stuffed paper in the cracks in the door, but the ghostly moaning continued, and I fell asleep in my clothes, the light still burning, until the small hours of the morning when I woke from a dream of kerosene tins brimful of whitebait, and a pair of hands slipping into the slithering, silver catch before making me a cupped offering.

A cold dawn light was breaking when I paid for my night's lodging and drove past the boarded-up tearooms on the main street and on to the river road that would hopefully take me to Tauwhare.

When I lived in Wellington in 1998, one of the first new friends I made was Geoff Park, a writer and research scientist with the Department of Conservation. In *Nga Uruora: The Groves of Life*, Geoff describes one of the last surviving stands of lowland forest in New Zealand. Dominated by kahikatea and teeming with native birds, Tauwhare is almost an island, the Mokau River enclosing it protectively and preserving its extraordinary biodiversity. That it had escaped the predatory expansion of European settlement in the nineteenth century and become a "Native Reserve" may have had something to do with the powerful tapu of the place—its association with the dead or with forest spirits—or sheer happenstance.

As an avid sea-kayaker, it had been only natural for Geoff to approach Tauwhare from the river. "From low on the water, the big kahikatea seem to guard the head of the estuary. Their forest is the last of its kind in the North Island, but there was a time when trees like them stood on the tidal flats of almost every river. Other than the ravaged hills and the fact that most of the bleached, stranded logs littering the river are willows, the scene is as close as you are going to get today to what was seen by the first canoe-load of people to come out of the waves and up an estuary."

I tried to walk in to Tauwhare from the road, but it was so muddy underfoot, and the forest so dense and drenched, that I soon retreated to my car.

I was about to leave Taranaki. By no stretch of the imagination had my visit been a homecoming. Rather, I had found myself looking past the accident of my being raised in the shadow of the mountain to a history of which I had known next to nothing as a boy yet which was the actual shadow under which I had grown up—the dark presence of dispossession, ignorance, and violence, a presence that still seeped into our lives, so that even my uncle Harold's fruitless search for his birth parents, his true identity, or for love seemed genealogically related to the cosmic injustice that had been done in that province years before he was born.

Though Geoff Park writes that "the relentless overwhelming" of the natural landscape by settler culture cannot be reversed, I had seen how readily mānuka, hebe, karamū, and punga reclaimed the land and how Māori had regained land rights in the nation that had marginalized and almost destroyed them. Firstness implies a tenacity that may put all successive events in the shade. It is as though there existed, like the original ecology, a natural justice that reasserts itself in the face of our feeble efforts to impose our will on a place that has, so to speak, a mind of its own.

As I drove on, I began to see that our return to the past is not always morbid; it is a means of repossessing our lives. Every morning, while shaving, my grandfather would recite Rudyard Kipling's "If." Perhaps this was his way of beginning every day as though it were the first and of perpetually redeeming the day before. Perhaps the poem took him back to the day he began his new life in New Zealand, exchanging the old country for the new in the hope that he might help build a Fabian utopia. "If you can watch the things you gave your life to, broken, / And stoop and build 'em up with worn-out tools: / If you can make one heap of all your winnings / And risk it on one turn of pitch-and-toss, /And lose, and start again at your beginnings / And never breathe a word about your loss . . ." But might not such small rituals also be, as Walter Benjamin suggests, the expatriate's attempt to inoculate himself against a nostalgia that continuously threatens to overwhelm him? Given that we can never forget our most formative years, is it true that as we approach old age, bewildered by a world that is changing too rapidly for us to keep pace, we search for the foundations beneath the rubble of what we have become, returning to our beginnings for a last loving look at a world that was once entirely ours? Perhaps, as Vincent O'Sulllivan writes:

There is a balance here
and its absence
I shall never quite bring off,

    there is a similitude
and simulacrum far back
as the guessed beginning.

There is a woman with an apple
barely bitten, she is saying,
"Welcome home."

Two Women

After reaching Hamilton, it took me a while to find an internet café where I could send an email to my wife and children. It also took me time to reorient myself to the hoardings and signs, the loud colors and cacophony of the city made even more overwhelming by the unforgiving light and the domesticated landscape. It was as though my experiences in Taranaki, including my night on the Mokau River, belonged to a remote time, more imagined than real, and that I had now entered an artificial and childlike place, constructed with a child's garishly painted building blocks.

The Korean owner assigned me a terminal under a malfunctioning fluorescent light. When I leaned back in my black vinyl chair, I hit a stroller in which a small child was licking an ice cream while her mother searched the World Wide Web. Unable to see my keyboard, I asked for another terminal nearer the door where the light was better. Then I rattled off my email, with a sketch of where I had been and what I had been doing, and a final few lines of affection for my family who, while never far from my thoughts, were in a place that seemed to bear no relationship with anywhere I had been.

This disturbing sense of separation from my real life was only increased when I left the internet café and tried to find my way to Hamilton East. Driving down broad streets where the grass was closely mown, shrubs trimmed, houses spick and span, and cars kept scrupulously clean, my old aversion to the obsessive tidiness and respectable veneer of bourgeois life suddenly made it hard to breathe, and I felt like fleeing back to Taranaki and taking the Forgotten World Highway, as I had earlier planned, into the rough-hewn back country between Tarata and Whangamomona.

In an email, Carrie had instructed me to look for a scruffy old house at the end of a driveway between two posh new houses. It was the sort of no-nonsense comment that had drawn me to her ten years ago when we were both living in Wellington.

Carrie met me at the door.

"Park your car in the driveway behind my ute," she said. "I bought it as a kind of salute to my late father. He loved his four-wheel drive." It was clear that Carrie still marched to her own drum. As she led me into the kitchen, she added, "There's the influence of the past for you!"

"You haven't changed," I said. "If anything you seem younger."

"It's just an illusion," Carrie said. "I keep fit by cycling daily around Bleakley Park, but my regime's been interrupted by a mysterious knee injury so I'm hobbling about with a cane and take industrial strength pain-killers. Go on through to the sitting room. I'll make us a pot of tea. Or do you prefer coffee?"

"Tea's fine. Herbal if you have it."

Beyond the window was the apple tree Carrie had described in one of her emails, "its white petals fluttering across the sunny lawn, exactly the same light, slightly sideways motion as snowflakes." And on the coffee table were several books relating to her work on the politics of science. David Nye's *Narratives and Spaces: Technology and the Construction of American Culture*, Bruno Latour's *Aramis, or the Love of Technology*.

Over the last few years, Carrie had given me invaluable help in my research on Māori reactions to genetic engineering. She had been working in Wellington on the controversial politics of GM—particularly the risks of using genetic technologies to control the introduced plant and animal species that threatened New Zealand's ecology and agriculture. The Australia brushtail possum, for instance, the country's most rapacious verte-brate pest, consumed thousands of metric tons of native vegetation each night, spreading tuberculosis to cattle and deer herds and costing the nation sixty million dollars annually. While some scientists were in favor of genetic technologies, several Māori submissions to the 2000 Royal Commission on Genetic Modification argued that this would constitute a dangerous and unprecedented intervention in the natural order of things. Like mixing waters from different catchments or sources, transferring genetic material across species boundaries violated *tikanga Māori* (the Māori way of doing things), disrupted the whakapapa and *mauri* (life essence) of those species, and destroyed a primordial balance between Ranginui (sky/father) and Papatūānuku (earth/mother). Underlying these anxieties was a collective memory of other violent intrusions in which Māori had lost their lands, livelihood, and sovereignty. As I wrote at the time, "Our wariness of new technologies must be seen in the light of our ambivalence toward the strange. Our attitudes toward both strangers and strange technologies will depend upon the degree to which we feel in control of them, as well as the degree to which such innovations are felt to augment rather than diminish our own sense of well-being."

As Carrie served tea, she talked about her current research on social responses to radical technological innovations. I responded by telling her of a friend in England who was mystified by the snail's pace with which human beings realize the potential of new technologies. Although computers offer us marvelous resources for independent research, enabling us to be more creative in finding knowledge relevant to twenty-first-century life, Gerard argues that in the UK, schools and curricula continue to be designed for an industrial age when pupils were gathered in a single classroom, physically separated from one another, talked at by a teacher who then required them to read from a textbook or write in a notebook.

"But there's so much comfort in the familiar, isn't there?" Carrie said.

"I don't want to prejudge conservatism as a sign of a closed mind," I said. "I think we have to understand why we sometimes feel compelled to cleave to the past, preferring the tried and true even when it has played us false." And we quickly agreed on the irony of how, after industrialization, the new urbanites began to romanticize the pastoral life that had offered them so little, railing against England's "dark satanic mills." I also told Carrie about Samuel Butler's letter in the *Christchurch Press* on 13 June 1863, inspired by his recent reading of Charles Darwin's *Origin of Species,* in which he expressed the alarming view that "we are ourselves creating our own successors" in the form of ever more sophisticated, self-regulating machines. "Day by day the machines are gaining ground upon us; day by day we are becoming more subservient to them, and the time will come when the machines will hold the real supremacy over the world."

Musing on Darwin's theory of evolution, and how easily his original ideas had been misapplied, I reminded Carrie of my fascination with the aura of firstness in human experience, whether this found expression in indigenous people claiming special rights on the basis of first settlement, adopted children yearning to reconnect with their birth parents, migrants nostalgic for a lost homeland, or the bereaved unable to get over the death of a loved one.

"When I got your last email," Carrie said, "I was halfway through Michael Ondaatje's *Divisadero*. After thinking about your thoughts on the past in the present, I picked up the Ondaatje where I'd bookmarked it the previous night. Serendipitously, it was the section called 'The person formerly known as Anna.' Here, I've left it marked to show you."

> All my life I have loved traveling at night, with a companion, each of us discussing and sharing the known and familiar behavior of the other. It's like a villanelle, this inclination of going back to events in our past, the way the villanelle's form refuses to move forward in linear development, circling instead at those familiar moments of emotion. Only the rereading counts, Nabokov said . . . For we live with those retrievals from childhood that coalesce and echo throughout our lives, the way shattered pieces of glass in a kaleidoscope reappear in new forms and are songlike in their refrains and rhymes, making up a single monologue. We live permanently in the recurrence of our own stories, whatever story we tell.

"I love the image of the villanelle," I said.

"But there's something else," Carrie said, "and that's the part we play in bringing back to life what is already behind us, and the question of what aspects of our ancestry we choose to dwell on."

Carrie told me about two close friends who habitually invoked the past in accounting for their present circumstances. "But anyone's past contains good and bad aspects," Carrie said, "and it is up to us which aspect we dwell on. My friends seem determined to zero in on the negative side of their histories, the parents who let them down, the misfortunes they suffered in early life. This then becomes a self-fulfilling prophecy, a ticket to victimhood. Yet both these people have talent and intelligence. One is musically gifted, but despite a wonderful opportunity to play in a hot little band here in Hamilton, he found—or created—reasons to dis the whole thing before he really got into it. The other is constantly in siege mode, waging some battle or another against the world. She gave up on relationships years ago after some ratbag broke her heart. This disaster, and a cold Catholic childhood, convinced her that things were stacked against her."

"Did you ever think this way?" I asked. "Did you ever see yourself as a victim?"

"I had to struggle not to," Carrie admitted. "Grievance mode can be very seductive. But I always had a classic example right in front of me of how futile and unproductive it can be. My mother saw herself in that way. Doomed to disappointment, trapped in a life so much less than what she'd wanted. Her solution was to make the most of her unhappiness, her sense of deprivation, by using it to manipulate everyone around her and constantly be the center of attention. And of course, everything was always someone else's fault."

"I remember you talking to me about this once. This sense of victimhood as a prolonged grieving. One has lost something, or it has been taken away, and you cannot have a good life unless this mysterious and absent property is returned to you. But in your own case, what made the difference, what turned things around?"

"The role models of my two grandmothers," Carrie said.

Carrie was also at pains to point out that she had been fortunate to be born in the 1950s, with the wider opportunities and experiences that feminism made possible throughout the next two decades.

"My father's mother was really feisty, really classy," Carrie said, grinning broadly. "She was part-Māori, though I doubt this ever figured in her sense of who she was. She died the same week I was born, so I never knew her face to face. But it's as though she is me. I am her in another life. I have her voice, her looks, her walk. When I was a teenager, my father and aunt were sometimes quite spooked by it. She loved stylish clothes, color, design, lots of books and pictures around her. This room we're sitting in, these book-lined walls, the photographs and flowers, it's all hers as much as mine."

"When did you first feel this identification?"

"It's always been there. Trouble is, my parents saw it in a negative light because she was a wild one. When I did things that were judged inappropriate or unladylike, they'd sigh, 'You're just like your grandmother.' And that was a put-down. But I came to see it as something entirely positive. I share her sense of music. Not polite classical music, the Mozart and Bach that my mother made me learn, but party music, dance music, good shit-kicking stuff that you can't help but beat your heels to. Remember how I've always sung and played in bands, years of doing rock gigs in rough pubs, and now having fun with the cowboy stuff here, country rock, Western swing? Every time I go out to the mike on stage my grandmother's right beside me with a big smile, getting right into it."

Carrie's parents expected their daughter to find a "nice" anaesthesiologist or lawyer, raise children, and live in an up-market villa in Epsom or Remuera. But for Carrie this mantra of bourgeois respectability rang false. "My childhood was a long wait for a chance to get away and make my own kind of reality. Biding my time, I hid in books. Years later, when I studied medieval poetry at Victoria, 'The Wanderer' was a revelation. 'Who liveth alone longeth for mercy, Maker's mercy. Though he must traverse tracts of sea, sick at heart, trouble with oars and ice-cold waters, the ways of exile—Wyrd is set fast.' It sharpened my sense that I could never conform to any kind of conventional, externally imposed code. I had to make my own way in the world, no matter how incomprehensible, bizarre, or downright unrespectable it would seem in the eyes of my family. So my mother and father were seriously disappointed when I left home at sixteen and became a rebel. Sex, drugs, and rock 'n' roll. It was the early seventies, what can I say? They didn't speak to me for many years."

"Tell me more about your grandmother."

"She was a Northland farmer's wife. This was in the twenties and thirties. A very buttoned-down era. But what a great, crazy time she had! Lots of affairs. On VJ night she danced on the bar of the biggest pub in Whangarei in her bra and knickers. That was New Zealand in those days. Wild versus respectable. Like each side of the Iron Curtain. There was no middle ground, you were either one or the other."

"What of your other grandmother?" I asked. "You said she was also an inspiration to you."

"She was even more outrageously defiant and reckless than my father's mother. She was the daughter of a Hungarian count, a cavalry officer, at the height of the Hapsburg Empire. The family owned a large estate in northeast Hungary, and she had all the ultrarefined upbringing of a young woman of her class and era. But she fell head over heels in love at the age of seventeen with a thoroughly inappropriate man much older than her, a part-Jewish gambler, the son of a shopkeeper. Parental opposition didn't daunt her, and she ran off with him, which meant complete disowning, never seeing her family again. Anyway, after some time, his debts—and we suspect also other darker events—caused him in turn to have to do a runner. With his creditors and adversaries hot on his heels, he left her with three littlies to support, fled to Hamburg and got on the first ship out of there. He thought he was on his way to America, but ended up in Napier with a party of Scandinavians bound for what became Norsewood. He got a small farm at a place called Kumeroa just east of Woodville, and a few years later she and the kids followed him out via London. The farm was not a success, just a two-room cottage, very basic, and four years and two more children later she died of pneumonia. She's buried in the old graveyard there, high on a bluff looking out over the Manawatu River. It's a lovely place, part of someone's farm now, very peaceful with wind through a pine plantation and hawks wheeling. Anyway, the resonances of her life have had a huge effect on me—the way she gave up everything, walking away from all that was expected of her, all that was predictable and comfortable, leaving her whole life and identity to follow her heart. And she did it not just once but twice!"

"I admire the way you bring your grandmothers back to life," I said, "not only in your telling but in your life choices. Somewhere, Borges writes that 'every writer creates his own precursors. His work modifies our conception of the past, as it will modify the future.' But it isn't only writers who resuscitate the past, is it? We all do, whether we know it or not."

"But the important thing is that we actively retrieve the positive," Carrie insisted, "and not get tangled up in the inevitable negatives. That we understand the point of listening to the past, to the truths that continue to sing in us and through us with our ancestors' voices, the gifts they offer us to help make our time here more rewarding. We may not be able to avoid their legacies, but we can at least take the best out of it. Rather than reiterating the hostile, mean-spirited judgments of others, or dwelling on the tragic aspects of their stories, it seems much healthier to be proud of my grandmothers, their passion and optimism, their eccentricities and sheer gutsiness. And it gives me some kind of reassurance, trying to navigate the erratic course of my own life."

* * *

It was almost noon the following day when I said goodbye to Carrie and found the road toward the Hauraki Plains. Though I was sad not to have been able to spend more time with Carrie, I was glad to leave the dank and level suburbs of Hamilton behind.

Once clear of the city, my thoughts turned to my great-grandfather, William McKeever, an Irish emigrant who fought against Māori in the Waikato and was decorated for his service and valor. Who was he to me? Does genealogy imply identity, or are we free to include or exclude at will those with whom we feel no kinship? In Carrie's view, our ancestry offers itself up to us and is, as it were, there for the taking. But the past is not like a road or mountain range, linear in the early November light. It is elusive, sinuous, and vague—a multitude of unrealized possibilities that only take shape when we conjure them, when we have a use for them in the here and now. I had been moved by Carrie's account of her two grandmothers, her wild exemplars. Carrie had reminded me that our lives are never entirely our own. They incorporate the many places we have lived, the many people we have known. Nor is this all, for we carry in our genes an unfathomable ancestry as well as traits whose origins we can never trace to a single source. Above all, however, Carrie had reminded me of the extent to which we can rearrange the furniture of our past and reorganize the figures in its landscapes, pushing some into the background, bringing others to the fore, denying some a place in our lives while honoring others as role models and allies. Just as we befriend and unfriend individuals on Facebook, so we reshuffle elements of our past to create a workable sense of self, a viable community.

But do we really choose such figures in the past as guides or guardians, or does our life come to mirror theirs more gradually, more imperceptibly, until in midlife, looking back, we imagine them as avatars of ourselves, embodying what we have become? Given such a narrative, it is all too easy to conclude that we hold our ancestors' destinies in our hands, consummating in our own lives what they left unfinished in theirs.

In any event, I took comfort in the thought of Carrie's maternal grandmother, who not only lost her Hapsburg heritage but also her name and her fortune. Did she regret the strange turn of events that brought her to a backwater rural settlement in the North Island of New Zealand? Did she glimpse the possibility that one of her granddaughters would create a life that wove together the best aspects of the sophisticated world into which she had been born and the pragmatic values acquired on the impoverished farm where she ended her days—a happy accommodation, like Carrie's anomalous bungalow, filled with books and music and sheltered by unruly trees, on a back section in Hamilton's most exclusive neighborhood?

The Road to Karuna Falls

I took the tortuous coastal road north from Thames, clay embankments on one side, gnarled pōhutukawa trees on the other, and the gulf beyond. I had asked Alan to email me directions to Karuna Falls, but by the time I reached the metal road that led from Waikawau Bay toward the commune, the landmarks were familiar.

Thirty years ago, Alan had sold his auto body shop in Feilding and moved to the Coromandel Peninsula. The family lived in a caravan while Alan built a house with kauri, matai, rimu, and vintage leadlighting salvaged from the demolition of a hotel and the St. John's Ambulance depot in Auckland. I had always envied Alan's abilities as a builder, fitter, and turner, motor mechanic, electrician, gardener, fisherman, and hunter, convinced, as are many New Zealanders, that practical skills are more important than intellectual or verbal gifts. Alan, however, had never shared this view, and so we found common ground.

The house was half hidden by regenerating bush, at the top of some river stone steps. Cabbage tree leaves littered the ground. On the deck was one of Alan's unique crayfish pots, which he made and sold to supplement his pension.

I peered through the open door. It took a while before my eyes grew accustomed to the gloom. Alan was kneading bread on the dining table.

"Gidday, Mike," he said, as if I had been away only a day.

Though our talk immediately turned to the years we had lived in the Manawatu, we soon went on to exchange news of our children and grandchildren, marveling at how quickly one generation succeeds another. Alan was also curious to know how far I had driven that day and what had brought me back to New Zealand.

I told him a little about my project, and we talked of two old friends from Manawatu days who had died early and unfulfilled. "It bothers me," I said, "that some of us seem to come unscathed through life while others, with just as much promise and talent, fall by the wayside. Is it simply luck that some of us survive, and even thrive, while others don't?" I asked Alan if the trick was to reinvent oneself, as he had, leaving one life behind, embarking on another.

Alan placed his tins of bread dough on a shelf above the coal range and covered them with a tea towel. Then he stoked the range and asked if I wanted a cup of tea. Only when we were seated outside on the deck, where a tui was feeding on an orange impaled on a nail, did he address my question.

Born out of wedlock to a woman in the military and immediately given up for adoption, Alan never knew either of his birth parents. It was only after their deaths that he traced his mother, met his half-siblings, and gleaned from them a sketchy knowledge of the woman who brought him into the world. But a conspiracy of silence prevented him from learning the name of his father. "Still, I had a happy childhood," Alan said, "despite the fact that Mum and Dad never told me I'd been adopted. I'd be taunted at school sometimes, because back then antisocial behavior was considered a sure sign of illegitimacy, but my parents never broke their vow to keep my origins from me.

"But that's all water under the bridge. It's like my decision to come up here. I started my real life here. What happened before didn't matter. I left all that behind. I decided this was where my life was going to start."

I told Alan that his story reminded me of Alistair Campbell, whose memoir I had read in Wellington. "You share the same surname," I said, "but you also share the same lack of bitterness about your early life, when so much that happened to you was utterly beyond your knowledge and control."

One of New Zealand's best-known poets and playwrights, Alistair was born on Penryn Island in 1925, the third child of a gregarious New Zealand trader and a Penryn woman. When his mother, Teu, died in 1932, Alistair's father, Jock, felt that he could not manage four children on his own, so he sent the two eldest to New Zealand to be cared for by relatives. Jock did not recover from the loss of his beloved Teu. Increasingly "distant and listless, and engrossed with cares that had nothing to do with" his children, he died in a Papeete hospital fourteen months after the death of his wife.

Despite the wishes of Teu's family that the children remain on Penryn, Alistair and his younger brother Billy were also sent to New Zealand, where they arrived in May 1933 with luggage labels attached to their lapels. And like luggage, they were dispatched by New Zealand Railways to the address of their father's mother, care of the Post Office, Waihi. There the orphans were reunited with their elder siblings, Margaret and Stuart.

Within a year they moved to Dunedin, where their frail grandmother, unable to cope, negotiated for the children to be admitted to an orphanage. It was here that Alistair learned English and discovered an aptitude for reading and writing and, later, a love of literature. His childhood on Penryn became a disconnected set of hazy images—of playing or quarreling with his siblings, of tropical storms, and of the night his nanny woke him, crying softly, and he watched, confused, as his father was carried on a stretcher down the steep path to the sea to begin his final journey.

It was not until 1974, when he was forty-nine, that Alistair recovered his lost link with Penryn.

Early that year, two young Penryn girls came to Wellington and began a search for their cousins, "the Campbell children who had been 'lost across the sea.'" After working through all the A. Campbells in the telephone directory, and being rebuffed by mystified or irritated responses, Rima and Pauline finally located their cousin. "At long last," Alistair would later write, "my grandfather's wish had been fulfilled. It was a fairy tale ending—or should I say, a beginning."

In the following weeks he met most of his Penryn kin living in New Zealand, and two years later—forty years after leaving the island—he made his "pilgrimage" to Penryn and began piecing together the lives of his parents and the aristocratic lineage to which he belonged.

I had always been moved by Alistair's belated but passionate embrace of his Polynesian heritage, as well as the poems inspired by his journeys back to Penryn. No hint here of a postcolonial narrative of historical wrongs, no cry for recompense, no talk of trauma, victimhood, or grievance. Like Alan, Alistair relates his story of separation and loss as one in which every ending is a prelude to a new beginning, rough seas assigned no greater significance than calm, a life recounted without acrimony, blame, or the need for redemption.

Yet, as a child, Alistair was the butt of racial taunts and bullying. He was aware of being anomalous in the eyes of his peers and felt guilty that he could sometimes pass for white. His elder brother Stuart was killed in the Second World War. Alistair suffered periods of "mental illness." And he would always regret the loss of Penryn Māori, his "mother tongue." For isn't it true that one's first language is fundamental to one's identity, and to lose this language or, worse, be punished for speaking it—as many Māori and Pacific Islanders were in New Zealand—is to lose your sense of self-worth as well as your relationship with the most pivotal people in your life?

Alistair always projected an air of imperturbability. But he drank heavily, and one heard rumors of his violent temper and of domestic mayhem.

* * *

That night I slept soundly, waking to the pallid daylight infiltrating my room and momentarily bewildered as to where in the world I was. At the main house, Ngaere and Alan were already up and about. We breakfasted together. Oatmeal porridge and yogurt. Toasted homemade bread, and honey from a local hive. "The yields are worse each year," Alan said. "Wasps and viruses are killing off the bees."

After breakfast, Alan suggested that since the weather was so good we should perhaps take the boat out and catch some fish. I said I would go with him as far as the bay, but would prefer to spend the morning on the beach.

"No worries," Alan said. And I believed him. Here one went about one's business without too much negotiation and no apologies. Ngaere would repair to her studio up the hill and work on her art projects. Alan would locate the offshore areas where snapper and kingfish were most likely to be found. I would take refuge in my thoughts.

After driving to the south end of the bay, Alan reversed the trailer into the water and quickly unshackled the boat. I threw my boots off and waded in, holding the boat against the incoming tide as Alan drove the Land Cruiser back to a parking spot along the track.

The sea was warmer than I'd expected. The boat knocked gently against the breaking wavelets. Alan wasted no time in clambering into the boat, starting the outboard and moving to full throttle. As if eager to go, the boat churned the water and rapidly disappeared into the shining metal of the sea.

I set out along the beach. Oystercatchers and dotterels skittered away across the sea-ribbed sand. Underfoot were tangles of seaweed and intact mussel, pipi, and cockle shells.

I sat down on the tideline and slipped the rucksack from my shoulders. I felt the sun on my face, heard the slipshod sound of the sea and the distracted cry of a nesting dotterel. My mind drifted. I was thinking of the gap between the inspiration I drew from places like Waikawau Bay and the satisfaction I had found in America, Europe, and West Africa. With every return home, the expatriate is reborn. It is not simply because you are returned to the landscapes of your early life; it is because the quotidian, momentarily bathed in a new light, appears exotic. And so you marvel that this place you could not live in because of its emptiness and insularity still has the power to remind you of who you really are. I scribbled in my notebook, "How can my being-here seem so completely natural, and the other places in my life, including the place I left only two weeks ago, seem so distant now, as if it were a previous incarnation? Yet, within days of leaving this place it will become quiescent again, like a dream."

* * *

That afternoon, Alan came home with enough snapper to make a meal. Candles were lit. The honeyed woodwork glowed. Alan's son Richard turned up, and a little later his wife Kate arrived with their small children.

Over dinner, Kate pandered to my preoccupation with origins by telling me how the human immune system hones its ability to combat disease by reacting to pathogens in early childhood. If a child is not exposed to pollens, animal hair, and germs, it will be less likely to develop resistance to them. Both polluted and antiseptic environments make us susceptible to autoimmune disorders in later life.

A medical doctor and passionate advocate of breastfeeding and good nutrition as well as the use of herbal remedies, Kate covered the north of the Coromandel Peninsula, which required her to make often grueling journeys to reach her clients. She knew them both medically and personally, taking time to listen to their stories and attend to their needs, many of which were not so much physiological as existential. As she described the disastrous effects of junk food, pesticides, and pharmaceuticals on human health, and the relatively straightforward ways in which we can prevent disease, I was moved by the pragmatism of Alan, Ngaere, Richard, and Kate. In the subdued light of the living room, it was easy to see them as pioneers. It was not only the surroundings that reinforced this impression—the wood-burning stove, the ironware, the tins of homemade bread, the bucket of local honey, the organic fruit from the commune orchard. It was their very appearance: their serviceable clothing from Kathmandu or Swanndri, their lack of cosmetic pretension, their ability to make do with basic ame- nities, their rough and ready language. Here you discussed fitting a wider diameter pipe to a stove, improvising a chimney cowl from a scrap of hammered tin, or replacing a worn wheel bearing on a Land Cruiser with the same intensity and ingenuity with which a group of Harvard profes- sors might debate the ethics of intervention in a foreign state. If you rarely touched on or inquired into the life of another mind, or a school of thought, or the nature of experience, it was not because these things were irrelevant; rather, time did not permit such departures from the mundane and the never-ending problems of getting by. As for social life, relationships were mediated more by doing things together than by sharing intimacies.

Kate was a mine of useful information. After preparing an infusion of kumarahou tea, she explained that the native plant was so named because its flowering presaged the kumara planting season. "It can also be used as a decongestant," Kate added, "the leaves to make an ointment or home brew, and the flowers crushed to make soap."

When I remarked the abundance of kumarahou growing among the mānuka, Kate told me that the plant preferred poor soils, hence its nick- name, poverty weed.

"Kumarahou, mānuka, kawakawa, horopito—these are plants that first appear on depleted soils. The same plants that heal the land heal us. They transform the clay into earth that can support more life."

Kate's insights into the deep ecology that linked human well-being to the well-being of the environment prompted me to ask her a question that had bothered me from my first years of fieldwork in West Africa—whether there was any natural limit to the capacity of the earth to sustain human life.

"If, as you say, longevity does not imply health, and that we live longer in modern societies only because of constant and costly medical interven- tions, is it perhaps counterproductive in the long run to intervene in the poor world to lower infant mortality and save lives when the costs of sus- taining those lives over the long term are beyond the means of third world governments, even when they are supported with foreign aid?"

Kate said this was a dilemma we had to live with. "Not to intervene is impossible. It would be too much like Hitler, getting rid of some people so that the lives of others will flourish. But the fact remains that we have so magnified the value of individual lives that we have lost any sense of ourselves as part of the stream of life itself. That stream is greater than any of us. And in that stream all the elements that comprise life on earth are constantly combining and permuting. It's like a paintbox—a finite set of colors whose recombinations create, over time, almost infinite varieties of forms or figures. It is hard for us to give up on the idea of ourselves as unique and irreplaceable. But some kind of balance has to be found between self-preservation and the preservation of life in the wider sense."

Kate's remarks transformed the way I had been thinking about my relationship to New Zealand and to the past. I had started out with the image of a human life as a river. Its course marked by a series of events in time. Now I saw it as a constellation. A skylight above my bed gave onto the star-filled night. Gazing into deep space, I realized how unproductive it was to see life lineally—as cause and effect or as sequences and series—before and after, beginning, middle, and end. Just as some stars are visible at certain times of the year and invisible at others, or some constellations are momentarily hidden behind cloud while others swim clearly into view, so different aspects of our lives emerge or disappear in relation to the changing environments of which we are a part. This metaphysical view is nicely summarized by Carole Hungerford, whose work had inspired Kate. Hungerford suggests that our lives may be compared with a coral reef. "Startling though the image may be, it is a way of saying that we provide a habitat for the many microorganisms which live on and within us, and in turn we depend on them for health. Just as we see ourselves as a species within a larger ecosystem, so another species may live within us, our bodies constituting their habitat . . . Even more confronting than sharing our bodies with gut and other bacteria is the fact that the very cells of our body, our DNA, host the remnants of the viruses that once invaded our ancestors and are now part of our own genetic makeup. Infinity stretches outwards and inwards in space, forwards and backwards in time."

* * *

When I left Karuna Falls, Alan apologized for the rough conditions, but preempted my response by observing that I was probably used to worse in West Africa. Indeed, the eroded clay roads that not even a four-wheel-drive vehicle could negotiate after heavy rain, and the lack of urban amenities, had reminded me strongly of my sojourns in northern Sierra Leone, my clothing smelling of woodsmoke, hands ingrained with dirt, hair uncombed.

"It's been great to see you," I said. "Let's not wait another ten years before we get together again!"

I knew that my feelings were reciprocated, that connections can be recovered after long separations, the gap between past and present closed as a ship's wake is healed by the overwhelming ocean.

Crossing the Hauraki Plains, I regretted with every passing mile the wilderness I was leaving. On either side of the road were mud-spattered herds in hoof-pocked paddocks, wooden batons on the fences awry like some alien musical score. I passed through typical tinpot towns that advertised fish and chips, meat pies, and Tip Top ice cream. Low, close-cropped hawthorn hedges were a constant reminder of the hysteria with which our Anglo pioneers sought to subjugate the land, separating themselves from the very wilderness in which I had momentarily rediscovered the accidented landscape of myself. Recalling my conversation with Kate, I imagined my life as a sheet of paper on which every experience had left a trace. I had only to twist this paper into a ball for those traces to be entirely reconfigured. Events that on the flattened paper were poles apart were now brought into close conjunction. Marks that had been in the foreground, only moments ago, were now lost without a trace. Other marks, faded by sun or rain, were now legible. All that had befallen me was ever present. If it was not in the forefront of my mind, it was nevertheless there, in potentia, and I had only to travel a few thousand miles for what had been in abeyance to enter my consciousness anew. This sense that my experiences were only ever displaced, not supplanted, was nothing short of liberating.

Where Do We Come From? What Are We? Where Are We Going?

To speak of firstness is also to broach the question of nostalgia—a longing for a lost home that may also imply a longing for a primal and more perfect state of being.

In Auckland, I had lunch with my sister Juliet in a Ponsonby café. Juliet spoke of our maternal grandmother, Amy Tempest, who left the safety and security of her home in West Yorkshire and traveled to the other side of the world to marry the brother of her closest friend, who had migrated to New Zealand in 1906. She never got over her loss of England. In the Taranaki town in which she spent most of her life, she named her house Shibden for the verdant valley she pined for. The furnishings of her house echoed the home in which she had been raised. Her brother's watercolors of the dales and moors hung in every room. And when, in her last years, she suffered a "nervous breakdown," it was as if the cumulative effect of years of struggling to adjust to a place that had failed her test of respectability and gentility finally proved too much for her to bear. "She suffered post-partum depression after the birth of each of her four children," Juliet said. "Jack's [her eldest son's] suicide may have been the last straw." I remembered Amy's diary, written during her voyage out in 1908, and the letter she wrote her mother on the eve of her wedding describing what she was going to wear— "everything white and cream except my garters which will be pale blue, and a pale blue ribbon through my camisole"—and ending with her articles of faith: "I often think about the talks we had together, Mother, about purity in woman. It is the greatest treasure she can hold. I must say I have found to my disappointment that some of the New Zealanders are lacking in home love and home influences. Home is their last consideration. They look upon it as a place to go when their pleasures are over. But ours is going to be an English home."

I asked Juliet what she knew of Amy's friend Emily, the sister of the man she married, whose story echoed Amy's.

Emily was a year younger than Amy, and her family, the Longbottoms, were poorer and less genteel than the Tempests. But Amy and Emily were both teachers. "This was the beginning of the friendship," Juliet said. Emily had been an exceptional pupil at Shelf Board School. When she completed her schooling at age thirteen, she stayed on as a pupil teacher and attended night school at Halifax Technical College. It was an hour's walk from her home to Halifax, and she would often study late into the night, drinking black coffee prepared by her young sister Alice, to stay awake. "This grueling schedule may have been the cause of a series of breakdowns she suffered," Juliet said, "though the earliest episode may date from the time she was teaching away from home, in Burnley in Wharfedale, where she was sexually assaulted." She suffered another breakdown in her forties and retired on a pension. After her next collapse, when she was sixty-six, she was admitted to a psychiatric hospital in Huddersfield where she died two years later, in 1948.

It was as though Amy and Emily were two sides of a single coin. Their destinies were entwined, despite their different backgrounds, the geographical distance between them, and the fact that one married and the other did not. That Amy never ceased to honor this affinity was evident when she named her first-born daughter (my mother) after her friend.

I tried to conceive of what it was like for Amy during the periods she spent in Tokanui Psychiatric Hospital in the mid 1950s, far from home, falling asleep in a dorm room filled with the damned, daily subjected to electroconvulsive therapy, and no doubt wondering whether this was a place of healing or horror and whether her prayers, her faith, could save her.

The hospital was built in 1912 and closed in 1998. The buildings are now derelict. Dead leaves fill the swimming pool. Dead vines cling to the brick walls. Broken windows are boarded up. Rats, mice, birds, and possums live in the ceiling spaces, shuffling and squealing like the ghostly reincarnations of the tens of thousands of human beings who inhabited the day rooms and locked dormitories.

After leaving Juliet, I drove to my sister Bronwen's house, where she brought out a box of photos and letters that documented the lives of our grandparents. Bronwen was particularly keen for me to see a photo of Amy's brother Walter. She said I resembled him. I wondered what such a resemblance might portend and whether we can read our own fates out of the detritus left in the wake of our forebears' lives. And my eyes filled with tears as I read the letters our grandfather, Fred, had written Amy expressing the loving hope that she would be home soon.

* * *

I spent my last day in New Zealand walking on the Whangaparaoa Peninsula. Again, I was struck by the juxtaposition of indigenous and imported flora—banks of hydrangeas growing alongside tree ferns and nikau palms; kniphofia, agapanthus, and nasturtium among native toetoe, flax, and kawakawa. Nothing suggested that some species were foreign, intrusive, or out of place. Indeed, a postcard image of a New Zealand beach would be incomplete without wild pōhutukawa and introduced araucarias framing the ocean.

Nor, I reminded myself, were the native birds of New Zealand really autochthonous. Originating in Gondwanaland or flying from Australia millennia ago, they made landfall on these islands and found themselves in paradise. Without mammalian predators to contend with, they no longer needed wings, and in due course many species lost the ability to fly. With the coming of the Māori one thousand years ago, and Europeans eight hundred years later, the defenseless birds quickly succumbed. Hunters drove the moa to extinction. Rats, cats, and mustelids decimated other species. And with the felling and burning of the lowland forests, others soon perished. Only in the vastness of Fiordland did the flightless takahē and kākāpō hold out, their numbers pitifully small, their future in the wild as yet uncertain.

Could I, without the means of flying from these islands, have flourished or found fulfillment? And what predators would have threatened my survival?

As I picked my way across a paddock of kikuyu grass to the sea, these questions nagged at me. The landscape was so utterly familiar, and yet I felt emotionally disengaged, a mere visitant. I had felt this way before, of course, most intensely in Taranaki. In fact, so strong was the sense that I had become a stranger to myself that I compared my experience to the Capgras Delusion, often associated with schizophrenia, in which one becomes convinced that a loved one has been taken over by an alien being. Despite the outward familiarity of the other, one cannot engage emotionally with him since one believes that he has been mysteriously replaced by a malevolent double. The delusion occurs in children, but fleetingly. You imagine you have been adopted or accidentally exchanged for another child at birth. You struggle to reconcile your emergent identity with the identity that others thrust upon you. You are never seen for what you are, for what you aspire to be, but as someone others want you to be for the sake of appearances, for their peace of mind. You feel existentially half-caste, connected by birth to one world yet by disposition to another.

This sense of being divided against myself quickly passed as I approached the sea. The shoreline consisted of a series of collapsed sandstone slabs. The edges of the layered rock had been bitten into by the ocean and resembled petrified stacks of pancakes. I found one that had been worn smooth. With the flat of my hand, I cleared the gnarled pōhutukawa bark and leaf litter from it, then sat and watched gulls diving for fish in the ultramarine water. One flew low in front of me, scooping its prey from just below the surface. I could hear the slap slap slap of wet wings as it made off with its catch.

* * *

My rental car was grimy from the back roads I'd traveled, streaked with mud and speckled with tar. Rather than risk incurring a penalty when I returned it to the depot, I decided to give the car a quick clean at the service station where I filled the petrol tank. With no one waiting at the pump and plenty of sudsy water at my disposal, I was able to give the car a thorough going over. But as I worked, some Māori garage hands exchanged comments, loud enough for me to hear, and when I'd finished, one called, laughing, "Hey, mate, you missed a bit underneath!" This made me marvel at my audacity and ask myself why I had felt free to do something I would never have dared do in the U.S. The answer was unsettling. The only person who might have reprimanded me was the cashier at the service station, but he was Indian. I had assumed a right for myself that I had withheld from him. I had behaved as if there were a difference between being a citizen of a place where you were born and raised and being a second-class citizen—a migrant or stranger. How else could I explain the alacrity with which I'd used the soapy water and squeegee to clean my car, not just the windows, with so little regard for the Indian cashier who, for all I knew, had been watching me and wondering whether to intervene? And what of the men whose disapproving remarks I had dismissed as good-natured banter? Were we united as tricksters, as jokers, whose power lay in bucking authority, getting around the law, going against the grain? Whatever the case, I had learned that one's sense of belonging had a shadow side, namely a sense that certain others did not really belong and that you could, if you wished, ride roughshod over them.

The young Punjabi cabdriver who drove me to Auckland airport the following day betrayed no such qualms. Kamilji said that he had dreamed of New Zealand from as long ago as he could remember. In his imagination, it was a place of rain, greenness, and social tranquility. I was reminded of images I had recently seen on TV, of a bombed out Taliban training school in Waziristan. On the plaster walls were naive paintings of idyllic landscapes, swans on placid lakes, houris, and lotus flowers. Through suicide, the young fighters imagined they would exchange their barren hills, mud-walled houses, and poverty stricken villages for Paradise.

After graduating, Kamilji applied for residence. "My wife loves this country even more passionately than I do," he said. "I will go home from time to time, to help my brother with his internet marketing business, but that's all. Here is where my wife and I want to raise our children. As far from the Punjab as we can get."

How ironic, I thought, that I should have grown up in the very rain-drenched Pacific utopia that Kamilji had dreamed of, but had left it in search of deserts, and that he had found through migration what many of his compatriots now hoped to attain through heroic self-immolation. Later, when I was airborne and scribbling these thoughts into my notebook, I wondered whether New Zealand remained the bedrock of my life not because it was the place where I first opened my eyes on the world, but because of the place I had assigned it in my imagination. I had seized upon its emptiness and remoteness as a symbol of my own estrangement.

Taking a Line for a Walk

I broke my journey home in San Francisco in order to attend an anthropology conference. On checking into my hotel, however, I discovered that the balance on my credit card was insufficient to cover the costs of my five-day stay as well as the additional charges deposit. After talking to the manager at the front desk, I managed to have the $500 deposit waived. But I had to give an assurance that I would not incur any extra charges by using the minibar, gym, telephone, room or laundry service, ordering a massage or watching pornographic movies. I had brought muesli, fruit, soymilk, and orange juice with me, and so I moved the bottles and cans in the minibar to make room for my supplies. Minutes later I received a call to ask if I had, contrary to my stated intention, used the minibar. I explained that I had not realized that moving a bottle in the minibar would register downstairs and my account be charged automatically. Obligingly, the caller told me that a small refrigerator would be delivered to my room at no extra charge to accommodate my orange juice. The minibar was then locked by remote control, with my bunch of bananas still inside. I felt too foolish to ask for the bar to be reopened.

It occurred to me that my sense of disorientation had less to do with jet lag than an inability to overcome my antipodean aversion to the pretensions of power, prestige, and profiteering. Perhaps this is why I called to ask if I could watch the television without any extra charge and whether I was free to use the soap, shampoo, and conditioner in the bathroom without penalty. "This is all complimentary, Mr. Jackson," I was told. "We hope your stay will be a pleasant one. Please do not hesitate to ask if we can be of any further assistance."

That night, feeling cut off from the world, I lay in semidarkness in my anonymous cubicle, twenty floors aboveground, counting the hours until dawn. The only sound was the soft unvarying rush of air through a vent as I surveyed my room—the brass light fittings, pink and oystershell walls, paintings of cherry blossoms, ceramic jars, and a tree outside a Parisian mansion. I walked to the window, drew back the curtains, and peered into the night. High-rise, mist-swathed buildings. Traffic moving in endless though interrupted procession in the street below.

With a day to kill before the anthropological conference began, I visited the San Francisco Museum of Modern Art where I became immediately entranced by the paintings and etchings of Paul Klee. His work reconnected me with my antipodean journey and gave me the idea of using the titles of his paintings for some of the chapter headings in my book. Klee's *Fata Morgana at Sea*, for example, brought me back to the illusion of Corsica—an image of the imaginary yet necessary nature of art, creating simulacra of the real that make it possible for us to address experiences that might otherwise defeat us. Several other works conspired to reinforce this idea: Diego Rivera's *The Flower Carrier,* in which a woman helps an overburdened man to his feet, taking the weight of his load; Pablo Picasso's *The Coffee Pot,* painted in Paris during World War II, the cup suggesting a female form, the phallic spout of the coffee pot opposing it, as fascism opposed the free and sensuous expression of life.

I spent the rest of the day exploring a city I had always wanted to see. It did not disappoint. Perhaps it was the strange juxtaposition of Australasian and North American flora that made me feel at home—the eucalyptuses, figs, phoenix palms, pines, and cedars. Perhaps it was the nonchalant and affable way strangers answered my questions about how to get to China-town or the Golden Gate Bridge. Perhaps it was the steep hills, and the sur-real, fogbound landscape in which buildings, trees, water, and traffic were partially submerged.

I walked for miles, hoping for a glimpse of the bridge. I guessed it to be out there somewhere in the bay, and I was hoping the mist would lift. A foghorn sounded morosely across the veiled water. When I asked a jogger if the fog was likely to burn off, he said, "It's not going to get hot enough. At least not today."

I never got to see the bridge. But I was content to drift, as I had in New Zealand, and see what happened. In a grocery store at Nob Hill, I over-heard a woman telling her companion that her brother had committed suicide seventeen years ago to the day. "I turned the corner this sum-mer," she said, "which makes me think I'm now ready to write a book about it." On a street corner at Russian Hill, I passed a woman pushing a friend in a wheelchair. The woman said, "Well, he didn't fit in with the kids." To which the woman in the wheelchair replied, "But you didn't fit in either."

That afternoon, the fog thickened and the daylight faded early. In my hotel room, I wrote up the notes I had taken during my rambles. I kept coming back to the image of the bridge. How could I cross the narrows between my recent antipodean travels and the dominant discourse of the conference at which I been invited to present a paper? How could I retain, in my writing, a strong sense of primary experience, unclouded by the sec-ondary elaborations with which scholars purport to explain the world? My disorientation could not be explained by jetlag alone. I was betwixt and between two hemispheres—geographic and cerebral—and struggling to reconcile opposing impulses. Even as I resisted the impulse to create coher-ence, arrive at an interpretation, identify a cause, or come to a conclusion, I came up against the limits of discursive prose. Perhaps it is enough to juxtapose telling and showing rather than try to fuse them, thus echoing the way in which past and present coexist in our consciousness without the tension between them ever being fully resolved.

The cover of a recent issue of *Psychology Today* depicted a cracked white candied heart with the words "First Love, First Loss" written in lipstick across it. The feature article spoke learnedly of "the primacy effect," of "the early-life memory bump," and of the "transference" of feelings developed in primary relationships (notably with one's parents) to all subsequent relationships. I preferred Maurice Merleau-Ponty's image of past time not as something that can be *known* but as a region where our lives are prepared.

That a human life unfolds lineally is as much a fiction as the idea that lives are like libraries, able to be labeled and classified, bookended by Birth and Death. These are ways we retrospectively bestow on life a semblance of order or the appearance of purpose and design. The same is true of the experience of firstness, which bears a family resemblance to Hannah Arendt's notion of natality—the perennial surprise of being in the world, new experiences continually befalling us whether we seek them or not. "This character of startling unexpectedness is inherent in all beginnings and in all origins," Arendt writes. But is there really any finite moment to which we can we assign such terms as *first* or *final*?

This train of thought led me back to Paul's Ricoeur's phrase "the enigma of anteriority" and his allusions to the gap between an identifiable beginning (for instance, the date of one's birth or the day James Cook made landfall in New Zealand) and all that prefigures such biographical and historical moments. Perhaps only poetry can do justice to the sense of mystery that surrounds our relationship to the past, the "haunted bay" from which "the godwits vanish toward another summer" or the half-light of our "diffident glory" in which "the sailor lives, and stands beside us, paying out into our time's wave the stain of blood that writes an island story."

We are shaped as much by our ancestry and our circumstances as by our own will, and we are, to paraphrase John Donne, inescapably a part of all mankind. We may think of ourselves as islands, but these are islands in the stream of genealogy and history, "a part of the maine." Though every person is unique, he or she also shares with countless others, close kin as well as distant strangers, the same DNA, the same evolutionary history, the same humanity. Like ice floes, our visible features belie submerged and barely visible forms.

And like an ice floe, our existence begins as a piece of a continent, only to drift and disappear into an ocean with the taste of human tears.

How can one compose a picture of an iceberg that includes its tip, its mass beneath the surface, its watery environment and its continual transformations? Is it not like attempting to capture simultaneously both the singularity of a human life and its similarity to the lives of others? In his famous essay on the storyteller, Walter Benjamin speaks of the traces of the storyteller that "cling to the story the way the handprints of the potter cling to the clay vessel"—an allusion to the potsherds unearthed by archaeologists whose accidental signatures locate an actual person within a historical period, a cultural context, or religious tradition. But a fingerprint is hardly a person, and one comes back to the question of whether, and to what extent, given the constraints of culture, class, and circumstance, we are the authors of our own lives.

Toward the end of his life, Ricoeur admitted misgivings about having always placed his personal life *sous rature,* avoiding subjective language because it seemed improvisatory and uncontrolled. In a sustained conversation with two close friends, Ricoeur decided, however, to merge the discursive spheres he had hitherto kept separate, allowing the "rule of life to overtake the rule of thought." And he recounts how, within two years of his birth in 1913, his father was killed in the battle of the Marne and his mother died soon after. He and his sister were adopted by their paternal grandparents and went to live in Rennes—a move that effectively cut the children off from their maternal kin. There is no doubt, Ricoeur observed years later, that this genealogical separation "exerted a very strong influence . . . and [was] at the same time very traumatic, since the maternal side was hidden. . . . I only understood the figure of the mother through the way my wife was perceived by her children. The word 'mama' was a word pronounced by my children but never by me." When his sister died of tuberculosis in 1932, Ricoeur was again made aware of how the past can hold one in thrall. Her "youth was in a sense eclipsed by mine," Ricoeur said. "I have regretted this all my life, with the impression that she received less than her due, while I received more than mine; I still struggle with the feeling of an unpaid debt, with the feeling that she suffered an injustice from which I benefited. This must have played an important role in my life: the 'unpaid debt' is a persistent theme, turning up frequently in my work."

Orphaned so young, denied the warmth and intimacy of a mother's love, and raised in a household of older people where reading and religious faith were fervent preoccupations, it is not surprising that Ricoeur should discover a sense of deep well-being in books and develop a bipolar fascination with philosophy and religion. Yet it is also tempting to see in the austere allure of scholarship a retreat from painful and possibly unresolved experiences of personal loss. Indeed, I see it as both poignant and ironic that the author of *Time and Narrative* should seldom refer to any story drawn from life in this monumental work and that his famed study of the hermeneutics of suspicion should focus on Freud's philosophical writings and almost completely ignore the clinical work that cuts closest to the bone. It would be crass to suggest that the course of Ricoeur's intellectual life was determined by traumatic events in his early childhood, but Ricoeur himself was surely mindful of the connection between his autobiographical disclosures and his comments on the origin that "always slips away at the same time as it surges up in the present under the enigma of the always-already-there."

It was my friend Davíd Carrasco who introduced me to Ricoeur's enigma of anteriority, a notion that helped him throw light on the Latino fascination with the interplay of personal identity and indigenous origins, between a historical situation and its mythical beginnings.

In his discussion of what he calls "Aztec moments," Davíd quotes a dinner companion who expressed the view that Chicanos don't just have senior moments, those moments of forgetting details of one's memory or some recent event. "We have Aztec moments, when we realize que los Indios de Mexico, los Aztecas, los Toltecas y los Mayas are part of our historias, who we are. We are not Españoles, we're mestizos and proud of our indigenista parts." Davíd and his dinner companions recalled conversations with parents and grandparents as well as childhood journeys to Mexico where they discovered their names and faces and family stories in Mexican museums, parks, villages, churches, mining towns, myths, and histories. "In each of our families," Davíd writes, "there was an Indio in appearance or in lineage. My father was called El Indio in his family because, like his mother Carlota Carranza Carrasco, he had what was perceived as the physiognomy of a Mexican Indian. In those days it wasn't a sign of pride. But for us around the table, having an Aztec moment meant that Chicanos are able to remember their native roots, to expand their sense of identity beyond either Anglo definitions or the black-white dichotomy that animates so much of race discourse in the U.S. And we felt pride in this remembering and were coming to realize that our mestizaje was both a complex social location but also a symbolic meaning from which we viewed the world with complex eyes."

Davíd's reflections on his mixed heritage brought me back to the question that had prompted my return to the country where I was born and raised. It is not that one remembers one's past exactly. Nor that one completely imagines it. Aotearoa and Aztlan are as historical as they are mythical. Let us say, then, that we draw on what we think we know of the past to create a sense of solidarity with others. And it is on the strength of this image of a primordial or foundational identity that we make claims for belonging and standing (*tūrangawaewae*), presence and recognition (*mana*), and well-being (*mauri ora*). But we can also invoke the past in making a case for disconnectedness and irremediable difference. Then our exclusive identity claims—ethnic, national, or personal—come up against the identity claims of others. What is first and fundamental for Māori may be incompatible with what is prior or a priori for Pākehā.

While Māori express firstness in autochthonous terms—as an umbilical connection with the land that gives them status as tangata whenua (*whenua* means both "land" and "placenta"), many Pākehā invoke rather different archetypes of belonging. When, as a child, I thought of the world to which I was naturally heir, I did not think primarily of family or lineage, but of a quiet bend in a local river, a pine plantation, a remnant stand of native bush, a hill from which, on a clear day, I could see the mountain. These elements defined a social microcosm of which I felt intimately a part. Winter and summer, I explored, charted, named, and absorbed this world of mine until there wasn't an acre I did not know by heart. This was at once my lifeworld and myself. Animate, attuned, and entangled. It's why I have always felt a deep affinity with Paul Cézanne. His paintings of Mont Sainte Victoire touch me like no others. These landscapes, like the landscapes my mother painted, are really abstract portraits—worlds not of rock and pine but of the flesh.

This mystical participation in nature was, I came to realize, not peculiar to me; it defined a national disposition.

Although New Zealand and Algeria are geographically distant, they share a similar colonial history. It is this history, Albert Camus suggests, that shapes a social imaginary in which landscape comes to figure as a central motif.

Writing in *Noces* about such places as Algiers, Tipasa, Oran, and Djemila, Camus frequently alludes to the cult of physicality that filled the cultural void in which the *pied noir* (French colonist) found himself. Having, on the one hand, no firsthand everyday knowledge of metropolitan France and, on the other, no practical understanding of Arab or Kabyle lifeworlds, the outsider tended to drift into a poetic mystical relationship with the physical landscape—the sun, the light, the sea, the mountains—and cultivate an idealized athleticism focused on sports and sexual prowess. The New Zealand in which I came of age was strikingly similar. Though my grandparents still spoke of England as a motherland to which one was both constitutionally and sentimentally tethered, I tended to see it as an antiquated, class-conscious, and distant country in which I could never feel at home. At the same time, I felt that indigenous Māori culture was, despite its exotic allure, equally beyond my reach. Perhaps this is why I grew up feeling not so much betwixt and between two cultural worlds as culture-less. As a result, I wavered between a "feminized" and poetic sensibility, anchored in the landscape, and a "masculinized" ethos whose ritual foci were contact sports such as rugby. But the authentic social belonging that finds its consummation in culture and community always lay elsewhere.

The affection and familiarity I feel toward my homeland is always commingled with a sense of disaffection, the origins of which are beyond my power to understand. Perhaps it has something to do with the terrible violence that accompanied the birth of the nation. Perhaps it reflects the isolation I felt as a child, always walking into the wind, going against the grain. I remember the deep affinity I felt for my grandfather, who struggled to overcome his working-class background while remaining loyal to a working-class ethic of the common man. As an intellectual, I often find myself in revolt against the arcane, abstract, and reductive conventions of the academy, but have never embraced the demotic view that common sense and intuition can be counted on to edify and enlighten or determine right from wrong. My New Zealand background made it easy for me to identify bullshit, but it did not prepare me to recognize wisdom. Perhaps I am simply observing that home is always a particular and familiar world—a place where one kicks over the traces, or from which one fares forth, looking for a wider world to call one's own. While one might outgrow the place where one began, one's offspring will find in a parent's accomplishments only another beginning or blind alley from which they, in turn, will feel compelled to move away in order to discover themselves.

* * *

On the night flight from San Francisco to Boston I dreamed I was in a large bed, trying to protect a small, premature, and naked infant from the other who shared my bed and kept turning and threatening to smother it. Curling my arm protectively around the fragile new life, I gazed on it with overwhelming love.

Afterword

> Historians are forever chasing shadows, painfully aware of their inability ever to reconstruct a dead world in its completeness. . . . We are doomed to be forever hailing someone who has just gone round the corner and out of earshot.
>
> —SIMON SCHAMA, *DEAD CERTAINTIES: UNWARRANTED SPECULATIONS*

If my feelings about my natal country have always been ambivalent, so too have my feelings about academe, which may account for why I have been such a wayward citizen of both. As an expatriate writer, I have found it as difficult to publish in New Zealand as it has been to secure a tenured university job and find funds for fieldwork. Undoubtedly, these difficulties reflect not only a life divided between two hemispheres, but an incessant switching between prose and poetry, ethnography and fiction. Though things may have been easier had I focused on one genre or settled in one country, my "reality hunger" would probably have been considered outré in literary as well as academic circles, despite David Shield's conviction that greater urgency now attaches "to the tale taken directly from life than one fashioned by the imagination out of life."

Rather than force myself to write in a style that might win academic kudos or popular acclaim, I repeatedly tell myself that one can only write what one is given to write. One can't create something foreign to one's nature or outside one's immediate experience simply because it may help advance one's career or cement one's reputation. Indeed, I have come to think that the deeper one goes into oneself, and the more honest one is about what one discovers in the course of this inward journey, the more likely it is that one will happen upon not the inner core of one's own singular being, or a language that does justice to life, but the truth of what it means to be human. In sharing this struggle, one's own journey through life becomes the journey of Everyman, and others may find in one's own travails a way of rethinking their own. Egotism and narcissism are by-products of remaining in the shallows of the self, distracted by the fads and fashions of one's time or the clamoring of the crowd. The deeper one goes, the more those fads and fashions fade, and the raised voices recede, until there remains only the profound silence of the now, broken only by the systole and diastole of the human heart.

This sense that writing simultaneously carries one deep into oneself *and* far beyond oneself was what won me over to words before I had read a single poem, discovered ethnography, or entered academe. Paul Ricoeur's arresting phrase "the enigma of anteriority" touches on the mystery of what draws us to one profession, person, or genre rather than another. "It is as though there were a dialectic of the origin and the beginning," Ricoeur writes. "The beginning should be able to be dated in a chronology, but the origin always slips away, at the same time as it surges up in the present under the enigma of the always-already-there." There are echoes here of Carl Jung's notion of the archetype, Aby Warburg's concept of *nachleben*, and Maurice Merleau-Ponty's comment, "My personal existence must be the resumption of a prepersonal tradition. There is, therefore, another subject beneath me, for whom a world exists before I am here, and who marks out my place in it." John Berger writes in a similar vein. "Experience is indivisible and continuous, at least within a single lifetime and perhaps over many lifetimes. I never have the impression that my experience is entirely my own, and it often seems to me that it preceded me. In any case experience folds upon itself, refers backwards and forwards to itself through the referents of hope and fear; and, by the use of metaphor, which is at the origin of language, it is continually comparing like with unlike, what is small with what is large, what is near with what is distant."

All these observations touch on the relationship between our own particular lives and what we may call life itself, whether in the space of the
world, the stream of time, or the ocean of humanity from whence we
emerge and wherein we ultimately vanish.

The great film director Abbas Kiarostami was once asked, "What films
or works of art influenced your direction as a filmmaker?" This was his
reply: "Life itself will create more changes in our field than the influence of
the films of others. Perhaps those who see many movies could acquire these
influences from other films, but as for myself, since my eyes are watchful
of life itself, and my senses are focused on my environment, I could say
without a doubt, *it is the experience of living and what goes on around me
and not the cinema nor literature that is most influential*."

That the stream of life is unpredictably and tragically interrupted is as
compelling as the fact that in spite of catastrophes, life goes on.

At thirty minutes past midnight on June 21, 1990, a violent earthquake
centered along the shores of the Caspian Sea in northwestern Iran laid
waste a twenty-thousand-square-mile area and razed entire villages in the
provinces of Zanjan and Gilan. Fifty thousand people, many of them asleep
at the time the earthquake struck, were killed, and hundreds of thousands
were left homeless. Into this devastated region, Abbas Kiarostami, accompanied by one of his sons, drives his small car in the hope that he can locate
the village where, four years before, he filmed *Where Is My Friend's Home*.
He is particularly anxious to find the local boy who played the key role in
his film. Kiarostami's 1992 film, *Life and Nothing More*, documents this
journey.

Playing on the French title of the film (*Et la vie continue*), Jean-Luc
Nancy suggests that it is in the nature of life to go on, regardless of what
interrupts its flow. Existence is not something, he remarks; it consists in
the truth that it continues, come what may, "neither above nor below the
moments, events, singularities, and individuals that are discontinuous, but
in a manner that is stranger yet: in discontinuity itself, and without fusing
it into a *continuum*." This "perseverance" of being, of which Spinoza speaks,
which Bergson calls "duration," does not necessarily contain any meaning,
for it is felt before any meaning, metaphysical or moral, is attached to it. In
Kiarostami's film, no reference is made to resilience, no consolation is
wrung from the fact that a couple get married not long after the disaster

(something that did not really happen), no one is blamed, no question of justice is broached, and no reasons are given for why some houses withstood the quake and others crumbled or why some died and some survived. Life, it is suggested, is a flow or passage, periodically interrupted or blocked, in which we are swept along despite ourselves, and despite our inability to say what it is that flows, or recall the past, or define the boundaries of the states through which we pass. And this life that transpires, in what we speak of as a specific place, a specific time, and a specific life, is "inside and outside us at one and the same time."

At one point, the father gives a ride to a man carrying a stone for a squat toilet. The man puts the stone on the roof rack of the car, but reaches his arm through the widow to hold the stone in place on the winding road. The father says, "You bought this on such a day?" to which his passenger replies, "The dead are dead. The living need this precious stone." This image, Jean-Luc Nancy says, is evidence of what it means to speak of life going on.

Life itself is clearly more than the identity terms with which we name it, encircle it, or grasp it. Though hesitant to name his influences, Kiarostami mentions Buster Keaton and Yasujirō Ozu. And though he remained in Iran after the 1979 revolution, when many other artists fled, he regards this not as a political or cultural act but as a natural thing to do. "When you are a tree that is rooted in the ground, and transfer it from one place to another, the tree will no longer bear fruit. And if it does, the fruit will not be as good as it was in its original place. This is a rule of nature. I think if I had left my country, I would be the same as the tree."

This raises a vexing question for any transplanted writer. For while one may find intellectual nourishment by putting down roots in foreign soil, the achievement of a cosmopolitan identity never erases the sense of having forfeited one's connection to one's natal place. This sense, that what you have gained cannot completely compensate for what you have lost, tugs at your heart forever. Recognition abroad is one thing, but it is one's reputation in one's homeland that matters most, which is why countless stories are told of school reunions that people attend in the hope of getting revenge for the wrongs they suffered as students or gaining recognition of their adult successes. In struggling not to feel embittered by my failures to get published in my homeland, I remind myself that other writers have had a far harder time of it than me, including writers who have not chosen to live abroad. The Iranian government has banned screenings of Kiarostami's films. "I think they don't understand [them] and so prevent them being shown just in case there is a message they don't want to get out. They tend to support films that are stylistically very different from mine—melodramas." Kiarostami is aware of the irony. "The government is not in my way, but it is not assisting me either. We lead our separate lives."

That Kiarostami is more than an Iranian filmmaker few would contest, and I wholeheartedly agree with Aminatta Forna, who writes against being labeled as a female writer, a gay writer, a black writer, or, in her case, an African writer. "All this classifying, it seems to me, is the very antithesis of literature. The way of literature is to seek universality. Writers try to reach beyond those things that divide us: culture, class, gender, race. Given the chance, we would resist classification." I am convinced, however, that despite her cosmopolitanism Aminatta's Sierra Leonean roots run as deeply as my New Zealand ones do in me, and it might be more accurate to say that the tension between particular and universal identifications, whether in literature or life, can never be fully resolved. Within my universalized self a particular self continues to lament: "Kowa yabar gida, gida ya barshi" (If you leave your home, your home will leave you).

The same tension lies at the heart of anthropology and history, for while both disciplines have evolved sophisticated methods for understanding the lives of others at other times or in other places, all intellectuals possess preunderstandings and prejudices, born of the time and place from whence they come. And so the question "Where do I belong?" always entails the question "To what or to whom am I beholden?" To what extent can I become other than the person I was born and raised to be? Is entering into the lives of others and giving voice to their experiences the way of realizing the Delphic injunction to know oneself?

Notes

Preface

Footprints and Futures—Association of Social Anthropologists of the UK and Commonwealth Annual Conference, Durham University, 4–7 July 2016, *Handbook*, 6.

The world of predecessors is by definition over and done with—Alfred Schutz, *The Phenomenology of the Social* World (1932), trans. George Walsh and Federick Lehnert (London: Heinemann, 1972), 208.

Like George Orwell, I had an aversion—George Orwell, "Politics of the English Language," in *Selected Essays* (Harmondsworth: Penguin, 1957), 147, 143–46 (153–54).

For Adorno, reification is a form of forgetting—"For all reification is a forgetting: objects become purely thing-like the moment they are retained for us without the continued presence of their other aspects: when something of them has been forgotten." Theodor Adorno and Walter Benjamin, *The Complete Correspondence, 1928–1940* (Cambridge: Harvard University Press, 1999), 321.

It is only very rarely, when I make a definite mental effort—George Orwell, *The Road to Wigan Pier* (Harmondsworth: Penguin, 1937), 30.

Within the reach of my direct experience—Schutz, *The Phenomenology of the Social* World, 163.

the uncanny (Unheimlich)—Sigmund Freud, "The Uncanny" (1919), in *The Uncanny*, trans. David McLintock (London: Penguin, 2003), 121–62.

The sentiment of pre-existence—A. L. Wigan, *The Duality of Mind* (London: Longman, Brown, Green and Longman, 1844). Twelve years later, John Draper, redefined Wigan's "sentiment of pre-existence" as "that strange impression, which all persons have occasionally observed in the course of their lives, that some incident or scene at the moment occurring to them, it may be of a quite trivial nature, has been witnessed by them once before, and is in an instant recognized." *Human Physiology* (London: Sampson Low, 1856), 331.

The presence of the original—Walter Benjamin, "The Work of Art in the Age of Mechanical Reproduction," in *Illuminations: Essays and Reflections,* ed. Hannah Arendt, trans. Harry Zohn (New York: Schocken, 1968), 217–51 (220, 222–23).

Tim O'Brien seeks to capture the paradox of war—Tim O'Brien, *The Things They Carried* (Boston: Houghton Mifflin, 1990), 87.

A problem proposed by Edmund Leach fifty-five years ago—"[I suggest] an interesting problem which is quite distinct from the purely philosophical issue as to what is the *nature* of Time. This is: How do we come to have such a verbal category as *time* at all? How does it link up with our everyday experiences?" Edmund Leach, "Two Essays Concerning the Symbolic Representation of Time," in *Rethinking Anthropology* (London: Athlone, 1961), 124–136 (124–25).

Consider, too, James Joyce's Ulysses—James Joyce, *Ulysses* (1922) (London: Picador, 1998), 592–93.

If culturally or historically specific modes of reckoning—Marshall Sahlins, *How "Natives" Think: About Captain Cook, for Example* (Chicago: Chicago University Press, 1995); Gananath Obeyesekere, *The Apotheosis of Captain Cook: European Myth-Making in the Pacific* (Princeton: Princeton University Press, 1992).

In such matters it never a question of either/or—"A careful examination of Obeyesekere (1992) and Sahlins (1995) suggests that they are partly talking at cross purposes. No matter how much evidence each presents to buttress his case, the other does not concur because each uses a different though related perspective to demonstrate different though related points." Robert Borovsky, "Cook, Lono, Obeyesekere, and Sahlins," *Current Anthropology* 38, no. 2 (1997): 255–282 (256).

Walter Benjamin's notion of the now (jetzeit)—Walter Benjamin, *The Arcades Project,* trans. Howard Eiland and Kevin McLaughlin (Cambridge: Belknap, 1999), 470.

More radically, Lauren Berlant—*Cruel Optimism* (Durham: Duke University Press, 2011), 66. James alludes to this, following E. R. Clay, as "the specious present," since every moment in the ongoing stream of time contains vestiges of past experience and anticipations of future events. William James, *Principles of Psychology* (New York: Dover, 1950), 1:609.

If as Michel de Certeau suggests—Michel de Certeau, *The Writing of History* (1975), trans. Tom Conley (New York: Columbia University Press, 1988), 2.

There are echoes here of Henri Bergson's notion of "inner duration"—Henri Bergson, "The Idea of Duration," in *Henry Bergson: Key Writings,* ed. Keith Ansell Pearson and John Mullarkey, trans. Melissa McMahon (New York: Continuum, 2002), 63.

Writing in her great memoir about those who survived Stalin's Gulag—Nadezhda Mandelstam, *Hope Against Hope: A Memoir,* trans. Max Hayward (Harmondsworth: Penguin, 1975), 455.

Lawrence Langer speaks of this as a movement from chronology to duration—Lawrence L. Langer, "The Alarmed Vision: Social Suffering and Holocaust Atrocity," in *Social Suffering,* ed. Arthur Kleinman, Veena Das, and Margaret Lock (Berkeley: University of California Press, 1997), 47–65 (55).

In Pig Earth—John Berger, *Pig Earth* (London: Writers and Readers Publishing Cooperative, 1979), 8.

E. E. Evans-Pritchard recounts a similar anecdote—E. E. Evans-Pritchard, *The Nuer: A Description of the Modes of Livelihood and Political Institutions of a Nilotic People* (Oxford: Clarendon, 1940), 108.

Rather than see history as valid and myth as illusory—Hayden White, *The Practical Past* (Evanston: Northwestern University Press, 2014), xi. Michael de Certeau makes a similar point: "History is probably our myth." De Certeau, *The Writing of History*, 21.

Hence Gaston Bachelard's famous observation—Gaston Bachelard, *The Poetics of Space*, trans. Maria Jolas (Boston: Beacon, 1969), 6.

Effects may precede causes and, to all intents and purposes, "bring about the past"—Michael Dummett, *Truth and Other Enigmas* (London: Duckworth, 1978), 319–50.

Contemporary allusions to slavery effectively bring the phenomenon into being—Shaw's superb ethnographic work among the Temne shows how the present and past "mutually configure" each other and how the habitus of the slave trade produced "oblique" effects and "practical memories" in contemporary cultural preoccupations with secrecy, suspicion, danger, theft, and witchcraft. Rosalind Shaw, *Memories of the Slave Trade: Ritual and the Historical Imagination in Sierra Leone* (Chicago: Chicago University Press, (2002). In a similarly nonreductive vein, Ferme argues that we should be alert to "the importance of understanding history not only as a site of causal explanations but also as a source of particular forms—symbolic, linguistic, practical—that social actors deploy to rework the social fabric in response to contingent events. These new social and cultural forms are the effect of a dialogical mediation between the present historical situation and a past repertoire of ideas with which social actors critically engage." Marian Ferme, *The Underneath of Things: Violence, History, and the Everyday in Sierra Leone* (Berkeley: University of California Press, 2001), 227).

Margaret Mead's famous "rap on race" with James Baldwin—Margaret Mead, *A Rap on Race* (Philadelphia: Lippincott, 1971), 188, 191, 167.

Experience is double-barreled—John Dewey reiterates James's argument in *Experience and Nature* (New York: Dover, 1958), 11, emphasizing that "the conception of experience as the equivalent of subjective private consciousness set over against nature, which consists wholly of physical objects, has wrought havoc in philosophy." Oakeshott concurs. "'Experience' stands for the concrete whole which analysis divides into 'experiencing' and 'what is experienced.' Experiencing and what is experienced are, taken separately, meaningless abstractions; they cannot, in fact, be separated." Michael Oakeshott, *Experience and Its Modes* (Cambridge: Cambridge University Press, 1933), 9.

The gambler may lose all track of time—As Schüll observes, the gambler plays not to win but to stay in a "zone where nothing else matters." Natasha Dow Schüll, *Addiction by Design: Machine Gambling in Las Vegas* (Princeton: Princeton University Press, 2012), 2. Walter Benjamin suggests that gambling creates an "intoxicating" sense of being-in-the-now, since every card dealt or every turn of the wheel of chance conjures a sense of a new beginning, independent of any previous condition, and free of the past. Benjamin, *The Arcades Project*, 512–13.

Time's wingèd chariot—Andrew Marvell, "To His Coy Mistress."

Nuer pastoralists have no word in their language—Evans-Pritchard, *The Nuer*, 102–3.

Death is always a matter of time—Heidegger speaks of Dasein's being-towards-death, though the potential to experience one's own extinction is inevitably contingent on the potential to experience the death of others. Martin Heidegger, *Being and Time*, trans. John Macquarie and Edward Robinson (New York: Harper and Row,

1962), 293–96. See also de Certeau, *The Writing of History*, in which he notes that our relation with death is simply another relation with time (5).

Regimes of historicity—See François Hartog, *Regimes of Historicity: Presentism and Experiences of Time* (2003), trans. Saskia Brown (New York: Columbia University Press, 2015), xvi–xvii.

diverse "tones of mental life"—Henry Bergson, *Matter and Memory*, trans. Nancy Margaret Paul and W. Scott Palmer (New York: Zone, 1988), 169.

Traditional Aboriginal conceptions of the Dreaming—"The Dreamings of Aboriginal Australia, as recognizable from the ethnographic record . . . appear archaeologically not out of time, but as having emerged at recognizable occasions in the past (likely gradually unfolding 3500–1400 BP)." Bruno David, *Landscapes, Rock-Art, and the Dreaming: An Archaeology of Preunderstanding* (London: Leicester University Press, 2002), 209.

Cyclical/linear—In a critique of Clifford Geertz's conception of Balinese time as "a motionless present, a vectorless now," Howe argues that Balinese are "perfectly capable of thinking in terms of linear/progressive time even when they are utilizing their traditional calendrical system . . . there is really no conflict between 'linear' and 'cyclical' (i.e., non-durational) time." L. Howe, "The Social Determinants of Knowledge: Maurice Bloch and Balinese Time," *Man* (n.s.), 16 (1981): 220–34. Cited in Alfred Gell, *The Anthropology of Time: Cultural Constructions of Temporal Maps and Images* (Providence: Berg, 1992), 74. See Lévi-Strauss on stationary/cumulative and cold and hot. Claude Lévi-Strauss, *Race and History* (Paris: UNESCO, 1952), 24–25; "The Scope of Anthropology," *Current Anthropology* 7, no. 2 (1966): 121; also Clifford Geertz, *The Interpretation of Culture* (New York: Basic Books, 1973), 404.

Rather, we need to speak of polyontologies—One of the most eloquent ethnographic arguments for this existential perspective is Devaka Premawardhana's essay "Conversion and Convertibility in Northern Mozambique," in *What is Existential Anthropology?* ed. Michael Jackson and Albert Piette (New York: Berghahn, 2015), 30–57. Tobie Nathan has made a compelling ethnopsychiatric case against reified or institutionalized notions of identity, preferring descriptions of "multiple, unstable identities subject to change within a lifespan, attributing equal value to each." Who, he asks, "can claim to be whom or what he or she is and nothing else?" "Across Space and Time: Identity and Transnational Diasporas," in *Transnationalism: Diasporas and the Advent of a New (dis)Order*, ed. Eliezer Ben-Rafael and Yitzhak Sternberg, with Judit Liwerant and Yosef Gorny (Boston: Brill, 2009), 181–94 (181–82). See also Michael Jackson, "Migrant Imaginaries and Multiple Lives," in *The Wherewithall of Life: Ethics, Migration, and the Question of Well-Being* (Berkeley: University of California Press, 2013), 201–8.

Bob Dylan would move from realist to surrealist imagery—Bob Dylan, "With God on Our Side," from *The Times They Are A'changin* (1964), and "My Back Pages," from *Another Side of Bob Dylan* (1964).

Time may not be unreal, as John McTaggart famously declared—John McTaggart, "The Unreality of Time," *Mind* 17, 68: 457–74.

However, as Johannes Fabian points out—Johannes Fabian, *Time and the Other: How Anthropology Makes Its Object* (New York: Columbia University Press, 1983).

Realism specializes in apparently unmediated experiences—Saul Bellow, "The Art of Fiction," interview with Gordon Lloyd Harper, *Paris Review* 36 (Winter 1966).

Herodotus shared this view—Hartog, *Regimes of Historicity*, 1.

Svetlana Boym's argument against seeing exile and expatriation as all-or-nothing phenomena—Svetlana Boym, "Off-Modern," in *Atlas of Transformation*, http://monumen taltotransformation.org/atlas-of-transformation/htm/o/off-modern/off-modern -svetlana-boym.html. See also Svetlana Boym, *The Future of Nostalgia* (New York: Basic Books, 2001), xvi–xvii.

Prologue

One sometimes happens on a scholarly essay—Thomas Schwarz Wentzer, "'I have Seen Königsberg Burning'": "Philosophical Anthropology and the Responsiveness of Historical Experience," *Anthropological Theory* 14, no. 1 (2014): 27–48.
Thomas quotes Walter Benjamin to convey this thought—Walter Benjamin, "Theses on the Philosophy of History," in *Illuminations: Essays and Reflections*, ed. Hannah Arendt, trans. Harry Zohn (translation modified by Thomas Schwartz Wentzer) (New York: Schocken, 1968), 254.

The Green Evening

The Te Kooti manhunt—was known as *Te Whai a Te Motu*—The Pursuit of the Island.
The Powelka Pandemonium—*New Zealand Truth*, 19 April 1910.

The Blind Impress

The Pawelkas settled near Oxford, North Canterbury—The names get Anglicized in New Zealand: Josef becomes Joseph; Alois becomes Louise, then Louisa; König becomes Koenig or King. Pawelka (or Pavelka) is the Czech diminutive of Paul (Pavel). In 1910 newspapers regularly misspelled the name Powelka.
Sixteen months after Mary Rosina's death—The redoubtable Rosina died in her eighty-fourth year (1913), a year and a half after Joe's disappearance.
The sense of having been pounded all over by invisible adversaries—James K. Baxter, "Notes on the Education of a New Zealand Poet," in *The Man on the Horse* (Dunedin: University of Otago Press, 1967), 121.

The Other Side of the Tracks

Ethnic Poles in Northern Germany—German-speaking immigrants in New Zealand. Gertraut Maria Stoffel, "The Austrian Connection with New Zealand in the Nineteenth Century," in *The German Connection: New Zealand and German-Speaking Europe in the Nineteenth Century*, ed. James N. Bade (Auckland: Oxford University Press, 1993), 21–34; Jerzy Woodzimierz Pobog-Jaworowski, *Polish Settlers in Taranaki, 1876–1976* (Wellington: National Library of New Zealand, 1976), 3–4.

Of the Woe That Is in Marriage

Of the Woe that is in Marriage—From the poem by Robert Lowell, first published in *Life Studies* (London: Faber and Faber, 1959).

It seems likely that Joe was guilty of petty larceny—Joe would be charged with stealing a lady's bicycle on 9 October from Ira Gordon, a painter and paperhanger who lived a few doors away.

It is now part of the Pawelka legend—The principal source is Albert William Organ's *The True Life Story of Joseph John Pawelka: His Crimes, Sentences, Prison Career, and Final Escape* (Wellington: Books and Papers, 1912). Other sources are W. H. Caron's and Jack R Sheehan's "Pawelka, the Gaol Breaker," in The *Kaiwarra Mystery . . . and More Famous Trials* (Wellington: National Magazines, 1935), 17–26; and Des Swain's *Pawelka* (Tauranga: Moana, 1989).

For the Rangitāne people, the word manawa-tu—Although *The Encyclopaedia of New Zealand* (1966, 2:395) claims that "the origin of the name Manawatu is obscure," the Rangitāne mythology is spelled out in J. M. McEwan's *Rangitane: A Tribal History* (Auckland: Heinemann, 1986), 16–17. For additional details, I am indebted to Te Pakaka Tawhai, personal communication, 29 June 1984.

Fires of No Return

Fires of No Return—In *Fires of No Return* is the title of a collection of poems by James K. Baxter (London: Oxford University Press, 1958). The image alludes to the Māori saying as long as a person lives on the land or returns to it regularly, a fire burns there (*ahi ka*). But if one goes away and does not return, the fire goes out (*ahi mataotao*).

In 1910, Palmerston is a town of 12,000—Palmerston North in 1910. George Conrad Petersen, *Palmerston North: A Centennial History* (Wellington: A. H. and A. W. Reed, 1973).

It is likely that this visitor was one of the thousands of vagrants—Petersen, *Palmerston North*, 143. See also, John A. Lee, *Roughnecks, Rolling Stones, and Rouseabouts* (Christchurch: Whitcoulls, 1977). On footloose young men as scapegoats, see Erik Olsen, "Towards a New Society," in *The Oxford History of New Zealand*, ed. Geoffrey W. Rice (Auckland: Oxford University Press, 1992), 261.

In Wellington I began reading Mikal Gilmore's A Shot in the Heart—Mikal Gilmore, *A Shot in the Heart* (New York: Doubleday, 1994), 133–34.

He is already the bogeyman parents use to frighten their errant children—Many older informants recalled how, when they were children, their parents warned them that Joe Pawelka would "get them" if they did not behave. According to Judith Binney, an earlier generation used Te Kooti in exactly the same way. Judith Binney, *Redemption Songs: A Life of Te Kooti Arikirangi Te Turuki* (Auckland: Auckland University Press, 1995), 4.

Fugue

Stanley Liddicoat—Stanley Liddicoat's name is given as Lidichen and Linton in other reports. Such journalistic imprecision is typical of both names and dates in newspaper articles covering the Pawelka story. In *The Manawatu Evening Standard*, 29 April 1910, the date of the theft of a steel from Dixon's butchery is given as 13 July 1909; in the *Records of the Magistrates Court* it is given as 6 July. While the *Standard* reports the theft of Ira Gordon's bicycle to have occurred on 9 October 1909, the *Records of the Court* state 1 November.

Pawelka's letter—*Evening Post*, 27 May 1910.

According to newspaper reports, Hanlon had been living in fear of the fugitive—One may suppose that Hanlon's intolerance of Joe Pawelka's failings reflected the self-congratulatory, vulnerable pride of the self-made man. Starting life as an Irish farm laborer, Hanlon migrated to New Zealand in 1879 at age 20. He married Lizzie Wilson's elder sister Jinny in 1883 and established himself as a carrier and entrepreneur. He owned "fine stables," the only hearse in the Ashhurst district, and the local coach. According to *The Cyclopaedia of New Zealand* (1897:208), his business as "about the best in the district."

Shots in the Dark

Was Joe Pawelka the man at Grover's Store—At his trial Pawelka is acquitted of the Farland burglary because of insufficient evidence.

Interviewed in hospital, McGuire says he "could not actually say it was Powelka"—Sergeant McGuire, whose bullet wound caused irreversible liver damage and septic peritonitis, dies at 6 A.M. on Thursday, 14 April. His funeral took place the following day at Pahiatua in torrential rain.

Joe Pawelka's alibi—Report by Sergeant Bowden, Feilding, 11 October 1911. PI 910/610 National Archives, Wellington.

No Quarter

Protest meetings were called and trade unions took up the case—I have made use of the following books in drawing this picture of Trade Unions and class divisions in New Zealand circa 1910: Laurie Barber, *New Zealand: A Short History* (London: Hutchinson, 1990), 87–99; Erik Olssen, "Towards a New Society," in *The Oxford History of New Zealand*, ed. Geoffrey Rice (Auckland: Oxford University Press, 1992), 254–84; Miles Fairburn, *The Ideal Society and Its Enemies: The Foundations of Modern New Zealand Society, 1850–1900* (Auckland: Auckland University Press, 1989); Tony Simpson, *A Vision Betrayed: The Decline of Democracy in New Zealand* (Auckland: Hodder and Stoughton, 1984).

We are not lumps of clay—Jean-Paul Sartre, *Saint Genet: Actor and Martyr*, trans. B. Frechtman (New York: Braziller, 1963), 49.

Escape

Indeed, it seems that he immediately set out to win the hearts—Albert William Organ, *The True Life Story of Joseph John Pawelka* (Wellington: Books and Papers, 1912), 75–76. The account of Pawelka's escape attempts is drawn from the police file (JPD 1911/15/2) that contains a detailed Department of Justice report on both the 17 August attempted escape and the successful 27 August escape.

Warder Eric Wallace raised the alarm—The following month, though absolved from "willful neglect," Warder Wallace was dismissed from the prison service.

Beyond the Call of Duty

Carlo Ginzburg begins his study of truth, falsity, and fiction—Carlo Ginzburg, *Threads and Traces: True, False, Fictive,* trans. Anne C. Tedeschi and John Tedeschi (Berkeley: University of California Press, 2012), 1.

Ray was a retired senior constable—Ray Carter, *Beyond the Call of Duty: A History of the Palmerston North Police District* (Palmerston North: Stylex Print, 1988).

Talking to Jack Hansen

When Bowden asked Hansen if he thought that Pawelka had left—Sergeant Bowden's report, Feilding, 11 October 1911. PI 1910/610 National Archives, Wellington.

Fitzgibbon asked if this view was founded on facts—Sergeant Fitzgibbon's report, Kimbolton, 28 October 1911. PI 1910/610 National Archives, Wellington.

Willie Hansen's derogatory remarks—*Manawatu Evening Standard,* 14 April 1910.

When in her nineties, Lula Parker-Betenson related the story—Lula Parker-Betenson, *Butch Cassidy, My Brother* (as told to Dora Flack) (Harmondsworth: Penguin, 1976), 1, 164, 168. For details of the Butch Cassidy story, see also Larry Pointer, *In Search of Butch Cassidy* (Norman: University of Oklahoma Press, 1977).

I was also reminded of Robyn Jensen's story—"The Girl Who Never Came Home: A Mother's Agony," review of Robyn Jensen's *Kirsa: A Mother's Story, New Zealand Herald Weekend Magazine,* 20 August 1994.

Still Life With Lading Lists

Pawelka at Gallipoli—I am grateful to Des Hurley for bringing to my attention an item that appeared in several New Zealand dailies in February 1916. On the strength of a letter from a soldier who reported seeing Pawelka in the Dardenelles, it was concluded that this must have been Joe. This was probably either wishful thinking or journalistic opportunism. Surely Joe's brother Jack, who was at Gallipoli before being invalided to England with enteric fever, would have known if his elder brother was also there. There is, I suppose, a remote possibility that Jack left the Dardenelles well before the evacuation on 20 December 1915, and that his brother Joe then appeared on the scene, to be spotted by an old mate and made the subject of comment in a letter written between September and December 1915.

A sobering statistic—New Zealanders in World War I. *An Encyclopaedia of New Zealand* (Wellington: R. E. Owen, 1966), 3:559–68.

Pawelka's possible aliases—I have checked twenty-five of the forty-two John Wilsons who served in the Australian armed forces in World War I, as well as one Joseph Wilson (d. Auburn NSW 1934, aged thirty-nine; Joe Pawelka would have been forty-seven in 1934). I have also checked all but one of the Joseph Wilsons (whose father's names were also Joseph) in the NSW Registry of Deaths. I have also checked the New Zealand War Register (1914–1918), but to no avail. As a footnote to this research, Joe Pawelka's cousin and namesake, Joseph Pavelka, was killed accidentally at White Rock in December 1912—the same year Joe left New Zealand—and another of Joe's cousins, Edward Pavelka, was killed in action in France in June 1916.

The Remaining Pieces

The sale of the section at Edwards Street—"Pawelka's Flight: Sensational Happenings Recalled by Land Sale," *Manawatu Evening Standard*, 13 January 1965.

Guilt and Shame

Kids would taunt her about being related to a murderer—Coincidentally, Marion Leahy (née Wilson), who shared these reminiscences with me, was the granddaughter of Sarah Wilson (née Spinks) who lived three doors from my grandparents' house in Inglewood. When telling me about Joe Pawelka, my grandfather would often mention "old Mrs Wilson who lives along the street," but it wasn't until I met Marion Leahy that I learned of her exact connection with Joe Pawelka. Sarah Wilson married James Wilson, one of Lizzie's older brothers. James Wilson died in 1944, Sarah eighteen years later in 1962.

Death's Secretary

A picture of wounded narcissism—Erich Fromm, *The Anatomy of Human Destructiveness* (London: Jonathan Cape, 1974), 200–5. But, of such clinical profiles, Oliver Sacks cautions, "The danger is that we may go overboard in medicalizing our predecessors (and contemporaries), reducing their complexity to expressions of neurological or psychiatric disorder, while neglecting all the other factors that determine a life, not least the irreducible uniqueness of the individual." Oliver Sacks, *An Anthropologist on Mars* (New York: Knopf, 1995), 165.

In 1987, broadcaster and freelance journalist Des Swain—Des Swain, *Pawelka* (Tauranga: Moana, 1989), 109, 110.

John Berger observes that—John Berger, "The Secretary of Death," in *The Sense of Sight: Writings by John Berger* (New York: Pantheon, 1985), 239–42. Berger is drawing on Walter Benjamin's comments in "The Storyteller" that "Death is the sanction of everything that the storyteller can tell. He has borrowed his authority from death." Walter Benjamin, *Illuminations: Essays and Reflections,* ed. Hannah Arendt, trans. Harry Zohn (New York: Schocken, 1968), 94.

George Santayana once observed that—George Santayana, *Life of Reason; or, The Phases of Human Progress* (New York: Scribner's, 1955).

Time and Space

Both history and ethnography are concerned with societies others then the one in which we live—Claude Lévi-Strauss, "Introduction: History and Anthropology," *Structural Anthropology,* trans. Claire Jacobson and Brooke Grundfest Schoepf (New York: Basic Books, 1963), 1–27 (18, 16).

Homogenous space and homogenous time—Henry Bergson, *Matter and Memory,* trans. Nancy Margaret Paul and W. Scott Palmer (New York: Zone, 1988), 211.

Thus, in Northern Luzon, the Illongot—R. I. Rosaldo, *Illongot Headhunting, 1883–1974: A Study in Society and History* (Stanford: Stanford University Press, 1980), 48.

duration is our most prescient sense of being-in-time—Although Veena Das, following Bergson, argues that duration "is the very condition of subjectivity" (Veena Das, *Life and Words: Violence and the Descent into the Ordinary* [Berkeley: University of California Press, 2007], 98), I cannot think of time without immediately becoming aware of *where* I am and what I *doing.*

Here and there readily become metaphors for now and then, and vice versa—Bergson, *Matter and Memory,* 128.

Bergson observed that "time, conceived under the form of an unbounded and homogenous medium"—Henri Bergson, "The Idea of Duration," in *Henry Bergson: Key Writings,* ed. Keith Ansell Pearson and John Mullarkey, trans. Melissa McMahon (New York: Continuum, 2002), 59.

Past events, processes, institutions, person, and things are no longer perceivable—Hayden White, *The Practical Past* (Evanston, IL: Northwestern University Press, 2014), xi.

That every individual life between birth and death—Hannah Arendt, *The Human Condition* (Chicago: University of Chicago Press, 1958), 184.

A few days after this dream was shared—Michael Jackson, *At Home in the World* (Durham: Duke University Press, 1995), 69.

According to Nugget, Wagon Joe's crooked arm and pockmarked skin—Jackson, *At Home in the World,* 58.

Then ashes I was; not yet was I born—Frederica de Laguna, *Under Mount Saint Elias: The History and Culture of the Yakutat Tlingit* (Washington, DC: Smithsonian Institution Press, 1989), 673, 699; cited by Gananath Obeyesekere, *Imagining Karma: Ethical Transformation in Amerindian, Buddhist, and Greek Rebirth* (Berkeley: University of California Press, 2002), 51, 52.

A Mapuche thunder shaman—Ana Mariella Bacigalupo, *Thunder Shaman: Making History with Mapuche Spirits in Chile and Patagonia* (Austin: University of Texas Press, 2015).

In Cuba, a Kongo-inspired society of affliction known as Palo—Todd Ramón Ochoa, *Society of the Dead: Quota Manaquita and Palo Praise in Cuba* (Berkeley: University of California Press, 2010), 1.

A person possessed by spirits in Mayotte—Michael Lambek, *Human Spirits: A Cultural Account of Trance in Mayotte* (Toronto: University of Toronto Press, 1993). In seeking to do justice to this lived experience of history, Lambek evokes the title of Ian Hacking's 2002 book, *Historical Ontology*. "Both/And," in *What is Existential Anthropology*, ed. Michael Jackson and Albert Piette (New York: Berghahn, 2015), 58–83 (74).

In the mountains of East Naxos, Greece—Charles Stewart, *Dreaming and Historical Consciousness in Island Greece* (Cambridge: Harvard University Press, 2012).

Historicity is the only way in which Being is accessible to me—Karl Jaspers, *Philosophie* (Berlin: Springer, 1932), 2:152.

What we call the beginning is often the end—T. S. Eliot, "Little Gidding," from *Four Quartets* (London: Faber and Faber, 1959), 58.

A great part of my life was going to be spent in trying to define—Marguerite Yourcenar, *Reflections on the Composition of Memoirs of Hadrian* (New York: Farrar, Strauss and Giroux, 2005), 320, 323, 324, 325, 330, 340.

Marguerite Yourcenar's Souvenirs Pieux—Translated as *Dear Departed: A Memoir,* trans. Maria Pouisa Ascher (London: Virago, 1997).

The being I refer to as me—Yourcenar, *Dear Departed,* 3.

Beyond the confines of individual history—Yourcenar, *Dear Departed,* 3. Elsewhere, she has noted: "It is *very important* that the reader *not* get the impression that the author is greatly or personally interested about her origins, since the whole quest is more sociological and historical than personal." Cited by Harold Beaver, "Remembering the World She Never Knew," *New York Times Book Review,* 1 March 1992, 13.

Recapture and recount her history—Yourcenar, *Dear Departed,* 53.

As Joyce Johnson put it—*Minor Characters: A Beat Memoir* (London: Virago, 1983), 237.

First Things First

what hold our histories have over us—Karl Marx, *The Eighteenth Brumaire of Louis Bonaparte* (London: Lawrence and Wishart, 1984), 10. "Men make their own history, but they do not make it just as they please; they do not make it under circumstances chosen by themselves, but under circumstances directly encountered, given and transmitted from the past. The tradition of all the dead generations weighs like a nightmare on the brains of the living."

Memory, like a good storyteller, is an artful liar—Cf. Sue Halpern: "Memory . . . is an expert storyteller." *I Can't Remember What I Forgot: The Good News from the Front Lines of Memory Research* (New York: Harmony, 2008), 66.

Braided Rivers

cars falling into holes—Roger Marshall, recalling the Christchurch earthquake. Phil Mercer, "Christchurch: Broken City Faces Life After Quake," 24 February 2011, http://www.bbc.co.uk/news/world-asia-pacific-12565923.

Sohrab and Rustam—dir. Vishram Bedekar (1963), music Sajjad Hussain.

Against the Grain

in Canterbury, he could not decide—In his discussion of chiasmus in Butler's work, Ralf Norrman argues that since "the two halves of a chiasmus are each other's mirror images, chiasmus is therefore likely to be typical of narcissistic people, who have problems with their relations to others, and most of all wish to see in others a reflection of themselves." *Samuel Butler and the Meaning of Chiasmus* (Macmillan: London, 1986), 6–7.

beyond the pale of civilization—Samuel Butler, *A First Year in Canterbury Settlement*, ed. A. C. Brassington and P. B. Maling (Auckland: Blackwood and Janet Paul, 1964 [1863]), 48.

some signs of human care—Butler, *A First Year in Canterbury Settlement*, 59.

far better adapted—Butler, *A First Year in Canterbury Settlement*, 50.

sheep, horses, dogs, cattle—Butler, *A First Year in Canterbury Settlement*, 35.

the solitude was greater than I could bear—Samuel Butler, *Erewhon or Over the Range*, ed. Hans-Peter Breuer and Daniel F. Howard (Toronto: Associated University Presses,1981), 74.

totally debarred from the intellectual society of clever men—Letter to his aunt, Mrs. Worsley, 1861; cited in Peter Raby, *Samuel Butler: A Biography* (London: Hogarth, 1991), 81.

Early settlers in the Matukituki Valley—John C. Aspinall, *High Country Sheep Station: A Bulletin for Schools* (Wellington: Education Department, School Publications Branch, 1976), 6–8.

It took time to get used—"Matukituki," in Michael Jackson, *Going On* (Dunedin: McIndoe, 1985), 58–59.

the insubstantial and curiously childlike buildings—Compare Samuel Butler's first impressions of Lyttelton: "scattered wooden boxes of houses, with ragged roods of scrubby ground between them." Butler, *A First Year in Canterbury Settlement*, 33.

Henry Lawson at Mangamaunu—Details drawn from W. H. Pearson, *Henry Lawson Among Māoris* (Canberra: Australian National University Press, 1968); and Charles Ferrall, ed., *Henry Lawson in New Zealand* (Wellington: Steele Roberts, 2011).

sentimental rot—Henry Lawson, "A Daughter of Māoriland," *Antipodean* 3 (1897): 4.

Pākehā attitudes to Māori—Henry Lawson to Hugh McCallum, June 25, 1897, Mitchell Library Uncat. MSS. Set 184, Item 7.

I was slow at arithmetic—Henry Lawson, "Fragment of an Autobiography," Mitchell Library MS. Published in *The Stories of Henry Lawson*, ed. Cecil Mann, 3 vols. (Sydney: Angus and Roberston, 1964).

Poor girl... but I shouldn't care to punish her—Henry Lawson to Hugh McCallum, in *The Stories of Henry Lawson.*

there is no creature whose inward being is so strong—George Eliot, *Middlemarch* (Harmondsworth: Penguin, 1985), 896.

As the loneliness of this place is affecting Mrs. Lawson's health—Henry Lawson, letter to the secretary of education, September 28, 1897. Cited in Pearson, *Henry Lawson Among Māoris,* 177.

a disillusioned and cruelly wronged man—Henry Lawson to George Robertson, March 28 1917, "Correspondence re Selected Poems of Henry Lawson," Mitchell Library MS., ii, 260. On Māori recollections of Lawson, see Pearson, *Henry Lawson Among Māoris,* 156–57.

dark and lonely—Henry Lawson, "The Old Mile Tree," Miscellaneous MSS, verse 1, 111, Mitchell Library, A 1869. Published in *Bulletin,* 23 November 1911, 44.

miserable little hell of New Pipeclay—Lawson, "Fragment of an Autobiography," vol. 2, fo. 139–40.

delicate, shabby, soul-starved—1913 "Fragment of an Autobiography," vol. 4, fo. 193.

Lawson was predisposed—Pearson, *Henry Lawson Among Māoris,* 152.

Bill Pearson himself—Paul Millar writes of Pearson as "diffident . . . hesitant, unsure of himself, vulnerable," and "quite outside the pale," thus echoing Lawson's descriptions of his childhood personality. Pearson was also bullied at school and "picked on" at home. He recognized Hans Christian Andersen's tale of the ugly duckling "as the story of myself." Paul Millar, *No Fretful Sleeper: A Life of Bill Pearson* (Auckland: Auckland University Press, 2010), 325, 192, 32, 31.

magnificently ugly . . . a calm and sensuous soul—The first comments are by Henry James, the second by Ralph Waldo Emerson.

there is no creature whose inward being—Eliot, "Finale," *Middlemarch.*

I sometimes wonder whether—Bill Pearson, from an unpublished interview with Jeffrey Paparoa Holman, 12 July 1999. Paul Millar also makes this connection between Bill Pearson's identification with Māori and his own sense of being excluded and disparaged. The Māori club became, for him, an alternative community, a place of "warmth and unconditional friendship." Millar, *No Fretful Sleeper,* 236–37.

I pulled out of the Māori club—Pearson, *Henry Lawson Among Māoris,* 113.

No Direction Home

No Direction Home—Bob Dylan documentary: *No Direction Home: Bob Dylan,* dir. Martin Scorsese (2005). The title is from Dylan's song, "Like a Rolling Stone" (*Highway 61 Revisited*).

why Lawson was so uninspired by the Inland Kaikoura range—One of Lawson's rare poetic evocations of the Kaikoura Coast is interleaved with nostalgic references to the Australian outback, "the wastes of the Never Never . . . where the dead men lie." Charles Ferrall, ed., *Henry Lawson in New Zealand* (Wellington: Steele Roberts, 2011), 117–18.

the idea of "originals" among the Mehinaku—Carla Stang, *A Walk to the River in Amazonia: Ordinary Reality for the Mehinaku Indians* (New York: Berghahn, 2009), 51–52.

Next I was a waitress and a bookshop assistant—Brigid Lowry, "My Writing Life," Brigid Lowry website, www.tasman.net/~penwoman/.

Sometimes it seems the most pleasurable job—Lowry, "My Writing Life."

Beginnings are not the same as origins—Paul Ricoeur, *Critique and Conviction: Conversations with François Azouvi and Marc de Launay*, trans. Kathleen Blamey (New York: Columbia University Press, 1998), 100.

This was the enigma of anteriority—Ricoeur, *Critique and Conviction.*

jute barons and jute industry—Samita Sen, *Women and Labor in Late Colonial India: The Bengal Jute Industry* (Cambridge: Cambridge University Press, 1999).

When the Roman jailers—Jean-Paul Clébert, *The Gypsies*, trans. Charles Duff (Harmondsworth: Penguin, 1967), 24–26.

Crossing Cook Strait

Crossing Cook Strait—James K. Baxter, *In Fires of No Return* (London: Oxford University Press, 1958), 58.

I've always tended to look back—Cited in Athol McCredie, "The Social Landscape," in *Witness to Change: Life in New Zealand*, ed. John Pascoe, Les Cleveland, and Ans Westra (Wellington: PhotoForum, 1985), 52. See also Les Cleveland, *Message from the Exterior, Six Decades* (Wellington: City Gallery, 1998).

John Mulgan's Man Alone (Auckland: Longman Paul, 1972).

Les Cleveland, *The Iron Hand: New Zealand Soldiers' Poems from World War Two* (Wellington: Wai-te-Ata Press, 1979).

But I could not persuade anyone in the battalion—Cleveland, *The Iron Hand*, 11–12. In his poem "The Long Way Back," Cleveland writes of the same moment: "A week ago the other survivors / Carousing rowdily in Rome / Declined to join this excursion" (51).

and all the other friends of friends—Cleveland, *The Iron Hand*, 52.

Back in New Zealand—Cleveland, *The Iron Hand*, 12.

a stripped-down, pragmatic mentality—David Brooks, "Where's the Trauma and the Grief?" *New York Times*, 15 August 2008.

If I were to attempt an epic of our military experience—Les Cleveland, "An Assiduous Industry," *New Zealand Books*, June 1997, 15.

combat soldiers have something in common with workers in hazardous civilian occupations—Les Cleveland, "Soldiers' Songs: The Folklore of the Powerless," *New York Folklore* 11, nos. 1–4 (1985): 79. See also Les Cleveland, *Dark Laughter: War and Song in Popular Culture* (Westport, CT: Praeger, 1994).

Ag Demetrios—The Church of Saint Demetrius, or Hagios Demetrios (Greek: Άγιος Δημήτριος), is the main sanctuary dedicated to Saint Demetrius, the patron saint of Thessaloniki, in Central Macedonia, Greece, dating from a time when it was the second largest city of the Byzantine Empire.

a Taoist view that sees the world as essentially (and demonically) chaotic—Michael Puett and Christine Gross-Loh, *The Path: What Chinese Philosophers Can Teach Us About the Good Life* (New York: Simon and Schuster, 2016).

Metaphor of the Table

My life as Me—Barry Humphries, *My Life as Me: A Memoir* (London: Michael Joseph, 2002), 75–77.

Banaba is our mother—Jennifer Shennan and Makin Corrie Tekenimatang, eds., *One and a Half Pacific Islands: Stories Banaban People Tell of Themselves* (Wellington: Victoria University Press, 2005), 128.

the loss of laughter and joy—Shennan and Tekenimatang, *One and a Half Pacific Islands*, 115.

We look on Rabi as synonymous with Banaba—Shennan and Tekenimatang, *One and a Half Pacific Islands*, 127.

Life is good—Shennan and Tekenimatang, *One and a Half Pacific Islands*, 71.

the first complete New Zealand pop song—Chris Bourke, *Blue Smoke: The Lost Dawn of New Zealand Popular Music 1918–1964* (Auckland: Auckland University Press, 2010), 155.

even as a child he was "extremely shy"—Bourke, *Blue Smoke*, 154.

one day, "halfway across the Indian Ocean"—James Thornton, "Ruru Karaitiana—Māori Songwriter," *New Settler* (1949): 17. Cited in Bourke, *Blue Smoke*, 103.

within half an hour he had written lyrics "in his head"—"Success in America: Dunedin Songwriter's 'Blue Smoke,'" *Otago Daily Times*, 5 April 1952, 11. Cited in Bourke, *Blue Smoke*, 103.

It is possible, however, that the tune—Les Cleveland, personal communication, 4 August 2011.

differed from the lines penned by Ruru Karaitiana—Les Cleveland recalls that Ngarimu's lines were identical with the lines he learned in Trentham Camp and the Middle East in 1943.

recorded more "slow sad waltzes"—Bourke, *Blue Smoke*, 161.

I don't know whether Ruru ever felt free to start—Jack Kelleher, "Blue Smoke," *Dominion*, 17 December 1970, 15. Cited in Bourke, *Blue Smoke*, 163.

Destruction and Hope

Destruction and Hope—Paul Klee, San Francisco Museum of Modern Art.

On April 15, 1945—Though echoing Keith's account of his father's experience, the following paragraph is closely based on Gavin Mortimer's account of the liberation of Celle and of Belsen. Gavin Mortimer, *Stirling's Men: The Inside History of the SAS in World War 11* (London: Weidenfeld and Nicolson, 2004), 322–24.

It is as if I walked into Dachau—Cited in Caroline Moorehead, *Martha Gellhorn: A Life* (New York: Vintage: 2004), 284.

His sense of continuity was powerful—Keith Ridler, "If Not the Words: Shared Practical Activity and Friendship in Fieldwork," in *Things As They Are: New Directions of Phenomenological Anthropology*, ed. Michael Jackson (Bloomington: Indiana University Press, 1996), 244.

while you are at the table—Paul Myerscough, "Diary," *London Review of Books*, 29 January, 2009, 35.

Distance Looks Our Way

Distance looks our way—Charles Brasch, "The Islands" (ii), in *Selected Poems,* ed. Alan Roddick (Dunedin: Otago University Press, 2015), 32.
Schweitzer's dismay—*On the Edge of the Primeval Forest* (Macmillan: New York, 1948). Schweitzer discusses briefly the conflicts between what he calls civilizing and colonizing interests (79) and makes observations on the timber trade without, however, remarking the negative repercussions of massive deforestation.

The Illusion of Corsica

Gregory O'Brien's recently published memoir—Gregory O'Brien, *News of the Swimmer Reaches Shore: A Guide to French Usage* (Wellington: Victoria University Press, 2007).
those who cannot remember the past are condemned to repeat it—George Santayana, *The Life of Reason; or, The Phases of Human Progress* (New York: Scribner's, 1905).
The solace of such work lies in this—Lawrence Durrell, *Justine* (London: Faber and Faber, 1957), 17.
Every day includes much more non-being than being—Virginia Woolf, *Moments of Being: Unpublished Autobiographical Writings* (London: Triad Grafton, 1978), 81.
the pollinating gift of facts—This and the following quotations concerning Norman Lewis appear in a review of a Lewis biography by novelist and essayist Andrew O'Hagen, "Candle Moments," *London Review of Books,* 25 September 2008, 23.
while some psychologists find evidence for the permanence of some memory traces—David F. Hall, Elizabeth F. Loftus, and James P. Tousignant, "Postevent Information and Changes in Recollection for a Natural Event," in *Eyewitness Testimony: Psychological Perspectives,* ed. Gary L. Wells and Elizabeth F. Loftus (Cambridge: Cambridge University Press, 1984), 124–41 (132–35).
to see people not only as they are but as they might be—Lyndall Gordon, *A Private Life of Henry James: Two Women and His Art* (London: Chatto and Windus, 1998).
In truth, everyone, in life—Letter of Henry James to Grace Norton (1880). Cited by Colm Tóibín, "A Man with My Trouble," *London Review of Books,* 3 January 2008, 15–18.
during a four day's passage—This and the following quotations are from Joseph Conrad's "Author's Note" to *Victory* (London: J. M. Dent, 1962), ix–xvii.

Return to the Manawatu

A cherry tree—Letter from Emilie Monrad in *Kaingahou: A Palmerston North Home for Many Families from the Monrads to the Present Day,* comp. Bodil and Gunner Petersen (Palmerston North: Manawatu Branch Committee of the New Zealand Historic Places Trust, 2001), 11.

He and his companions—Val A. Burr, on behalf of the Scandinavian Club of Manawatu, *Mosquitoes and Sawdust: A History of Scandinavians in Early Palmerston North and Surrounding Districts ('Scandia 11')* (Palmerston North, 1995), 49.

The People of the Four Winds—"The mixed Māori population of Pukekohe have given themselves a name—Nga Hau E Wha (The Four Winds)—which expresses their varied backgrounds. The Four Winds of Māoridom appear to have been caught in the stronger current of change, and it is worthwhile considering the direction in which they are blowing." B. Kernot, "Which Way Are the Winds Blowing." *Te Ao Hou* 42 (March 1963): 20.

torn between two languages, one expressive, the other critical—Roland Barthes, *Camera Lucida: Reflections on Photography* (1980), trans. Richard Howard (New York: Farrar, Straus and Giroux, 2010), 8.

what Walter Benjamin calls "the unique existence," or the "aura" of the original—Walter Benjamin, "The Work of Art in the Age of Mechanical Reproduction," in *Illuminations: Essays and Reflections,* ed. Hannah Arendt, trans. Harry Zohn (New York: Schocken, 1968), 221–22.

it was Thomas Wolfe who famously said, "You can't go home again"—Thomas Wolfe, "The Quest for the Fair Medusa," from *You Can't Go Home Again,* excerpted in Maxwell Geismar, *Selections from the Works of Thomas Wolfe* (London: Heinemann, 1952), 505, 557.

Burned Places

Burned places—Most Taranaki towns were built in bush clearings after the native forest was axed and fired. The Gaelic etymology of Inglewood, my hometown, is from *aingeal,* "fire," hence "a fire-cleared space in a forest."

He and a friend Bill Webb would go across the bridge—Julia Millen, *Ronald Hugh Morrieson: A Biography* (Auckland: David Ling, 1996), 120.

a revue called Topsy Turvey—Allan Thomas, *Music Is Where You Find It: Music in the Town of Hawera, 1946: An Historical Ethnography* (Wellington: School of Music, Victoria University of Wellington/Music Books New Zealand, 2004), 61–64.

Te Hawera *means burned place in Māori*—John Houston, *Māori Life in Old Taranaki* (Wellington: Reed, 1965), 180–81.

In the 1940s and 1950s, Māori lived in the small settlement of Taiporohenui—Thomas, *Music Is Where You Find It,* 36.

Fires in Morrieson's fiction—Fires connected with insurance scams and illicit gambling also appear in *Came a Hot Friday.* Millen, *Ronald Hugh Morrieson,* 156–57.

Revenant

That's the bad part about golf—Johnny Miller, commenting on Retief Goosen (on the eve of his fortieth birthday), about to putt on the sixteenth green at the PGA Transitions Championship, Sunday, 22 March 2009.

Te Āti Awa

Te Āti Awa—The generic name for the iwi occupying their ancestral homelands in Taranaki.

Between the abstract poles of dominance and subordination—Ranajit Guha, *Dominance and Hegemony: History and Power in Colonial India* (Cambridge: Harvard University Press, 1997), 20–23.

The simple fact—Hannah Arendt, "Labor, Work, Action," in *The Portable Hannah Arendt*, ed. Peter Baehr (New York: Penguin, 2000), 180.

strikes out on its own and affects others—Hannah Arendt, *The Human Condition* (Chicago: University of Chicago Press, 1958), 190.

the chaotic uncertainty of the future—Arendt, *The Human Condition*, 237.

Life is a constant struggle between progression and regression—Te Pakaka Tawhai, "He Tipuna Wharenui o te Rohe o Uepohatu," MA thesis, Massey University, Palmerston North, New Zealand, 1978, 16.

the milder and quieter reception within the lighted house at night—Te Rangi Hiroa (Peter Buck), *The Coming of the Māori*, 2nd ed. (Wellington: Whitcombe and Tombs, 1966), 373.

ancient explanations and ancestral wisdom (kōrero tahito) are invaluable—Te Pakaka Tawhai, "He Tipuna Wharenui o te Rohe o Uepohatu," 14. Judith Binney makes the same point, observing that "narratives born of social and political crises are preserved in memory not so much as records of those times but as tools by which to act in the present. When cast in predictive form, an 'orthodox' structuring for many oral societies, they may also change the present, and the future." Judith Binney, *Stories Without End: Essays 1975-2010* (Wellington: Bridget Williams, 2010), 325.

the past is never dead—William Faulkner, *Requiem for a Nun* (New York: Random House, 1951), 73.

For Māori, the past is seen as that which lies before one—Binney, *Stories Without End*, 72.

I will not agree to our bedroom being sold—cited in *The Taranaki Report*—Waitangi Tribunal, *Kaupapa Tuatahi* (Wellington: Government Printer, 1996), 3.6.

As the troops advanced—Waitangi Tribunal, *Kaupapa Tuatahi*, 4.5.

In 1863, the army, now vastly outnumbering Māori—In 1860, there were eight hundred British troops in Taranaki. A year later the number had risen to thirty-five hundred; by 1865 it was almost five thousand. Te Āti Awa fighters seldom numbered more than five hundred, and in his first campaigns Titokowaru was outnumbered twelve to one. Waitangi Tribunal, *Kaupapa Tuatahi*, 4.10.

I hitch up my horse and pass to the front—Cited in Dick Scott, *Ask That Mountain: The Story of Parihaka* (Auckland: Heinemann, 1975), 11.

Te Whiti-o-Rongomaia and Tohu Kakahi—Both men attended the Reverend Johannes Frederic Riemenschneider's mission school at Warea, built and managed a flourmill there, and arranged horticultural and building schemes until 1865, when Warea's school, homes, mill, and cultivations were destroyed by government troops. They then made their decision to establish Parihaka.

it cannot be assumed that grievance dissipates—Waitangi Tribunal, *Kaupapa Tuatahi*, 5.9.

The fact that one group—Michael King, *Being Pākehā Now: Reflections and Recollections of a White Native* (Auckland: Penguin 1999), 11.

As far as I am concerned—King, *Being Pākehā Now*, 235.

But pointing out that all New Zealanders are immigrants—J. G. A. Pocock argues that both Māori and Pākehā immigrated to New Zealand under duress—escaping marginalization in their original homelands, victims of social injustice, exiles from Eden. Whether their origin stories are called history or myth, they provide common ground for conversations between two peoples whose histories have driven them together. "Once the Pākehā stop seeing their first ancestors as heroic barbarians and see them as dispossessed exiles from paradise instead, dialogue with the tangata whenua becomes possible. The question is whether either group will retain a discourse of liberty, or merely self-pity." J. G. A. Pocock, "Tangata Whenua and Enlightenment Anthropology," *New Zealand Journal of History* 27, no. 1 (1992): 28–53 (44–45). Anne Salmond makes a similar argument in *Two Worlds: First Meetings Between Māori and Europeans, 1642–1772* (Honolulu: University of Hawaii Press, 1991).

the aspiration of many Māori to be Māori first and New Zealanders second—King, *Being Pākehā Now*, 132.

This is not only because those who proclaim to be autochthonous—In the Cameroons, for instance, "Beti and Bulu people now proudly proclaim to be autochthones—'born from the soil'—of the forest area in the south of the country. Yet the same Beti/Bulu may clinch arguments over to whom the forest 'really' belongs with the simple statement 'La forêt est à nous puisqu'on l'a conquise' (the forest is ours because we conquered it), referring to their epic immigration from the savannah southward into the forest 150 to 200 years ago." Peter Geschiere, *The Perils of Belonging: Auchthony, Citizenship, and Exclusion in Africa and Europe* (Chicago: Chicago University Press, 2009), ix–x.

Symbolic Landscape

Symbolic Landscape—Diego Rivera, San Francisco Museum of Modern Art.

From low on the water—Geoff Park, *Nga Uruora: The Groves of Life: Ecology and History in a New Zealand Landscape* (Wellington: Victoria University Press, 1995), 119.

the expatriate's attempt to inoculate himself against a nostalgia—Walter Benjamin, *Berlin Childhood Around 1900*, trans. Howard Eiland (Cambridge: Belknap, 2006), 37.

There is a balance here—Vincent O'Sullivan, *Blame Vermeer* (Wellington: Victoria University Press, 2009).

Two Women

Two Women—Fernand Léger, San Francisco Museum of Modern Art.

our wariness of new technologies—A paraphrase of Michael Jackson, "Familiar and Foreign Bodies," in *Existential Anthropology: Events, Exigencies and Effects* (New York: Berghahn, 2005), 131.

on the slowness with which new technologies are taken up—Gerard Macdonald, "The Political Economy of Schooling," in Gerard Macdonald and David Hursh, *Twenty-First Century Schools: Knowledge, Networks, and New Economies* (Rotterdam: Sense, 2006).

Samuel Butler's letter—"Darwin Among the Machines," *Christchurch Press*, 13 June 1863. Republished in *The Note-Books of Samuel Butler*, ed. Henry Festing Jones (New York: Dutton, 1917), 42–47.

All my life I have loved traveling at night—Michael Ondaatje, *Divisadero* (New York: Vintage International, 2007), 136.

every writer creates his own precursors—Jorges Luis Borges, "Kafka and His Precursors," trans. James E. Irby, in *Labyrinths*, ed. Donald A. Yates and James E. Irby (Harmondsworth: Penguin, 1970), 236. Borges acknowledges T. S. Eliot's earlier phrasing of this view in his essay "Tradition and the Individual Talent," in *Points of View*, ed. John Hayward (London: Faber, 1941), 25–26.

we can rearrange the furniture of our past and reorganise the figures in its landscapes—Echoes of this idea inform Michael White's remarkable work on the process of "remembering" in narrative therapy, *Maps of Narrative Practice* (New York: Norton, 2007), ch. 3.

The Road to Karuna Falls

distant and listless, and engrossed with cares—Alistair Campbell, *Island to Island* (Christchurch: Whitcoulls, 1984), 75.

the Campbell children who had been "lost across the sea"—Campbell, *Island to Island*, 9.

It was a fairy tale ending—Campbell, *Island to Island*, 9.

Kumarahou, mānuka, kawakawa, horopito—For further details, see Murdoch Riley, *Māori Healing and Herbal: New Zealand Ethnobotanical Sourcebook* (Paraparaumu: Viking Sevenseas, 1994).

Startling though the image may be—Carole Hungerford, *Good Health in the Twenty-first Century: A Family Doctor's Unconventional Guide* (Melbourne, Scribe, 2006), 412.

Where Do We Come From? What Are We? Where Are We Going?

Where do we come from? What are we? Where are we going?—Paul Gauguin (1897), Museum of Fine Arts, Boston.

Emily had been an exceptional pupil at Shelf Board School—Following the 1870 Education Act, schools were established under the control of locally elected school boards. Although fees could be charged, the schools were financed by government grants and subsidized by local government rates. Education was provided for children from five to ten.

The hospital was built in 1912 and closed in 1998—Lester Thorley, "Return to Tokanui," *Waikato Times*, July 8, 2006.

I had seized upon its emptiness and remoteness as a symbol of my own estrangement—Dyer makes a similar observation in his book on D. H. Lawrence. "Lawrence himself said more or less the same thing in *Kangaroo*. The autobiographical figure, Richard Lovat Somers, 'wearied himself to death struggling with the problem of himself and calling it Australia.'" Geoff Dyer, *Out of Sheer Rage: Wrestling with D. H. Lawrence* (New York: Picador, 2009), 114.

Taking a Line for a Walk

Taking a line for a walk—Paul Klee, *Notebooks,* vol. 1: *The Thinking Eye,* trans. R. Manheim (London: Lund Humprires, 1961), 105.

a recent issue of Psychology Today—Jay Dixit, "Heartbreak and Home Runs: The Power of First Experiences," *Psychology Today* 43, no. 1 (January/February 2010): 61–69 (62).

a region where our lives are prepared—Maurice Merleau-Ponty, *The Structure of Behavior,* trans. Alden L Fisher (Boston: Beacon, 1967), 222.

Hannah Arendt's notion of natality—Hannah Arendt, *The Human Condition* (Chicago: University of Chicago Press, 1958), 177.

the enigma of anteriority—Paul Ricoeur, *Critique and Conviction: Conversations with François Azouvi and Marc de Launay,* trans. Kathleen Blamey (New York: Columbia University Press, 1998), 100.

the godwits vanish toward another summer—Charles Brasch, "The Islands" (ii), in *Selected Poems,* ed. Alan Roddick (Dunedin: Otago University Press, 2015), 32.

the sailor lives, and stands beside us—Allen Curnow, "Landfall in Unknown Seas," in *Early Days Yet: New and Collected Poems 1941–1997* (Auckland: Auckland University Press, 1997), 15"

cling to the story the way the handprints of the potter cling to the clay vessel—Walter Benjamin, *Illuminations: Essays and Reflections,* ed. Hannah Arendt, trans. Harry Zohn (New York: Schocken, 1969), 92.

rule of life to overtake the rule of thought—Ricoeur, *Critique and Conviction,* 2.

exerted a very strong influence—Ricoeur, *Critique and Conviction,* 4.

always slips away at the same time as it surges up in the present—Ricoeur, *Critique and Conviction,* 100.

In his discussion of what he calls "Aztec moments"—David Carrasco, "Aztec Moments and Chicano Cosmovision: Aztlan Recalled to Life," in *Moctezuma's Mexico: Visions of the Aztec World,* ed. David Carrasco and Eduardo Matos Moctezuma, rev. ed. (Boulder: University of Colorado Press, 2003).

Writing in Noces *about such places as Algiers, Tipasa, Oran, and Djemila*—Albert Camus, "Nuptials" (1938), in *Lyrical and Critical Essays,* trans. Ellen Conroy Kennedy (New York: Vintage, 1970), 62–105.

Coda

The tale taken directly from life—David Shields, *Reality Hunger: A Manifesto* (New York: Knopf, 2010), 200.

My personal existence must be the resumption of a prepersonal existence—Maurice Merleau-Ponty, *Phenomenology of Perception* (London: Routledge and Kegan Paul, 1962), 254.

Experience is indivisible and continuous—John Berger, *Pig Earth* (London: Writers and Readers Publishing Cooperative, 1979), 6.

Indiana University cinema interview with Abbas Kiarostami, July 21, 2014, *An Abbas Kiarostami Interview: An IU Cinema Exclusive* https://www.youtube.com/watch ?v=neYgsuUC8pw.

Existence is not something—Jean-Luc Nancy, "On Evidence: Life and Nothing More, by Abbas Kiarostami," *Discourse* 21, no. 1 (Winter 1999): 76–87 (83).

inside and outside us at one and the same time—Henri Bergson, "Concerning the Nature of Time," in *Henri Bergson: Key Writings* (2002), 205–19 (205).

This image . . . is evidence of what it means to speak of life going on—Stuart Jeffries, "Landscapes of the Mind," an interview with Abbas Kiarostami, *Guardian*, November 19, 2005, http://www.theguardian.com/film/2005/apr/16/art.

When you are a tree that is rooted in the ground—Jeffries, "Landscapes of the Mind."

All this classifying, it seems to me, is the very antithesis of literature—Aminatta Forna, "Don't Judge a Book by Its Author," *Guardian*, February 13, 2015, www.theguardian .com/books/2015/feb/13/aminatta-forna-don't-judge-book-by-cover.

Kowa yabar gida, gida ya barshi—I am grateful to Emily Williamson for sharing this Hausa saying with me.

Acknowledgments

The Blind Impress

Warm thanks are due to Shamian Firth of Dunmore Publishing, Auckland, New Zealand, for her editorial expertise and support when *The Blind Impress* was originally published in 1997. I would also like to thank Juliet Batten, Les and Mary Cleveland, Bryn and Isabelle Jones, Judith Loveridge and Keith Ridler, Bronwen Nicholson and Brian Boyd, Jennifer Shennan and Allan Thomas for their unfailing friendship and hospitality to me in New Zealand. For their generous help and goodwill, I owe a great deal to John and Maria Bryce, Ray Carter, Jack Hansen, Anne Harris, Richard Hill, Desmond Hurley, Fay Jaquiery, Stewart Lusk, and Marion Leahy. Acknowledgement is also made for permission to quote materials from the following sources:

National Archives, Wellington: *Police Department File* 1910 on Escaped Prisoner John Joseph Pawelka (National Archives, Pl 1910/610); *Criminal Record Book* No. 11 of the Magistrates Court, Palmerston North, covering the period 5 May 1909 to 25 October 1910 (National Archives, Box 855 MOY W 3298); *Trial and Sentencing File*: Rex versus Joseph John Pawelka, Supreme Court of NZ, Palmerston North (National Archives, Box 734 MOY W3298); Passenger Lists, Auckland outward, Jan-July 1912 (National Archives SS 1 311).

Alexander Turnbull Library, Wellington: *Manawatu Evening Standard, New Zealand Truth, Evening Post,* and *New Zealand Times.*

The Enigma of Anteriority

I wish to thank the Center for the Study of World Religions at Harvard Divinity School for the Faculty Grant that funded my fieldwork and travels in Aotearoa New Zealand and Australia in 2008 and 2011. I am also deeply grateful to the following friends, family, and colleagues for their hospitality, support, and shared stories, as well as their generosity in allowing me to publish passages from private conversations: Brian Boyd, Alan Campbell, Ngaere Campbell, Richard Campbell, Dr. Kate Campbell, Christie Carlson, David Carrasco, Les Cleveland, Mary Cleveland, Ronda Cooper, Martin Edmond, Kathy Golski, Jack Golson, Beth Jones, Ruth Jones, Anne Harris, Jeffrey Paparoa Holman, Heidi Jackson, Helen Jackson, Juliet Jackson, Louisa Jackson, Margaret Jackson, Miles Jackson, Judith Loveridge, Brigid Lowry, Ewen Macdonald, Karl Maughan, Susan Lloyd McGarry, Bronwen Nicolson, Anne Noonan, Susan Norrie, Gregory O'Brien, Mahara Okeroa, Vincent O'Sullivan, Peter Oxley, Geoff Park, Emily Perkins, Rachel Perkins, Michael Puett, Nigel Rapport, Keith Ridler, Larry Rueter, Jennifer Shennan, Cris Shore, Birgitte Refslund Sorensen, Don Swearer, Allan Thomas. Last but not least, I warmly acknowledge Penelope Todd's and Raymond Huber's invaluable editorial guidance during my writing of an earlier version of "The Enigma of Anteriority" (published as an ebook entitled *Road Markings: An Anthropologist in the Antipodes* (Dunedin: Rosa Mira, 2012).

Index

Holocaust, xvi–xvii, 176–77, 275n
Home: expatriation and, 237; identity and,
  252; returning to, 41, 183, 224–25. *See
  also* Pawelka, John Joseph, family home
  of
Homesickness, 116–17; home, returning to,
  and, 41; settlers and, 139
Hometown, returning to, 205–9
Homophobia, 144
Homosexuality, 144
Hope, 180
Houdini, Harry, 67
Howe, L., 264n
Human rights, displacement and, 182
Humphries, Barry, 170
Hungerford, Carole, 239
Hysteria, Pawelka causing, 46–47

Identity, 264n; Capgras Delusion and, 243;
  genealogy and, 229–33, 248; home and,
  252; indigeneity and, 250–51; landscape
  and, 251–52; language and, 225–26;
  Latino, 250–51; past, constructed from,
  228–33; Pawelka and, 40–41, 61;
  universality and, 255–59
"If" (Kipling), 224
"I Have Seen Königsberg Burning"
  (Wentzer), 3–5
Imagination: history and, 84; memory and,
  23, 85. *See also* Past, acting
  imaginatively on
Immigrants, 199–200; Māori and, 194–97;
  New Zealand and, 193–94, 218–19,
  243–45, 279n; second-class citizens,
  perceived as, 244. *See also* Danish
  immigrants; *Manuhiri*
Immune system, childhood and, 237
Indigeneity: identity and, 250–51; New
  Zealand and, 242–43, 251, 279n. *See also*
  Tangata whenua
Individuality, soldiers maintaining,
  163–64
In Fires of No Return (Baxter), 266n
Inglewood, New Zealand, 205–7, 209;
  etymology of, 277n; Māori and, 19, 208
Invention, facts and, 191

Involuntary memory, 135
Iran, 257–59
Iron Hand, The (Cleveland), 160–61

Jackson, Jesse, 180
Jackson, Michael, 8, 193, 219–20
James, Henry: art and, 192–93; writing
  and, 17
James, William, xviii, 262n
Jaspers, Karl, 125
Jensen, Robyn, 80
Jesus, xv; crucifixion of, gypsies and,
  155–56
Johnson, Joyce, 128
Joyce, James, xv–xvi
Jung, Carl, 256

Kakahi, Tohu, 217, 278n
Kangaroo (Lawrence), 280n
Kant, Immanuel, 4
Karaitiana, Ruru, 172–75. *See also* "Blue
  Smoke"
Karma, 149
Keaton, Buster, 258
Kelleher, Jack, 174
Kiarostami, Abbas, 257–59
Kimbolton, New Zealand, 11–13, 30–32;
  Pawelka convalescing in, 23–24;
  Pawelka hiding in, 72–73, 110; Pawelka
  on, 16–17; Pawelka supported in, 14, 44,
  50
King, Michael, 218
Kingi, Wiremu, 18, 215–17
Kinship, 157
Kipling, Rudyard, 224
Klee, Paul, 246
Knowledge: culture and, 123; history and,
  122–23; space and, 121; time and, 121;
  White and, 122–23
Kooti, Te, 7, 266n
Kramer, Josef, 177
Kuranko: space and, 122; time and, 122
Kuruwarri. See Traces

Labyrinth, Minoan, 65, 190
Lambek, Michael, 271n

xviii, 263*n*; grievances and, 218; knowledge and, 121; Kuranko and, 122; music and, 128; objectivity and, xv–xxi; space and, 121–22; subjectivity and, xv–xxi. *See also specific topics*
Time and Narrative (Ricoeur), 250
Time past, ethnography and, xxii
Time travel, memory and, 207
Tlingit, reincarnation and, 125
Toi whenua, xxiv
Towns, small, 95; insularity decreasing in, 87; Pawelka and, 17–18, 32
Traces: Aboriginal people and, 124; history and, 65; Pawelka and, 65–66
Tragedy, media and, 80, 101–2, 186
Trauma, 160–62; childhood and, 168–70, 174–75, 249–50; chronology and, xvii; colonialism and, 170–72; losing and, 206–7; memory and, 116–17, 133; recovery and, 163–66, 172; slavery and, 170–71; storytelling and, 210
Trial, Pawelka, 56–59, 110, 267*n*
Trompe l'oeil, 192
Truth: museums and, 91; narrative and, 65, 80–81; phenomenology and, xiv–xv. *See also* Happening truth; Story truth
Tupu (unfolding), 213
Turangawaewae (belonging), 114
Turning points, decisive, 38
Typhoid, Pawelka contracting, 23

Ulysses (Joyce), xv–xvi
Uncanny *(Unheimlich),* xiv
Unionization, New Zealand and, 60
Universality, identity and, 255–59
Uptightness, New Zealand and, 178

Vagrants, Pawelka and, 33
Vengeance, 168–70
Vernacular, New Zealand and, 146
Victoria (Queen), 13, 185
Victory (Conrad), 193
Vigilantes, Pawelka and, 47–48
Violence: New Zealand and, 9–10; witnessing and, 86–87, 91, 160–66, 176–77

Waitangi Tribunal, 218
"Wanderer, The," 230
War, death and, xv. *See also* Boer War; Prisoners of war; Taranaki War; World War I; World War II
Warburg, Aby, xix–xx, 256
Wentzer, Thomas Schwarz, 3–5
West Africa: death and, 125; past as perceived in, 123
Where Is My Friend's Home, 257
Wherowhero, Potatau Te, 211–12
White, Hayden: history and, xvii–xviii, 122–23; knowledge and, 122–23; myth and, xvii–xviii
Whitebait, 221
Whiti-o-Rongomaia, Te, 217, 278*n*
Wigan, A. L., xiv, 261*n*
Wilder, George, 60
Winfrey, Oprah, 180
Winning, firstness and, 206
Witnessing, violence and, 86–87, 91, 160–66, 176–77
Wolfe, Thomas, 202
Women, marriage, taken advantage of in, 197–98
Woolf, Virginia, 190
Workhouses, xii
World turned upside down, 204
World War I: Egypt and, 88; New Zealand and, 88–89; Pawelka and, 68–69, 71, 88–89, 91, 108, 268*n*, 269*n*
World War II, 3–5, 116–17; Americans and, 188; France and, 187–88; New Zealand and, 160–66, 172–73, 176–77
Writing, 190–91; academic, 247, 255–56; Borges and, 231; expatriation and, 122, 255, 258; experience captured in, 247; healing and, 149; James, H., and, 17; organically, 150–51; origins and, 192–93, 271*n*; the self and, 256

Yasujirō Ozu, 258
"You Are My Sunshine," 209
Yourcenar, Marguerite, 127–28; Hadrian (Emperor) and, 126; origins and, 271*n*
Youth (Conrad), 130, 132

GPSR Authorized Representative: Easy Access System Europe, Mustamäe tee 50, 10621 Tallinn, Estonia, gpsr.requests@easproject.com